Key Directions in Legal Education

Key Directions in Legal Education identifies and explores key contemporary and emerging themes that are significant and heavily debated within legal education from both UK and international perspectives. It provides a rich comparative dialogue and insights into the current and future directions of legal education.

The book discusses in detail topics including the pressures on law schools exerted by external stakeholders, the fostering of interdisciplinary approaches and collaboration within legal education and the evolution of discourses around teaching and learning legal skills. It elaborates on the continuing development of clinical legal education as a component of the law degree and the emergence and use of innovative technologies within law teaching. The approach of pairing UK and international authors to obtain comparative insights and analysis on a range of key themes is original and provides both a genuine comparative dialogue and a clear international focus.

This book will be of great interest for researchers, academics and post-graduate students in the field of law and legal pedagogy.

Emma Jones is a Senior Lecturer in Law in the School of Law, The University of Sheffield, UK, and a Senior Fellow of the Higher Education Authority.

Fiona Cownie is Professor of Law Emerita in the School of Law, Keele University, UK, a Principal Fellow of the Higher Education Academy and a Senior Research Associate of the Institute of Advanced Legal Studies, London University, UK.

Legal Pedagogy

Series Editor: **Kris Gledhill**, Auckland University of Technology, New Zealand

This series consists of high-quality monographs, each of which explores best practice in an aspect of the law school curriculum. Books cover teaching methods and curriculum design in the main areas of law, how to integrate themes and areas of jurisprudential thought, and wider questions about legal education more generally. With contributions from around the world, this series explores innovative thinking and practice within the context of a generally conservative branch of academia, with the aim of promoting discussion as to how best to teach the various aspects of the law degree and ensure the ongoing validity of the law degree as a whole. Typical topics addressed include the value of variety in teaching methods and curriculum design, how best to incorporate educational research, the role for more practical courses, and the need to ensure that law schools provide degrees of relevance to the needs of students and of society.

The books in this series will be of great interest to academics, researchers and postgraduates in the fields of law and education, as well as teachers of law who may be interested in revising curricula and need guidance in doing so. In addition, the legal profession, and in particular those who regulate entry into the profession, will find much to interest them within the series.

Books in this series:

Re-thinking Legal Education under the Civil and Common Law
A Road Map for Constructive Change
Edited by Richard Grimes

Reimagining Contract Law Pedagogy
A New Agenda for Teaching
Edited by Warren Swain and David Campbell

Key Directions in Legal Education
National and International Perspectives
Edited By Emma Jones and Fiona Cownie

For more information about books in this series, please visit www.routledge.com/law/series/LEGPED

Key Directions in Legal Education

National and International Perspectives

Edited by
Emma Jones and Fiona Cownie

Routledge
Taylor & Francis Group
LONDON AND NEW YORK

First published 2020 by Routledge

2 Park Square, Milton Park, Abingdon, Oxon OX14 4RN
605 Third Avenue, New York, NY 10017

Routledge is an imprint of the Taylor & Francis Group, an informa business

First issued in paperback 2021

British Library Cataloguing-in-Publication Data
A catalogue record for this book is available from the British Library

Library of Congress Cataloging-in-Publication Data
A catalog record has been requested for this book

ISBN: 978-1-138-33005-4 (hbk)
ISBN: 978-1-03-217504-1 (pbk)
DOI: 10.4324/9780429448065

Typeset in Bembo
by Taylor & Francis Books

To all our students, past and present, remembering our shared experiences of legal education

Contents

Contributors

Emma Jones (Co-Editor) is a Senior Lecturer in the University of Sheffield School of Law. She is currently developing courses that explore the role of digital lawyering and provide critical perspectives on the legal profession. Her research focuses on legal education and the legal profession, with a particular emphasis on the role of emotion and well-being and her monograph *Emotions in the Law School: Transforming Legal Education Through The Passions* is published by Routledge. She is a member of the executive committee for the Association of Law Teachers and the steering group of the Legal Education Research Network. She previously worked as a solicitor in private practice and is a qualified teacher.

Fiona Cownie (Co-Editor) is Professor of Law Emerita at Keele Univesity, UK, and is a leading expert on legal education, having published widely in the area for several decades. Her approach to research is interdisciplinary, and she is a Fellow of the Royal Society of Arts and a Fellow of the Academy of Social Sciences. From 2013–2017 she was Pro Vice Chancellor (Education and Student Experience) at Keele University in the UK and she is a Principal Fellow of the Higher Education Academy. Professor Cownie is currently writing a biography of the first female professor of law in the U.K.

Seán Arthurs is the Senior Manager of Education Initiatives for the National PTA, a lawyer, teacher and lifelong learner. He holds a Doctorate in Education Leadership from Harvard, a BBA (University of Notre Dame), a JD (University of Cincinnati), a Master of Arts in Teaching (University of Portland), and an LLM in Advocacy (Georgetown). Dr Arthurs has worked as a judicial clerk, Legal Aid attorney, human rights volunteer, litigation associate and high school teacher. When he is not attending school, Dr Arthurs is learning and laughing with his two inquisitive children who remind him frequently about how little he knows.

Anthony Bradney is Emeritus Professor of Law at Keele University and a Senior Research Fellow at the Institute of Advanced Legal Studies,

University of London. He has published widely on a number of topics including university legal education, law and religion and law and popular culture.

Mandy Burton is Professor of Socio-Legal Studies at the University of Leicester. Her research and teaching lies mainly in the fields of family law, criminal law and criminal justice. She has carried out numerous empirical projects examining the law in action in domestic abuse cases, as well as other serious sexual and violent crimes. Mandy adopts interdisciplinary and collaborative approaches in both her research and teaching. She is also committed to policy relevant research and making an impact on how the law responds to domestic abuse.

Ubaldus de Vries is Associate Professor and Director of Education at Utrecht University, the Netherlands. In his research, de Vries bridges social theory and jurisprudence, addressing questions in the field of sustainability, risk and responsibility and global justice. In addition, he seeks to integrate research into teaching and experiments with new didactical ways to strengthen the academic nature of legal educations. His latest publications are (with John Fanning) *Law in the Risk Society* (eleven international publishers, 2017) and (with Bart Van Klink) *Academic Learning in Law* (Edward Elgar, 2016).

Rachael Field is a Professor in the Law Faculty at Bond University on the Gold Coast, Australia. She is a member of the Executive of Bond's Centre for Professional Legal Education and Co-Director of the Bond Dispute Resolution Centre. Her areas of research expertise include legal education, dispute resolution, family law and domestic violence. Rachael is an Australian Learning and Teaching Fellow and a Senior Fellow of the Higher Education Academy. She founded the Australian Wellness Network for Law in 2010 and co-founded the Australian Dispute Resolution Research Network. Rachael has volunteered at Women's Legal Service in Brisbane since 1993, and has been president of the Service since 2004. In 2013 Rachael was named Queensland Woman Lawyer of the Year.

Richard Grimes qualified as a solicitor in 1977 and worked initially in a law centre and later as a full-equity partner for a provisional law firm, handling, principally, publicly funded cases. He has since worked in a number of universities in the UK and overseas and for the last 25 years has devoted his time to developing experiential means of learning about law and the legal system that focus on the application of theory to practice. He is now a visiting professor at Charles University, Prague, and is an independent legal education and access to justice consultant.

Jessica Guth is a Reader at Leeds Law School, Leeds Beckett University. She is the former Chair (now Treasurer) of the Association of Law Teachers and has previously also held committee or sub-committee roles on the Socio-

Legal Studies Association Executive Committee and the Society of Legal Scholars Education Sub Committee. Prior to joining Leeds Law School, Jess was the Head of Law at the University of Bradford. Jessica's research is focused on legal education generally and she has particular interests in the lived experiences of legal academics as well as in feminist and queer approaches to law and law teaching and the development of legal skills.

Debarati Halder is presently engaged as Professor of Legal Studies at Unitedworld School of Law, Karnavati University, Gandhinagar, Gujarat, India. She is the founder-Managing Director (Hon.) of the Centre for Cyber Victim Counselling (www.cybervictims.org) and founder-secretary of the South Asian Society of Criminology and Victimology (www.sascv.org). She has authored several books and scholarly peer reviewed articles on cybercrimes against women and legal issues, therapeutic jurisprudence and cyber victimology. She is an expert resource person for several government and non-government stakeholders including UNICEF, the National Commission for Women in, India and Facebook. She has been awarded a WebWonderWomen award for her work on law and policy regarding women's rights from the Ministry of Women and Child Developments, Twitter and Breakthrough India. She can be reached at debaratihalder@gmail.com.

Hugh McFaul is a Director of The Open University Law School's Open Justice Centre, leading on public legal education issues. He has worked to develop innovative community-based experiential learning opportunities for OU students with national and international partners. He is particularly interested in harnessing the potential of online technologies to support the social justice agenda by increasing levels of public legal literacy and has experimented with virtual reality technology to support and engage his students.

Jan H. F. Meyer is an Honorary Professor, and a former Professor of Education, in the School of Civil Engineering at the University of Queensland, Australia. He has two symbiotic research interests: the theoretical underpinning of university teaching; and student learning well-being at under- and postgraduate levels. Much of his earlier research focused on the quantitative modelling of individual differences in students' learning, particularly in the transition from school to university. Later work focused on helping students to develop their metalearning capacity in, and beyond, this transition. Jan is the originator of the notion of a 'threshold concept' and proposed the basic idea with Ray Land in a seminal paper in 2003. The subsequently-developed Threshold Concepts Framework has integrated and extended his research interests into new domains. Recent work contributes in both practical and theoretical terms to previously alluded, to but relatively under-researched, aspects of the Framework; namely, the professional development of university teachers and the affective experiences of student learning.

Michael Palmer is Emeritus Professor of Law at the University of London (SOAS) and Senior Research Fellow at both the Institute of Advanced Legal Studies (IALS) and the Hong Kong Institute of Asia-Pacific Studies (HKI-SAPS) at the Chinese University of Hong Kong. Between 2009 and 2016 he was an Associate Dean and then Dean of a mainland Chinese law school.

Francine Ryan is a Senior Lecturer and the Director of The Open University Law School's Open Justice Law Clinic, whose innovative feature is that it is an entirely online service. Francine's research focuses on the impact of technology on the future of legal education and the legal profession; she is particularly interested in the integration of technology into legal education to support access to justice and to help students prepare for a rapidly changing workplace.

Ekokoi Solomon is a barrister and solicitor of the Supreme Court of Nigeria. He is a constitutional scholar and law lecturer at the Faculty of Law, University of Uyo, Nigeria. His main fields of research are constitutional law and theory and legal education. He teaches the Nigerian legal system and other law courses at the Universy of Uyo, Nigeria, and has published in local and international journals. He holds an LLB degree from the University of Calabar, Nigeria, an LLM degree from the University of Uyo, Nigeria and is currently a PhD candidate at the University of Calabar, Nigeria.

Caroline Strevens is Reader in Legal Education, Head of the Law Department at the University of Portsmouth, UK and Chair of the Association of Law Teachers. Her academic career was preceded by a career in legal practice as a solicitor. Caroline's primary research area is legal education including experiential learning and more recently she has been investigating how principles of positive psychology may influence well-being of staff and students in higher education. Her most recent publication, entitled 'Perceptions of Wellbeing in Law Teachers', was published in *The Law Teacher*. Caroline continues to work with international collaborators investigating the well-being of law students, legal academics and junior lawyers.

Andy Unger is Associate Professor in Law and Head of the Law Division in the School of Law and Social Sciences, London South Bank University. He teaches human rights, medical law and ethics and law and technology. He is currently leading the revalidation of the LSBU law courses in the light of the introduction of the Solicitors Qualifying Examination and other changes to professional qualification.

Dawn Watkins is Professor of Law, University of Leicester, UK. Her varied research and teaching interests are in law and the humanities and in legal education, especially public legal education, and she is strongly committed to pursuing interdisciplinary and collaborative approaches in both these fields.

She is currently leading the FORTITUDE research project funded by the European Research Council. Its aim is to improve children and young people's legal capability, drawing on theories of play. She is a National Teaching Fellow of the Higher Education Academy.

Ling Zhou is a Research Associate at the Hong Kong Institute of Asia-Pacific Studies (HKIAPS), Chinese University of Hong Kong. She was awarded her DPhil in law at the University of Oxford in 2018. Her main research interests include civil justice and dispute resolution, socio-legal studies, and consumer protection. At the HKIAPS, Dr Zhou also researches issues in constitutional and administrative law.

Acknowledgements

Our thanks to all the authors who have contributed to this collection for their support. Our thanks also to Kris Gledhill, editor of the Legal Pedagogy series, for his encouragement.

Introduction

Emma Jones and Fiona Cownie

Entanglements and entrapments in the law school: legal education, change and relationality

This book is about contemporary legal education. Its view is international, across geographical boundaries and continents. Its contributions draw lessons from the past and provide predictions (or exhortations) for the future. Its contents vary from pedagogy to skills, from well-being to technology. Each topic contains two companion chapters, one written from the perspective of the United Kingdom (UK) and one from that of a different country. In places, there are explicit comparisons drawn between jurisdictions, in others there are more implicit questions raised about similarities and differences, commensurability and compatibility.

Despite this diversity of topics, approaches and comparisons, regardless of the countries involved, the undergraduate or postgraduate nature of the qualification and the different voices included, there is a key unifying feature across all contributions and discussions, namely, the law student. The law student features in every chapter within this volume. This is sometimes as a part of case studies, as in de Vries' discussion of interdisciplinary initiatives involving law schools (Chapter 4). At other points it is in terms of what legal education is, and should be, providing for students, as in the discussion by Unger in Chapter 1 and Palmer and Zhou in Chapter 2, a theme also found in Bradney's exploration of 'What are university law schools for?' (Conclusion). In other contributions, the focus is on specific facets of the law student's law school experience, from experiential learning as discussed by Grimes and Arthurs (Chapters 7 and 8) to the role and use of skills as considered by Guth and Solomon (Chapters 11 and 12). Without law students, legal education in arguably its most familiar form, that of the university law school, would not exist. That is not to denigrate the vital role of legal academics in shaping the law school in countless ways. It is also not disregarding the fact that there are myriad other forms of legal education present in contemporary society, such as public legal education, citizenship (or similar) within compulsory schooling and informal legal learning, through articles, social media and Massive Open Online Courses. However, it is the university law school that is the focus of this volume and at its heart are law students. The student body forms a collection of individuals who have chosen (for whatever reason) to study law and who will spend a sustained period of time engrossed in its rules and norms, its culture and expectations.

The concept of relationality within legal education

In the preceding paragraph, I describe students as being at the "heart" of the law school for a particular reason. Around St Valentine's Day in the year of writing (festival of romance, greetings cards and last-minute chocolates), I saw an interesting meme on social media. It was an image of a person labelled 'Me', on bended knee, presenting an engagement ring to a woman labelled 'My law degree'. While there are several ways of interpreting this meme, what piqued *my* interest was the notion of the student as being in a relationship with their degree. I found this interesting, because it seemed to challenge some of the commonly held conceptions of the contemporary law student. In Chapter 9 of this volume, Strevens rightly points out that we live in an era in which students are often characterised and addressed as consumers. There is an assumption that students are rights orientated and employability focused, perhaps because that reflects so many of the neoliberal policies and explicit and implicit messages that are now enmeshed in higher education (Zepke, 2015, 2014). However, what was engaging about this meme was that it suggested something more (at least for some) than a functional, instrumental form of approach on the part of a law student. It hinted at a deeper engagement, an emotional attachment, to law as a discipline as well as to the law degree as an educational experience and the law school itself.

To suggest or discern an attachment to or engagement with law and legal education on the part of law students should not really be surprising. After all, it is usual for any individual to have their emotional responses and reactions mediated and influenced by their surroundings, their activities and those around them (Feldman Barrett, 2017). If an individual has committed themselves to becoming a law student, in the environs of a university law school, such emotional reactions and responses are inevitable and indeed inescapable. They will shape, and be shaped by, the law students' daily interactions, learning and relationship with both the law and other stakeholders in the law school (Jones, 2019). Such emotions and affect (feelings and preferences) will, in turn, contribute to the web of relationships that the individual creates (or, in some cases, fails to create) throughout their time in legal education. At its broadest this can encapsulate not only relationships with fellow students, legal academics and other staff within the law school and wider university, but it may also encompass a relationship with the discipline and experience of law itself as the law student's sense of identity develops (see, for example, Sommerlad, 2007). These relationships may be positive in terms of both learning and well-being, as when a law teacher provides an appropriately nurturing environment

(Bromberger, 2010). However, they may also be negative, as when students fail to develop a sense of belonging or social connectedness (Bergin and Pakenham, 2015; Tani and Vines, 2009). To develop this notion further than its starting point of one individual on bended knee solely addressing a (somewhat glamorous) personification of the law school, it is possible to conceptualise a law student as being at the centre of a web of relationships and connections throughout their legal studies – a form of spider diagram with intricate and interwoven lines and elements. A university law school will provide, and be inextricably enmeshed within, a range of relationships, entanglements and entrapments each with emotional and social facets and influences.

This form of attachment or interconnectivity can be best encapsulated by terms such as relationship centred and relational – terms that focus on the concept of relationality. With regard to lawyering, Brooks and Madden have described a relationship-centred approach as one that 'includes all approaches that focus on understanding and relating to the client in context, with a narrative that goes beyond the legal controversy and includes the many people and systems with which the client interacts' (2009, p.26). They are creating a vision of the legal profession that acknowledges the complexities of the relationships that are centred around the client and provide the context within which the more rigid, prescribed procedures and processes of the justice system take place. Brooks has also argued for a form of relational approach to clinical legal education in the context of the United States of America (US), defining it as one that explicitly identifies and explores the 'relational dynamics' inherent in interactions between students and their supervisors (2006, p.215). The advantages and opportunities (as well as the challenges) provided by clinical legal education programmes are well illustrated within this volume through the contributions of Richard Grimes and Sean Arthurs (Chapters 7 and 8). However, there is no reason why such a relational approach should begin and end in quasi-lawyering situations. Indeed, there is a strong argument that, within university law schools, legal education as a whole requires a relational approach. In other words, an approach acknowledging the relationships and connections within the law school as valuable and important and which seeks to factor these into the choices, decisions and conversations that arise both within and about legal education. Discussing the notion of a relational ontology in education more broadly, Lange suggests that it includes:

> [T]he contexts, properties, and patterns of interactions in which an individual is embedded, not just the worldview of an individual. It would address as much of the relational network as possible – geographic place and other non-human relations in that place, the myriad of work, personal, and familial relations brought into the room by learners, and the larger cultural, social, economic, and political relations as well as cosmic mythology and spiritual relations that exist at the historical moment. (2018, p.291)

This type of relationality is antithetical to traditional notions of legal education. The law has commonly been presented as the epitome of objective, reasoned rationality, disparaging personal relationships, emotions and the wider affective domain and characterising them as irrational and thus irrelevant (Grossi, 2015; Maroney, 2006). It has failed to acknowledge the importance of such relationships, emotions and affect, despite the overwhelming body of evidence from neuroscience and psychology that demonstrates the ways in which cognition is influenced by (and influences) relationships and affect (Damasio, 2006). Within legal education, it is perhaps unsurprising therefore that the focus has been on ignoring or suppressing the more relational aspects of human life, notably emotion and affect (Bromberger, 2010; Jones, 2019). More broadly, it is individualistic notions such as 'thinking like a lawyer' and particular forms of intellectual analysis and reasoning that are commonly prized, even deified, within law schools (James, 2008a). Arguably this results in the normalisation of a specific lexicon of language and behaviour which is rigid, narrow and impoverished (Mertz, 2007). This means that the broader connections and interactions surrounding an individual are disregarded, because they fall outside that particular, narrow legal prism. In relation to lawyering, Stier (1992) contrasts the notion of a relational approach with that of an 'instrumental' approach that is impersonal and focuses on using clients as tools to achieve success (see also Pearce and Wald, 2012). The traditional approach to legal education is arguably similarly instrumental in approach and thus only values the individual student's intellectual capabilities, those 'qualities of the mind' (Quality Assurance Agency, 2015) which law chooses to prize and prioritise. Such an approach denies or excludes the role of relationality within both law and education by rejecting the essence of what makes us human and eschewing the value of relationships and relationality.

To what extent does the traditional approach still dominate law schools? To what extent has the situation changed in contemporary legal education? There are interesting tensions and conflicts at play here, often influenced by wider policy discourses and narratives in higher education. For example, the neoliberalisation and marketisation of universities has led (as Strevens discusses in Chapter 9) to a seeming privileging of the student voice, often through formalised feedback-gathering exercises on either an institutional or national scale (such as the National Student Survey within the UK). This could be seen as beneficial in terms of relationality, in as much as it emphasises the viewpoint of the student (including law students), requiring their perspective to be heard (Zepke, 2014, 2015). However, at the same time, there is evidence that the results of such feedback can be skewed by other issues; for example, the gender of the academic teaching a course has been found to impact on the types of comments provided, with male academics receiving higher teaching evaluations from male students (Mengel, Sauermann and Zölitz, 2019). At one level, this demonstrates that relationality cannot be interpreted as a one-way flow of information and views. Instead, it needs to involve a process of dialogue and learning by all involved to enable discussion and exploration of wider issues such as gender (Brooks, 2016). At the same time, this example illustrates how one of the reasons for the difficulties that can be found within discourses around the student voice lies within the origins of its development. The neoliberal academy seeks to use emotional and affective reactions and responses, not to foster relationality but to promote economic productivity (Burke, 2015; Lynch, 2006). For universities to produce appropriately qualified knowledge production workers, and ensure their own survival, they must meet the demands of students and cater to the increasing prevalence of discourses around employability that often dominate discussions of the purpose of higher education (Frankham, 2016). In other words, the purpose of the contemporary emphasis on feedback-gathering is not to foster greater or more open dialogue, and thus nurture closer relationships. Instead, it is part of a broader agenda that focuses on individual productivity and gain and requires universities to play a full role in facilitating this wider economic prosperity. It does not place the student at the heart of higher education, because it does not acknowledge that there is such a heart.

One of the advantages of taking a relational view of higher education generally is the way in which it challenges such neoliberal discourses. At the same time, while focusing on the law school and the law student, it is necessary to consider what specific importance and value such relationality has within contemporary legal education. This is particularly the case when a snapshot of legal education across jurisdictions tends to suggest that law schools are already thriving (see, for example, the Legal Education and Training Review, 2013, para. 2.11). Law can be characterised as a discipline with high student numbers and relatively low running costs, making it popular with higher education institutes and (being perceived as) offering a certain status to those who chose to study it (Twining, 1994). Although such a broad-brush summary masks increasing disparities and challenges arising both within and between jurisdictions, overall law schools can be characterised as a success story on a range of measures. However, it is also clear that law schools are facing a range of challenges and demands and being compelled to address a series of changes at present. These mean that continued success cannot be taken for granted or assumed, but it also suggests a potential and ability for a relational conceptualisation to assist in navigating change and uncertainty. This volume itself, with its focus on key directions for legal education, demonstrates a range of these imperatives and pressures and the possible role of relationality within them.

Relationality within the university law school

In Chapter 1, Unger discusses the proposed introduction (in 2021) of the Solicitors Qualifying Examination in England and Wales. This will remove the requirement of a qualifying law degree, or its equivalent, for qualification into the solicitors' profession, thus potentially diminishing some of the university law school's appeal for prospective legal professionals. However, at the same time, as Unger argues, it allows for university law schools to develop distinct, innovative and effective pedagogies for law teaching by freeing themselves of the requirements of the qualifying law degree. What will these new pedagogies be and how will they reframe the current degree? The answer has to be, at least in part, that these will be shaped by the relationships within the law school, with its students, its legal academy, its broader stakeholders in the local community and the wider university. If a layer of regulation and procedure is removed, the gap that remains should be filled with the form of inclusive and open dialogue that is core to a relational approach (Brooks, 2016). Of course, there will be wider imperatives stemming from broader policy agendas and financial pressures in higher education too, but a relational approach can pervade many levels. These levels can include individual teaching pedagogy, in particular, through the notion of relational pedagogy where the teacher's or academic's interactions with their students become the foundation for developing flourishing communities for learning and development (Reeves and Le Mare, 2017; Saevi, 2011). Another level encompasses a broader engagement with external (or broader) internal pressures, by including relationality as an embedded element within decisions and choices and as a marker of progress and success. There is arguably a sentient warning about the dangers of ignoring relationality within Unger's companion chapter, Chapter 2, which focuses on legal education in the Chinese context. In this chapter, Zhou and Palmer discuss the limited relationship between legal education and the legal profession, and the lack of embedding of professional skills that has resulted from this. This is particularly problematic given Chinese law schools' potentially pivotal role in the training of legal professionals. The strong political-legal domination of the state seems to suggest an eschewing of relationality that has perhaps contributed to this lack of dialogue and disregard for the connection between law as an academic discipline and the realities of legal practice. The dictates of the wider system have led to a failure to appreciate the real and potential connections and relationships that exist between different parts of both legal education and the wider legal framework. This provides an indication of the benefits of acknowledging and exploring relationality alongside political-legal concerns.

It is this type of wider connection that is the focus of Burton and Watkin's contribution in Chapter 3 and de Vries' companion discussion in Chapter 4. The focus on interdisciplinary approaches and collaboration illustrates relationality at a conceptual level, demonstrating how university law schools can draw on, work with and connect to other disciplines. Burton and Watkins acknowledge that challenges arise in ensuring that such approaches and collaboration are nurtured within law schools, not least because of the tradition of doctrinalism and the influence of market forces. However, their argument is that interdisciplinarity and collaboration are vital components of legal education, regardless of whether a law degree is viewed as having academic or vocational purposes. The contribution of de Vries provides an overview of a number of interdisciplinary initiatives that draw on disciplines such as politics, psychology and economics, as well as placing law in a societal context. Perhaps the most inspirational example given is the use of poetry to encourage students to reflect on the relationship between the rule of law and authoritarian leadership. For de Vries, such programmes not only facilitate the ability of law students to find their own voice; they also enhance the relationality that can occur between legal education and the legal profession, and contribute to the development of a new type of legal practitioner who possesses greater criticality and openness. De Vries' reference to teams of lecturers suggests that connections can also be fostered between academics within and across disciplines. On some occasions, he notes that such interdisciplinarity may also involve law students working directly with students of other disciplines (for example, law and geography students working together on an environmental law programme). The reflexivity he urges readers to embed within such approaches can be used to foster a broad appreciation of the relationships and connections surrounding and enmeshing individual students as well as those within both the law school and the discipline of law, an essential quality for navigating change.

Alongside the rise of interdisciplinary approaches and collaboration (however far from linear that has been), in recent years legal education has had to adapt to the proliferation of new technologies within society. The contributions by Ryan and McFaul (Chapter 5) and Halder (Chapter 6) in this volume demonstrate two strands of this phenomenon. First, there are the ways in which law engages with the role and impact of technology within society as a whole. Second, there are the ways in which technology can affect the design and delivery of the law degree itself within university law schools. Both of these strands arguably have implications for a relational approach within legal education. With regard to the first, Ryan and McFaul provide a broad-brush overview of how technology and society interact, with a specific focus on the UK. They refer to the impact of technology on legal services, in particular in relation to dispute resolution. Halder's chapter discusses a number of key legal cases in India that also demonstrate the ways in which technology is interacting with a range of aspects of daily life. Such discussions and examples demonstrate the need to acknowledge the role of technology within human relationships and connections in the contemporary age, from the use of social media for networking and campaigning to the fascinating example of the triple *talaq* (a form of instant divorce) being sent via telephone or other media, effectively severing a relationship without any form of face-to-face contact. Halder's exploration of some of both the positive and negative interactions that technology can foster within relationships demonstrates both that any critique of technology needs to consider its impact on human relationships and, conversely, that human relationships and connections cannot be considered without factoring in the role technology now plays (Malpass, 2012).

The second thread, that of technology within legal education, is well illustrated by Ryan and McFaul's case study of The Open University's Open

Justice Centre in the UK and Halder's discussion of the use of legal databases and other technology within Indian law schools. Both explicitly demonstrate the importance of technology within university law schools. I would also argue that, implicitly, they both illustrate the need to consider the interaction between technology and relationships. As technology alters the way students connect and relate to their peers, their teachers and the wider law school, we need to critically evaluate and reflect on the impact of this. For example, what does it mean for the well-being of those navigating new technological advances? How does the use of new forms of communication influence the types and strength of connections that are formed? What can legal academics do to ameliorate the potential negative impacts and accentuate the positive? Without asking such key questions, there are dangers that technological innovations will be embraced within the law school without questioning whether there is a potential human cost involved, or a need for adaptation to preserve key relationships.

Clinical legal education provides a strong example of the importance of relationality in legal education. It is referred to in a number of chapters in this book (including by Unger in Chapter 1 and Ryan and McFaul in Chapter 5). The contributions of Grimes (Chapter 7) and Arthurs in this volume (Chapter 8) specifically discuss the role of clinical legal education within university law schools. Grimes, with a particular focus on the UK, traces key definitions, challenges and opportunities, including identifying a number of potential models of clinical legal education and exploring the different balances that can be struck between education and service. In the companion chapter, Arthurs considers the US context and identifies key trends influencing the development of the field, including the potential for it to be integrated within the wider law school curriculum. It is arguable that much clinical work is, or should be, imbued with relationality (Brooks, 2006). When dealing with clients, in clinic and in legal practice, much of the focus is on communicating, building dialogue and fostering rapport and empathy (Gerdy, 2008). Experiential learning itself is a process that involves not just the cognitive, but also the affective, including strong emotional components in an individual's response to their experience (see, for example, Abe, 2011). The work and experience of clinical legal education can potentially highlight connections between legal education and the legal profession and enhance law students' understanding of the importance of relational approaches. The pedagogies and practices it will often use can both reveal the importance of relationality and also assist in fostering and developing it further. It is therefore perhaps unsurprising that several authors in this volume suggest that there is the potential for clinical legal education to play a greater, and more embedded, role within law schools. This is not only a valuable response to change, but also a way of fostering change that acknowledges and appreciates relationality.

Given its relational aspects, it is fitting that, after exploring clinical legal education, the subsequent two chapters in this volume move on to explore well-being within legal education. One of the key arguments for the acknowledgement of emotions and affect and the shift towards a relational paradigm within legal education is its potentially beneficial impact on well-being (James, 2008b; Jones, 2019). This is well demonstrated by the increasing recognition in many jurisdictions, particularly the US and Australia, that law schools can be damaging to their students' mental and physical well-being, often because it has tried so hard to disregard non-cognitive facets of its law students' lives and character (Sheldon and Krieger, 2004; Towness O'Brien et al., 2011). Strevens (Chapter 9) identifies that the current messages being conveyed, intentionally and explicitly, to law students, are likely to diminish intrinsic motivation and foster extrinsic motivation in a way which self-determination theory indicates is detrimental to well-being. The aforementioned neoliberal notion of the student as a consumer is one of these messages. The characterisation of these discourses as a series of messages illustrates the lack of relational dialogue that this market-driven environment is propagating. The companion chapter, by Field and Meyer (Chapter 10), also draws on self-determination theory in order to explore the interconnection between well-being and the curriculum of the law degree. The focus here is on the way in which threshold concepts can be used to integrate and promote well-being. What is key within these two chapters is the way in which well-being is demonstrated to be influenced by many aspects of the law school experience. It thus demonstrates the need for a relational approach to extend beyond one aspect (such as student satisfaction) and imbue the entirety of the university law school, including curriculum and pedagogy. The current issues with well-being have arguably arisen, at least in part, because of a failure to acknowledge and respond to this facet of legal education in the past, and they therefore appear to lend weight to the argument that any change must encompass well-being and relationality.

The final set of companion chapters focuses on the role and development of legal skills within university law schools. In the UK context, Guth's chapter (Chapter 10) explicitly identifies the affective domain as an area that has been neglected to date within skills development, providing an additional link with other chapters in this volume. It also makes a strong case for the explicit teaching of skills to undergraduates studying law and explores the way in which the skills debate encompasses a range of influencing factors, including a number discussed in different contexts in previous chapters, such as technology and the increasing focus on employability. In the Nigerian context, Solomon discusses the issues that have arisen because of (what he perceives as) a lack of integrated and appropriate skills training to date, emphasising the importance of skills teaching to entrants into the legal profession. Together, these chapters illustrate the importance of the skills agenda on an international scale. With regard to relationality, they demonstrate the need to acknowledge this in the skills that are being identified and fostered in a way that will then facilitate a wider awareness and understanding of the need for relational approaches and an acknowledgement and utilisation of emotion and affect.

The conclusion to this volume addresses the fundamental question of what a university law school is for. When considering relationality, this is a vital question because it will determine the answer to the equally important question 'On what basis are we going to evaluate success?' If university law schools can be viewed as being relatively successful (by most measures) to date, then how are we going to determine whether that continues into the future? Is it sufficient to conclude that law schools are meeting their mission if it can be demonstrated that their numbers and cash flow are buoyant? It is possible that, at an institutional level, this form of metric can and does suffice. However, returning once again to the focus on people and relationships, it seems highly unlikely any law student would ascribe success to these measures. For law students, it may be that a more relevant assessment of success is based on the likelihood of obtaining a career in the legal profession as a result of their studies. In a jurisdiction such as the US, where law is a postgraduate, more vocationally orientated programme of study, this may have some feasibility. However, in a jurisdiction such as the UK, although a majority of law students appear to begin their studies with this aspiration (Hardee, 2012), it is only a minority of law students who will go on into legal practice (see, for example, the Law Society of England and Wales, 2017). While, as Unger illustrates in this volume (Chapter 1), there remain close and complex links between law schools and the legal profession, to measure success on this metric alone would either seem to suggest law schools are unsuccessful (in the UK, at least) or to disregard the majority of their graduates. As noted in preceding paragraphs, there is a wider emphasis on employability now running through higher education policy and discourse that could suggest that a broader measure of vocational success is appropriate. However, to focus solely on this would arguably diminish the value of the law school. It would give legal education little credence or value for its own sake, but simply position it as a conduit for knowledge production. Therefore, it is hard to see how such a measure can be adequate, let alone sufficient (Guth and Ashford, 2014).

Fung, when exploring the question of what a university is for generally, suggests that:

> There are perceived tensions within universities between those who see education predominantly in terms of training for the benefit of economic success, whether that of the individual or society, and those who conceive of education as being a more rounded set of cultural practices which are fundamentally about human development and 'becoming', human relations, and the development of a 'good' society. (2017, p.9)

We therefore return to my earlier critique of traditional legal education as focused solely on students' intellectual capabilities or qualities. If employability alone does not suffice, does solely intellectual, cognitive development instead become the measurement of success? Interestingly, on any measure of employability this falls down as disregarding the so-called 'soft skills' that have clear emotional and affective components and are increasingly being emphasised by employers, including law firms (Andrews and Higson, 2008; Jones, 2018). However, I would argue that, more importantly, such a wholly cognitive focus is flawed on many other levels, too. It ignores the emotional, relational components of law that pervade all aspects of the law school and that can add key insights into our understanding of law students and legal education more generally. Bradney's discussion in this volume's conclusion argues that a law school's primary duty is towards its university. He suggests that this encompasses not only financial support but, more importantly, a need to ensure that law contributes to the intellectual life at the centre of higher education. His argument is clear and compelling, but I would suggest we need to determine what is perceived and understood as intellectual in a way that encompasses relationality and uses this as a way to identify and navigate to the heart of higher education, a place where cognitive and non-cognitive are valued as legitimate and important parts of a university's mission. From the single law student seeking a closer relationship to her law degree, to the entanglements of law school stakeholders and the entrapments of neoliberalism, a relational prism is key to navigate the challenges and opportunities that lie ahead.

References

Abe, J. A. A. (2011). Positive emotions, emotional intelligence, and successful experiential learning. *Personality and Individual Differences*, 51(7), 817–822.

Andrews, J. and Higson, H. (2008). Graduate employability, 'soft skills' versus 'hard' business knowledge: a European study. *Higher Education in Europe*, 33(4), 411–422.

Bergin, A. and Pakenham, K. (2015). Law student stress: relationships between academic demands, social isolation, career pressure, study/life imbalance and adjustment outcomes in law students. *Psychiatry, Psychology and Law*, 22(3), 388–406.

Bromberger, N. (2010). Enhancing law student learning – the nurturing teacher. *Legal Education Review*, 20(1–2), 45–57.

Brooks, S. L. (2016). Teaching relational lawyering. *Richmond Journal of Law & Public Interest*, 19(4), 401.

Brooks, S. L. (2006). Using therapeutic jurisprudence to build effective relationships with students, clients and communities. *Clinical Law Review*, 13(1), 213–230.

Brooks, S. L. and Madden, R. G. (2009). Relationship-centered lawyering: social science theory for transforming legal practice. *Revista Juridica Universidad de Puerto Rico*, 78(1), 23–42.

Burke, P. J. (2015). Re/imagining higher education pedagogies: gender, emotion and difference. *Teaching in Higher Education*, 20(4), 388–401.

Damasio, A. (2006). *Descartes' Error*. London, Vintage.

Feldman Barrett, L. (2017). *How Emotions are Made: The Secret Life of the Brain*. London, Pan Macmillan.

Frankham, J. (2016). Employability and higher education: the follies of the 'productivity challenge' in the Teaching Excellence Framework. *Journal of Education Policy*, 32(5), 628–641.

Fung, D. (2017). *A Connected Curriculum for Higher Education*. London, UCL Press.

Gerdy, K. B. (2008). Clients, empathy and compassion: introducing first-year students to the 'heart' of lawyering. *Nebraska Law Review*, 87(1), 1–61.

Grossi, R. (2015). Understanding law and emotion. *Emotion Review*, 7(1), 55–60.

Guth, J. and Ashford, C. (2014). The Legal Education and Training Review: regulating socio-legal and liberal legal education. *The Law Teacher*, 48(1), 5–19.

Hardee, M. (2012). *Career Expectations of Students on Qualifying Law Degrees in England and Wales*, The Higher Education Academy, https://www.heacademy.ac.uk/knowledge-hub/career-expectations-students-qualifying-law-degrees-england-and-wales (accessed 4 August 2019).

James, C. (2008a). Lawyers' wellbeing and professional legal education. *The Law Teacher*, 42(1) 85–97.

James, C. (2008b). Lawyer dissatisfaction, emotional wellbeing and clinical legal education. *Legal Education Review*, 18(1–2), 123–137.

Jones, E. (2019). *Emotions in the Law School. Transforming legal education through the passions.* Abingdon and New York, Routledge.

Jones, E. (2018). Making practice more affective: emotional intelligence as a legal meta-competency. *European Journal of Current Legal Issues*, 24(1).

Lange, E. A. (2018). Transforming transformative education through ontologies of relationality. *Journal of Transformative Education*, 16(4) 280–301

Law Society of England and Wales (2017). *Trends in the Solicitors' Profession Annual Statistics Report 2017*, https://www.lawsociety.org.uk/support-services/research-trends/annual-statistics-report-2017/ (accessed 4 August 2019).

Legal Education and Training Review (2013). *Setting Standards. The Future of Legal Services Education and Training Regulation in England and Wales*, http://www.letr.org.uk/wp-content/uploads/LETR-Report.pdf (accessed 4 August 2019).

Lynch, K. (2006). Neoliberalism and marketisation: the implications for higher education. *European Education Research Journal*, 5(1), 1–12.

Malpass, J. (2012). The place of mobility: technology, connectivity, and individualization. In Wilken, R. and Goggin, G. (eds.). *Mobile Technology and Place.* Abingdon and New York, Routledge, pp. 26–38.

Maroney, T. A. (2006). Law and emotion: a proposed taxonomy of an emerging field . *Law and Human Behaviour*, 13(2), 119–142.

Mengel, F., Sauermann, J. and Zölitz, U. (2019). Gender bias in teaching evaluations. *Journal of the European Economic Association*, 17(2), 535–566.

Mertz, E. (2007). *The Language of Law School: Learning to 'Think Like a Lawyer'.* Oxford and New York, Oxford University Press.

Pearce, R. and Wald, E. G. (2012). Rethinking lawyer regulation: how a relational approach would improve professional rules and roles. *Michigan Stage Law Review*, 513–536.

Quality Assurance Agency (2015). *Subject Benchmark Statement Law*, http://www.qaa.ac.uk/publications/information-and guidance/PubID=2966#.VhtqPexVhBc (accessed 4 August 2019).

Reeves, J. and Le Mare, L. (2017). Supporting teachers in relational pedagogy and social emotional education: a qualitative exploration. *International Journal of Emotional Education*, 9(1), 85–98.

Saevi, T. (2011). Lived relationality as fulcrum for pedagogical–ethical practice. *Studies in Philosophy and Education*, 30, 455–461

Sheldon, K. M. and Krieger, L. S. (2004). Does law school undermine law students? examining changes in goals, values, and well-being. *Behavioral Sciences and the Law*, 22, 261–286.

Sommerlad, H. (2007). Researching and theorising the process of professional identity formation. *Journal of Law and Society*, 34(2), 109–217.

Stier, S. (1992). Reframing legal skills: relational lawyering. *Journal of Legal Education*. 42, 303.

Tani, M. and Vines, P. (2009). Law students' attitudes to education: pointers to depression in the legal academy and the profession? *Legal Education Review*, 19, 3–39.

Towness O'Brien, M., Tang, S. and Hall, K. (2011). No time to lose: negative impact on law student wellbeing may begin in year one. *International Journal of the First Year in Higher Education*, 2(2), 49–60.

Twining, W. (1994). *Blackstone's Tower. The English Law School.* London, Stevens & Sons/Sweet & Maxwell.

Zepke, N. (2015). What future for student engagement in neoliberal times? *Higher Education*, 69(4), 693–704.

Zepke, N. (2014). Student engagement research in higher education: questioning an academic orthodoxy. *Teaching in Higher Education*, 19(6), 697–708.

Part I

Legal education and external stakeholders

In the following two chapters, Unger and Zhou and Palmer reflect on a number of different pressures exerted on law schools and on individual legal academics in both the UK and China by actors who are located outside academia. While the socio-political situations of these jurisdictions are very different, in both of them law schools and legal academics face challenges that require astute political handling if legal education is to retain any significant degree of autonomy.

Chapter 1

Legal education future(s) – the changing relationship between law schools and the legal profession

Andy Unger

Introduction

At first glance, it would appear that since law schools in China are operating in the context of a very different political system from those in England and Wales, they would not have much in common when it came to a consideration of the pressures exerted on legal education by external actors. However, in broad terms, law schools in both jurisdictions are faced with pressures to change the education they deliver in order to satisfy the agendas of political actors outside their immediate environment. As Zhou and Palmer comment in their analysis of Chinese legal education in the following chapter:

> [I]t is perhaps better to see China as possessing a 'political-legal' culture rather than a legal culture. The continuing traditional influence of strong government, and the dominant position of the Chinese Communist Party in the administration of justice, mean that law and the legal system have strongly political and administrative dimensions. (Zhou and Palmer, this volume)

In England and Wales, the pressures on law schools to deliver outcomes specified by external players, while not exactly the same as those felt by Chinese law schools, are nevertheless numerous.

The changing relationship between law schools in England and Wales and the legal profession

Both higher education and the legal profession are undergoing a shift away from traditional professional self-regulation towards regulation by market forces. The legal profession has seen the loss of traditional monopolies, the introduction of competition and the loss of much of the Legal Aid system (Abel, 1988, 2003, Green and Sandbach, 2016). Higher education has undergone a process of massification with rates of participation rising from around one-fifth to nearly one-half in the last 30 years. The proportion of school leavers going on to some form of higher education is currently 49.8% (Department of Education, 2018). The benefits of that expansion in terms of diversity and social inclusion are obvious, but there have also been significant drawbacks. The increasing number of students going to university has raised the question of who should pay for higher education and the answer in England and Wales has been the students themselves, with university fees rising to full cost at £9,250 and the government introducing a student loan scheme hoping to ensure that all students can afford their education (Student Finance England, 2019). The question of value for money has in turn led to two further developments. The first is an increased emphasis on employability as the object of higher education, rather than the wider liberal education goals articulated by Robbins (1963). The second has been the introduction of business management techniques to ensure quality of provision, so that we are all now familiar with concepts such as outcomes-focused course design and the idea of academic freedom has been tempered by the 'reasonable management request'.

The result of these changes has been the marketisation of higher education in England and Wales with employers and students encouraged to make informed choices based on key sources of data such as the National Student Survey, the Destination of Leavers of Higher Education Survey and now the new Teaching Excellence Framework (TEF) (Office for Students, 2019) to complement the longstanding Research Excellence Framework (REF). TEF rankings of teaching quality in institutions as gold, silver or bronze are drawn from a range of data, including course completion, the National Student Survey and Destination of Leavers in Higher Education and they may soon impact the level of fees that universities can charge for their courses. These data, compiled into league tables for universities and individual courses, can have measurable, but generally modest, impacts on student recruitment when rankings change (Broecke, 2015). Regardless of the degree of their impact and even if other factors are more significant, league table rankings certainly inform management strategy in many English and Welsh universities (Catcheside, 2012).

The legal profession has also been introduced to competition and external quality controls by the Legal Services Act 2007 (Boon, 2010). In its first year of operation, the Legal Services Board (LSB), established by the Act to oversee the regulation of all legal services by the respective 'Approved Regulators' (including the Bar Council, the Chartered Institute of Legal Executives, the Council for Licensed Conveyancers and the Solicitors Regulation Authority), described itself as 'the independent body responsible for overseeing the regulation of lawyers in England and Wales. Our goal is to reform and modernise the legal services market place by putting the interests of consumers at the heart of the system, reflecting the objectives of the statute that created us, the Legal Services Act 2007' (Legal Services Board, 2011).

The Solicitors Qualifying Examination

It is in this context that the Solicitors Regulation Authority (SRA) has outlined radical changes to the way in which solicitors will qualify from September 2021, proposing the introduction of centrally set and assessed examinations of legal knowledge and procedure, ethics and legal skills, to be known as the Solicitors Qualifying Examination (SQE). The framework for the proposal has already been approved (LSB, 2018) and, although final approval is still outstanding, the general expectation is that SQE will go ahead from autumn 2021. Few UK law schools can afford to ignore these changes.

The Bar Standards Board is introducing similar changes for barristers (Bar Standards Board, 2019), but they are less radical and retain the existing stages of qualification envisaged by the Ormrod Report; academic, professional (comprising institutional training and 'in-training') and continuing education or training (Ormrod, 1971, para. 185). The Ormrod requirement for a graduate profession led to the establishment of what has become known as the qualifying law degree as the first stage of qualification for barristers or solicitors. Law schools are free to offer any law syllabus they choose, taught and assessed as they see fit, provided the degree has been validated as required within their university and the wider HE sector. But for the course to be recognised for the purposes of professional qualification it must meet the professions' stated requirements for a qualifying law degree, which were until recently articulated in a joint statement (Joint Academic Stage Board, 2012). At present, aspiring barristers and solicitors go on to take the bar professional training course or the legal practice course to be taught and assessed in the legal knowledge, procedure, ethics and skills appropriate to their chosen branch of the profession. Finally, candidates undertake supervised work experience as pupil barristers or trainee solicitors to complete their initial professional training. This chapter will focus on the changes to the way in which solicitors will qualify in the future (SRA, 2017).

The SRA proposals abandon the requirements for a qualifying law degree, the legal practice course and a training contract. These are replaced by the requirement for a degree (or equivalent), not necessarily in law, and passing two centrally set assessments – the Solicitors Qualifying Examination Stages 1 and 2. Intending solicitors must also undertake qualifying work experience supervised by a solicitor, although the solicitor's role is limited to ensuring they have an opportunity to learn from experience. Finally, candidates must pass character and suitability requirements. The proposed SQE Stage 1 assesses 'functioning legal knowledge' in three multiple choice question papers: 1) business, dispute resolution, contract, tort, 2) property, wills, solicitors' accounts and 3) public law, legal system, regulation, criminal. There is also a legal skills assessment on legal research and writing (SRA, 2019). All assessments are centrally set and assessed. SQE 2 comprises five skills assessments that must be taken and passed in two practice contexts of the candidate's choice, making a total of ten assessments. The skills are: client interviewing, advocacy/persuasive oral communication, case and matter analysis, legal research and written advice and legal drafting. The practice contexts are: criminal practice, dispute resolution, property, wills and the administration of estates and commercial and corporate practice. SQE 2 assessments are likely to last one hour and involve the use of simulated clients. Both SQE 1 and SQE 2 assessments will include unflagged ethical questions. The SRA will provide candidates with their scores for each of the modules, but will not provide grades for the examinations beyond 'pass' or 'fail' (SRAuthority, 2019). The SRA expects that many candidates will take SQE Stage 1 before their work-based experience and SQE Stage 2 at the end of their work experience. However, some city law firms have already indicated their intention to get their trainees to pass SQE 1 and SQE 2 as early as possible at the start of their work-based experience so that as much of their training as possible can focus on the specialisms they will practise (Law Society Gazette, 2018a).

Concerns about the Solicitors Qualifying Examination

One key difference between the proposals and the current arrangements is that a law degree or equivalent is no longer required for qualification. Another is that in future neither the law schools nor the profession are to be involved in the certification of competence to practise (SRA, 2017). At present, the law schools certify sufficiency of legal knowledge (by awarding a qualifying law degree or a graduate diploma in legal studies) and sufficiency of procedural knowledge and professional skills (bar vocational course, legal practice course) and professional practitioners certify fitness to practise following supervised 'in-training' as a pupil barrister or trainee solicitor. During the consultation process, the SRA expressed concern about differential pass rates on LPC courses and assumed that the reason must be differential assessment standards (as opposed to entry standards or teaching standards) (SRA, 2016a). It did not expressly say but might be assumed to have been equally worried about incompetent solicitors being able to sign off incompetent trainees to become incompetent solicitors of the future. In any event, it has taken control of the assessment of day one competence itself and hired a private training company, Kaplan, to administer the SQE for it (Law Society Gazette, 2018b). This is a significant reduction of professional self-regulation and does not appear to carry the profession's support (Hall, 2017). No one doubts the right and responsibility of the SRA to act in the public interest to ensure that newly qualified solicitors demonstrate high and consistent standards of competence, but many of the stakeholders consulted by the SRA have expressed considerable concern as to whether the SQE is a necessary reform or fit for purpose. Concerns include loss of status as a graduate profession (particularly with regard to competitor law firms internationally), a refusal to benchmark the QAA against the national qualifications framework and whether the SQE is, in effect, a lowering of entry standards. Another concern is the inability for candidates to qualify in specialist areas ranging from employment law and family law to intellectual property and mergers and acquisitions (SRA, 2016b). Despite the project being entitled 'Training for Tomorrow', the idea of a general practitioner of law is anomalous, since modern solicitors are all specialists to a greater or lesser extent and likely to be considered negligent if they were not (Legal Services Consumer Panel, 2010, para. 4.13). Finally, there are a number of concerns that the proposals will have a negative impact on equality of entry into the profession. It is not clear that the proposals will be any cheaper and the structure and nature of the assessments may have a negative impact on diversity by favouring candidates with aptitude for and experience of the assessment methods relied on and, particularly, those that can afford additional tuition and revision support (City of London Law Society, 2018a).

A recent special edition of the journal, *Law Teacher* (2018, Vol. 4), entitled 'From LETR to SQE: reforming legal education and training in England and Wales', provides a detailed review of the SQE and identifies many of the concerns that the law schools have. Mason and Guth in their editorial 'Re-claiming our discipline' condemn the SRA reforms as inappropriate: 'In our view not only are they significantly flawed in terms of their regulatory objective and pedagogy but they also do significant violence to law as an academic discipline' (Mason and Guth, 2018). Mason warns that the structure of SQE 1 reduces law and the truth of legal propositions to the ability of a candidate to predict the application of legal thought by others. He called this 'bleak legal realism' (Mason, 2018). Guth and Dutton warn that SQE-focused degrees will be dull, lacking options and theory, a poor preparation for legal practice and have the potential to make the inequalities inherent in the legal education system worse (Guth and Dutton, 2018). Morrison warns that multiple choice assessments may stifle creativity in learning and assessment (Morrison, 2018). Hall warns that MCQ assessments have the potential to 'trivialise content and threaten validity' (Hall, 2018). Bradney warns that any law school claiming that its LLB offers advantages in passing the SQE may have to justify its claim to the Advertising Standards Authority and points to two recent complaints against the University of Law as an illustration (Bradney, 2018).

Even the authors of the Legal Education and Training Review (which preceded the SQE proposals) doubt whether the SQE can deliver its intended benefits:

> Critics of competence-based approaches have long raised concerns about the ability of competence frameworks to capture the richness of high level professional learning, and highlighted risks of both under- and over-inclusiveness. All of these problems may flow from the current design of the SQE. First, the breadth of the knowledge component (particularly in the SQE1) continues to lock training into a model of preparation for general practice that no longer exists. Combined with breadth assessment through primarily multiple choice questions, and we have a model that can be said to ensure baseline competence in only the most rudimentary sense.

> Secondly, while many of the core professional skills (research, oral and written communication, advocacy) are constants, newer capabilities are becoming critical. The Report highlighted commercial and social awareness (which is, at least in the commercial context, captured by the new outcomes), but capacities such as a proper understanding of legal tech, project management, and 'design-thinking' are all examples of 'new' areas of competence currently being emphasised in practice ... Thirdly, there is little to suggest that the SRA has done anything to address, particularly through its assessment design, the impoverished focus on ethics and professionalism, and particularly the need for a broader education in professional values high-lighted by the Report. (Ching et al., 2018)

Julian Webb has additionally observed that the SQE approach does little to enable students to obtain a broad range of competences, including the capacity for emotional intelligence, ethical and values-based reasoning, critical and creative thinking, and the ability to deal with high levels of complexity and uncertainty. He says that 'by underplaying such attributes we do our students few favours, either intellectually or in terms of employability' (Webb, 2017).

The SQE proposals bundle up the legal knowledge required to pass a qualifying law degree with the procedure required to pass the LPC into the SQE Stage 1 and then test skills in the SQE Stage 2. The net effect is, potentially, to reduce the breadth and depth of legal knowledge required to become a solicitor. The SQE Stage 1 comprises online multiple choice questions (the consultation document suggests 120 questions per three-hour paper) and appears to focus on straightforward legal issues set in the context of legal practice and procedure. Currently, qualifying law degrees must satisfy the requirements of the Quality Assurance Agency (QAA) Law Benchmark (2015), whose requirements for law degree outcomes include: 'viii) ability to recognise ambiguity and deal with uncertainty in law' and 'ix) ability to produce a synthesis of relevant doctrinal and policy issues, presentation of a reasoned choice between alternative solutions and critical judgement of the merits of particular arguments' (Quality Assurance Agency, 2015). By contrast, the SRA says that the depth and breadth of legal knowledge required of candidates in any of the assessments is that of 'functioning legal knowledge'. This means that a candidate should be able to identify relevant core legal principles or rules, whether derived from cases, statutes or regulatory sources, and apply them appropriately and effectively to client-based and ethical problems and situations encountered in practice. Candidates will not be required to recall case names or cite statutory authority except where specified (SRA, 2019). It is not clear how legal complexity and ambiguity can be assessed by questions that take an average of 90 seconds to answer (SRA, 2017, para. 52 of the SQE consultation). The effect is likely to encourage students to focus on the application of straightforward principles of law in everyday practice situations without sufficient regard to complexity and ambiguity as required by the QAA Law Benchmark. It doesn't make clear when a prospective solicitor might be expected to study appellate as opposed to first instance law. Students qualifying without having taken a law degree will be less prepared for practice at the highest standard of competence while students who qualify with a law degree may be thought to have engaged in unnecessary time and expense if they study subjects and topics outside the SQE syllabus. This is likely to impact on professional standards or diversity or both.

Work-based experience is to become 'an opportunity to learn from experience'. In the consultation document, the SRAs say it will not require firms to make any judgments about whether a candidate is competent to be a solicitor. Instead, it will test their competence by the SQE Stage 2 assessments. It will only require the supervising solicitor to sign a declaration that the candidate has had the opportunity to develop some or all of the competences in the Statement of Solicitor Competence through the required period of workplace experience (SRA, 2017, para. 100). By contrast, under current arrangements every trainee solicitor undertaking a Training Contract has a supervisor who has responsibility for the development of their professional skills in terms of structure, supervision and feedback, not just for providing an opportunity to develop competence and to ensure their competence for their role. It is the supervising solicitor who signs off the final stage of qualification (SRA, 2016a). The net result is that there is no requirement for the teaching or supervised practice and development of legal skills. Candidates can simply obtain two years of paralegal work and train to pass the SQE 2 skills test. The question is whether the SQE 2 assessments are sufficient in themselves to ensure candidates fully develop the necessary legal skills for competent practice. The model of Objective Structured Clinical Examinations (OSCEs) is drawn from medical training, but UK doctors take a five-year medical degree that includes academic medical education, extensive supervised clinical practice and work-based learning, so the comparison would seem to be inapposite. As can be seen above, many legal academics and practitioners doubt that the SQE can ensure the full competence of a day one solicitor as set out in the Statement of Solicitor Competence (SRA, 2015). If it cannot, the SQE will effectively lower standards, at least by comparison with current best practice. There are also significant concerns about diversity, including the potential cost of the SQE, currently estimated to be £3,000–£4,500 for a single attempt of SQE 1 and 2 (SRA, 2018c), in addition to significant course fees. The advantages to students who can afford additional tuition and assessment practice and resits are obvious. This, together with the narrow assessment strategy and the potential emergence of a two-tier hierarchy between academic and vocational law degrees suggests that there are grounds for significant concern about the future of legal education and training in England and Wales. The SRA no longer claims that the flexibility of the SQE will improve diversity of access to the profession. Neither does it claim any more that the SQE will necessarily be cheaper than the current arrangements.

If the SQE is not cheaper, does not assist diversity nor raise standards, one might wonder what it is for and why it is needed. One possible answer is that the effect, intended or not, may be to make it easier to qualify and set up practice and thereby to increase competition in the legal services market. In a parallel consultation on standards and regulation, the SRA considered allowing newly qualified solicitors to open their own law firms immediately on qualification (SRA, 2018a). In response to feedback concerned about the removal of the requirement for the newly qualified solicitors to remain under the supervision of an experienced solicitor for three years post-qualification, the SRA compromised by requiring that they must employ at least one solicitor with three years or more experience if they want to establish their own firm immediately (SRA, 2018b, para. 50). This substantially undermines the effectiveness of the rule, because now the more experienced solicitor may be an employee rather than a manager. This rule change is explicitly concerned with removing barriers to competition. Whilst there is no doubt that advice deserts are emerging (Law Society Gazette, 2019) and only the very wealthy can afford access to justice (Green and Sandbach, 2016), we will have to wait and see whether the SQE and related reforms have any positive impact on competition and whether such competition will actually improve access to justice. Mason suggests not, that access to justice can only be affected marginally, and often not directly, by regulators (Mason et al., 2012).

The threats and opportunities posed by SQE for law schools

The SQE presents a number of threats and opportunities for law schools in England and Wales. On the one hand, the dropping of the requirement of a qualifying law degree (or GDLS) may mean that students choose to study other degrees and prepare for the SQE by themselves or by taking a specialised tutorial course, such as the courses offered by Barbri for the New York Bar exams and now the SRA Qualified Lawyers Transfer Scheme (Barbri, 2019). On the other hand, the requirement for a degree and the legal knowledge required to pass the exams mean that it is likely that many candidates will continue to choose to study a law degree. Further, student loans are available for LLB and LLM courses but not for courses aimed exclusively at preparation for the SQE. In terms of cost and flexibility, degree apprenticeships are an obviously attractive option. However, it is not clear whether law firms are currently recruiting a significant number of school leavers onto full degree apprenticeship routes. Data on solicitor apprenticeship starts are not disaggregated from those for business, administration and other law apprenticeships (Parliament. House of Commons, 2019, 4.2) but looking at legal recruitment websites suggests that paralegal and CILEx apprenticeships are more popular (Chambers Student Guide, 2019; LawCareers.Net, 2019).

The great opportunity for law schools is the freedom to design law degrees outside the traditional QLD requirements. The BSB will still require a QLD but will be satisfied by any degree that meets the QAA law benchmark. This means that law schools are free to redesign their courses with distinct pedagogies and move out of the shadow of the professional bodies' historic insistence on core foundation subjects and preference for unseen examinations. If desired, more time can be made available for theory, skills, social welfare law, international and comparative law, commercial awareness and commercial specialisms and/or emerging areas such as law and technology. Different teaching and learning strategies can be deployed or extended and law schools can now rethink their assessment strategies if they choose. As Phil Race, among many others, insists, assessment in higher education is broken and we spend too much time assessing the wrong things and, even, the wrong people in ways that obstruct rather than assist learning (Race, 2014).

However, although the most common response from law schools has been to condemn and turn their back on the SQE, it will be a brave and confident school that ignores it entirely. Although less than half of all law graduates eventually qualify as lawyers, many more start their studies with qualification as at least an option in mind. A law degree that addresses professional practice and skills and the SQE syllabus and assessment methodology may be attractive to them, especially if it does not sacrifice the other important elements of a degree education. Some law schools will carry on exactly as they are or take the freedom to develop academically interesting degrees that are not yoked to the requirements of professional qualification. Others may choose to develop degrees that prepare students fully or partly for the SQE and the other qualifying examinations. Market forces in the form of student choice (and student satisfaction) may mean that law schools that are neither sufficiently prestigious nor addressing professional practice in some way may be squeezed in terms of recruitment. Some may then have to change their courses out of necessity.

So far, very few law schools have expressed an intention to develop law degrees that prepare graduates exclusively to take the SQE immediately on graduation. As can be seen, many legal academics think that such degrees will have very little to recommend them other than the potentially significant saving of a year of time and fees on the road to qualification. Most law schools that choose to address the SQE are likely to develop courses that address it alongside other outcomes and aim to give their students a head start when they begin their postgraduate (or fourth year) of SQE studies. This approach mitigates some of the concerns about SQE degrees but raises the old debate about whether a law degree is a liberal arts education or a preparation for practice. However, the two need not be mutually exclusive choices. Guth and Ashford have argued for 'a more nuanced understanding of liberal legal education: one which does not oppose the teaching or exploration of practice relevant subjects or the learning of professional knowledge and skills; but one where these are acquired, if indeed they are, because they facilitate or come with the wider learning that constitutes a liberal education' (Guth and Ashford, 2014). Equally, Yorke contends persuasively that employability is not inconsistent with good academic learning (Yorke, 2006). If the SQE effectively lowers standards and does 'significant violence to law as an academic discipline' (Mason and Guth, 2018), it could be an exciting proposition to deploy innovative and effective pedagogies to redress the deficit and to build a 'multifunctional' law school as Twining suggested 25 years ago (Twining, 1994). For law schools already committed to or interested in clinical legal education, there is an opportunity here to expand or develop experiential learning as part of a strategy to engage students in law, theory and practice in a way that also begins their preparation for the new professional assessments should they wish to take them.

There are many rich resources for law schools willing to take up the challenge. Recent examples include Paul Maharg's vision of a pragmatist law teaching practice built around experience, ethics, technology and collaboration (Maharg, 2016), Grimes' survey of experiential learning best practice around the world (Grimes, 2018) and the extended argument from Thomas et al. that clinical legal education is the learning of the law and its implementation in the real world through action and reflection that has educational, public interest and employability benefits (Thomas et al., 2018). Developments in the United States are also interesting. The American Bar Association (ABA) Standards and Rules of Procedure for Approval of Law Schools 2014–2015 now require a minimum six credits of experiential learning for qualifying postgraduate law degrees and this has given a boost to simulation, clinic and placement modules (American Bar Association, 2015). Clearly the ABA is moving in a direction different from that of the SRA. In the UK, York University and University of Northumbria are interesting examples of what can be achieved in terms of integrating problem-based learning and clinical legal education into academically rigorous degrees. Paul Maharg's current project is the Simulated Client Initiative, which aligns with the prospective SQE 2 assessments (Maharg, 2019). Dunn, Roper and Kennedy (2018) have begun to consider if and how clinical legal experience might count towards qualifying work experience. Law schools intending to offer courses that address the SQE will need to develop appropriate SQE 1 MCQ question banks and there is currently a collaborative project among several law schools to work on this together. So, although the legal profession, particularly the SRA, is distancing itself from law schools and taking qualification back into its own hands, there are reasons to expect that, at least in some law schools, legal practice may take up a larger space in the curriculum than it has in the past.

Comparing law schools in England and Wales to those in the People's Republic of China

As will be seen in the following chapter, law schools in the People's Republic of China face similar challenges to those in law schools in England and Wales. The chapter will introduce the familiar theme of a centrally set qualifying examination and a debate about the extent to which law schools should prepare their students for legal practice, set in the context of a (for many) unfamiliar socialist, civil legal system. Since the end of the Cultural Revolution, the PRC has pursued a policy of introducing 'the Rule of Law with Chinese characteristics', meaning the rule of law without the separation of powers or any limits on the constitutional supremacy of the Chinese Communist Party (Castellucci, 2007). For an interesting, English-language discussion of this topic by Chinese scholars, see of Rule of Law in China: Spotlight Issues (2016). The Chinese experience casts a comparative light on our own debates about regulation and independence as we move beyond traditional professional peer regulation (Deech, 2012; Deech, 2019), showing a cross-cultural recognition of the importance of lawyers and judges in maintaining social stability and promoting prosperity, which, as we know from recent examples, is not to say that the independence of lawyers is complete or uncontested in either jurisdiction (Amnesty International, 2018; Amnesty International, 2017).

References

Abel, R. (1988). *The Making of the English Legal Profession*1800–1988. London, Beard Books (republished 2005).

Abel, R. (2003). *English Lawyers between Market and State: The Politics of Professionalism*. Oxford, Oxford University Press.

American Bar Association (2015), *Standards and Rules of Procedure for Approval of Law Schools*, www.americanbar.org/content/dam/aba/publications/misc/legal_education/Standards/2014_2015_aba_standards_chapter3.authcheckdam.pdf (accessed 5 May 2019).

Amnesty International (2018). *Third Anniversary of the Lawyers Crackdown in China: Where are the Human Rights Lawyers?*, https://www.amnesty.org/en/latest/campaigns/2018/07/china-human-rights-lawyers-crackdown-third-anniversary/ (accessed 6 June 2019).

Bar Standards Board (2019). *Future of Bar Training*, https://www.barstandardsboard.org.uk/media-centre/press-releases-and-news/bsb-agrees-further-key-elements-for-the-future-of-bar-training/ (accessed 5 May 2019).

Barbri (2019). *Barbri Online Preparation for the SRA Qualified Lawyers Transfer Scheme*, https://barbriqlts.com/ (accessed 5 May 2019).

Boon, A. (2010). Professionalism under the Legal Services Act 2007, University of Westminster School of Law Research Paper No. 11–15. *International Journal of the Legal Profession*, 17(3), 195–232.

Bradney, A. (2018). The success of university law schools in England and Wales: or how to fail. *The Law Teacher*, 52(4), 490–498.

Broecke, S. (2015). University rankings: do they matter in the UK? *Education Economics*, 23(2), 137–161.

Castellucci, I. (2007). Rule of law with Chinese characteristics. *Annual Survey of International & Comparative Law*, 13(1), Article 4, https://digitalcommons.law.ggu.edu/cgi/viewcontent.cgi?article=1112&context=annlsurvey
(accessed 6 June 2019).

Catcheside, K. (2012). What do universities actually gain by improving league table performance?, *The Guardian*, 16 March, https://www.theguardian.com/higher-education-network/blog/2012/mar/16/league-table-performance (accessed 10 May 2019).

Chambers Student Guide (2019). *Legal Apprenticeship Vacancies*, https://www.chambersstudent.co.uk/where-to-start/newsletter/legal-apprenticeship-vacancies (accessed 10 May 2019).

Ching, J., Maharg, P., Sherr, A. and Webb, J. (2018. Legal education and training review: a five-year retro/prospective, *The Law Teacher*, 52(4), 384–396.

City of London Law Society (Education Committee) (2018a). *CLLSSubmission to the Legal Services Board on the SRA's Application for the Approval of Amendments to its Regulatory Arrangements in Respect of the Introduction of the Solicitors Qualifying Examination*, https://www.legalservicesboard.org.uk/what_we_do/regulation/pdf/2018/CLLS_Letter_28_Feb_2018_SRA_SQE_Application.pdf (accessed 12 May 2019).

City of London Law Society (2018b). *City of London Law Society Letter to the SRA*, http://www.citysolicitors.org.uk/attachments/article/104/Training%20Committee%20-%20Timing%20of%20the%20SQE%20Stage%202%20Examination%20-%2008%2010%2018.pdf (accessed 12 May 2019).

Deech, Baroness (2012). *The Legal Profession – Regulating for Independence, Gresham College Lecture*, http://www.gresham.ac.uk/lectures-and-events/the-legal-profession-regulating-for-independence (accessed 6 June 2019).

Department of Education (2018). *Government Statistics on Participation in HE*, https://www.gov.uk/government/collections/statistics-on-higher-education-initial-participation-rates accessed 10 May 2019).

Dunn, R., Roper, V. and Kennedy, V. (2018). Clinical legal education as qualifying work experience for solicitors. *The Law Teacher*, 2(4), 439–452.

Green, L. and Sandbach, J. (2016). Justice in free fall: a report on the decline of civil legal aid in England and Wales. *Legal Action*, December 2016/January 2017, 9–11, https://www.lag.org.uk/?id=201911&fromsearch=true#iosfirsthighlight (accessed 10 May 2019).

Grimes, R. (ed.) (2018). *Re-thinking Legal Education Under the Civil and Common Law: A Road Map for Constructive Change*. Abingdon, Routledge.

Guth, J. and Ashford, C. (2014). The legal education and training review: regulating socio-legal and liberal legal education? *The Law Teacher*, 48(1), 5–19.

Guth, J. and Dutton, K. (2018). SQE-ezed out: SRA, status and stasis. *The Law Teacher*, 52(4), 425–438.

Hall, E. (2018). Glass houses: how might we decide on a 'good enough' assessment to become a solicitor? *The Law Teacher*, 52(4), 453–466.

Hall, E. (2017). Notes on the SRA report of the consultation on the Solicitors Qualifying Exam: 'comment is free, but facts are sacred'. *The Law Teacher*, 51(3), 364–372.

Joint Academic Stage Board (2012). *Joint Academic Stage Board Handbook*, https://www.barstandardsboard.org.uk/media/1472203/joint-academic-stage-board-handbook_-_nov_2012.pdf (accessed 20 April 2019).

LawCareers.Net (2019). *Legal Apprenticeship Vacancies*, https://www.lawcareers.net/Starting-Out/Law-Apprenticeships-Guide/LegalApprenticeshipVacancies (accessed 10 May 2019).

Law Society Gazette (2019). *Society Exposes 'Catastrophic' Advice Deserts*, https://www.lawgazette.co.uk/practice/society-exposes-catastrophic-housing-advice-deserts/5070051.article (accessed 10 May 2019).

Law Society Gazette (2018a). https://www.lawgazette.co.uk/law/firms-ponder-city-specific-training-to-prepare-for-super-exam/5068012.article (accessed 12 May 2019).

Law Society Gazette (2018b). https://www.lawgazette.co.uk/law/super-exam-provider-revealed-but-costs-still-unknown/5067132.article (accessed 11 May 2019).

Legal Services Board (2018). *Legal Services Board Approves Framework for SRA'sNnew Admission Requirements for Solicitors*, https://www.legalservicesboard.org.uk/news_publications/LSB_news/PDF/2018/20180327LSB_Approves_SRA_SQE_Application.html (accessed 10 May 2019).

Legal Services Board (2011). *Annual Report and Accounts*, https://assets.publishing.service.gov.uk/government/uploads/system/uploads/attachment_data/file/247574/1056.pdf (accessed 12 May 2019).

Legal Services Consumer Panel (2010). *Quality in Legal Services*, http://www.legalservicesconsumerpanel.org.uk/publications/research_and_reports/documents/ConsumerPanel_QualityinLegalServicesReport_Final.pdf (accessed 10 May 2019).

Maharg, P. (2019). *Simulated Client Initiative*, http://paulmaharg.com/tag/simulated-client-initiative/ (accessed 10 May 2019).

Maharg, P. (2016). *Transforming Legal Education: Learning and Teaching in the Early Twenty-first Century*. Abingdon, Routledge.

Mason, L. (2018). SQEezing the jurisprudence out of the SRA's super exam: the SQE's bleak legal realism and the rejection of law's multimodal truth. *The Law Teacher*, 52(4), 409–424.

Mason, L. and Guth, J. (2018). Re-claiming our discipline. *The Law Teacher*, 52(4), 379–383.

Mason, S. (2019). *Independent Review of Legal Services Regulation: The Structure of Legal Services Regulation, Working Paper LSR-4, UCL Centre for Ethics and Law*, https://www.ucl.ac.uk/ethics-law/sites/ethics-law/files/2._irlsr_wp_lsr-2_scope_1810_0.pdf (accessed 6 June 2019).

Mason, S., Marley, O. and Dunn, S. (2012). *Improving Access to Justice: Scope of the Regulatory Objective*, https://stephenmayson.files.wordpress.com/2013/08/mayson-marley-dunn-2012-access-to-justice.pdf (accessed 12 May 2019).

Morrison, D. (2018). The SQE and creativity: a race to the bottom? *The Law Teacher*, 52(4), 467–477.

Observer (2017). *Ministers 'Undermined Law' over Iraq War Crimes Allegations*, https://www.theguardian.com/law/2017/jul/22/iraq-war-crimes-ministry-of-defence (accessed 6 June 2019).

Office for Students (2019). *What is the Teaching Excellence Framework*, https://www.officeforstudents.org.uk/advice-and-guidance/teaching/what-is-the-tef/ (accessed 10 June 2019).

Ormrod, Lord Justice (1971). *Report of the Committee on Legal Education, Presented to Parliament by the Lord High Chancellor by Command of Her Majesty*, March 1971 (Cmnd, 4595). London, HMSO.

Parliament. House of Commons (2019). *Apprenticeship Statistics: England (House of Commons Library Briefing Paper No. 06113)*, http://researchbriefings.files.parliament.uk/documents/SN06113/SN06113.pdf (accessed 10 May 2019).

Quality Assurance Agency (2015). *QAA Law Benchmark*, http://www.qaa.ac.uk/docs/qaa/subject-benchmark-statements/sbs-law-15.pdf?sfvrsn=ff99f781_8 (accessed 11 May 2019).

Race, P. (2014). *Making Learning Happen*, 3rd ed.. London, Sage.

Robbins, Lord (1963). *Higher Education: Report of the Committee Appointed by the Prime Minister under the Chairmanship of Lord Robbins, 1961–1963* (Cm. 2154). London, HMSO.

Rule of Law in China: Spotlight Issues (2016). *Rule of Law in China.* Beijing, Foreign Language Press.

Solicitors Regulation Authority (2019). *SQE Assessment Specification*, https://www.sra.org.uk/sra/policy/sqe/pilot/sqe-assessment-specification.page#blueprint (accessed 27 April 2019).

Solicitors Regulation Authority (2018a). *Looking to the Future: Phase Two of our Handbook Reforms*, http://www.sra.org.uk/sra/consultations/lttf-phase-two-handbook-reform.page (accessed 9 May 2019).

Solicitors Regulation Authority (2018b). *Post Consultation Responses*, http://www.sra.org.uk/sra/consultations/lttf-phase-two-handbook-reform.page (accessed 9 May 2019).

Solicitors Regulation Authority (2018c). *SQE to be Introduced in Autumn 2021*, https://www.sra.org.uk/sra/news/press/sqe-launch-2021.page (accessed 10 May 2019).

Solicitors Regulation Authority (2017). *Consultation: A New Route to Qualification: the Solicitors Qualifying Examination and Consultation Responses*, https://www.sra.org.uk/sra/consultations/solicitors-qualifying-examination.page (accessed 9 May 2019).

Solicitors Regulation Authority (2016a). *Authorised Training Provider Information Pack*, https://www.sra.org.uk/trainees/resources/authorised-training-provider-information-pack.page (accessed 9 May 2019).

Solicitors Regulation Authority (2016b). *Training for Tomorrow: Assessing Competence. Consultation on a Proposal to Introduce the Solicitors' Qualifying Examination: SRA Response and Analysis of Responses*, https://www.sra.org.uk/sra/consultations/t4t-assessing-competence.page (accessed 16 May 2019).

Solicitors Regulation Authority (2015). *Statement of Solicitor Competence*, http://www.sra.org.uk/solicitors/competence-statement.page (accessed 10 May 2019).

Solicitors Regulation Authority (2007). *Day One Outcomes for Solicitors*, https://www.sra.org.uk/sra/news/day-one-outcomes-refined.page (accessed 12 May 2019).Student Finance England (2019). https://www.gov.uk/student-finance (accessed 25 April 2019).

Thomas, L., Vaughan, S., Malkhani, B. and Lynch, T. (eds.) (2018). *Reimagining Clinical Legal Education.* Oxford, Hart Publishing.

Twining, W. (1994). *Blackstone's Tower: The English Law School.* London, Sweet & Maxwell.

Webb, J. (2017). Preparing for practice in the 21st century: the role of legal education and its regulation. In Bergmans, B. (ed.). *Yearbook of Legal Education.* Berlin, Berliner Wissenschafts-Verlag, pp. 11–48.

Yorke, M. (2006). *Employability in Higher Education: What it Is – What it Is not, Higher Education Academy*, https://www.heacademy.ac.uk/knowledge-hub/employability-higher-education-what-it-what-it-not (accessed 10 May 2019).

Chapter 2

Changing legal education in China – the political legal system, academic study and professionalism

Ling Zhou and Michael Palmer[1]

Introduction

In search of economic growth, greater social stability and more regular engagement with the outside world, in the People's Republic of China ('China' or 'PRC'), a substantial body of legislation was enacted from the late 1970s onwards, including laws, regulations and implementation measures. A legal profession has emerged, and legal agencies have been revived and renovated so that they might better enforce the emerging corpus of law. The embrace of the rule of law in the 1982 Constitution as revised in 1999 also encouraged a growth in legal education so as to provide the personnel to staff the expanding legal institutions and to enhance legal consciousness throughout society.

Legal education in China has a complex relationship with the more general legal reform process initiated in 1979. In particular, there is no clear and positive relationship between formal legal education, on the one hand, and the administration of justice and professional practice of law, on the other. The former is seen as being mainly focused on *faxue* (法学) or 'academic law' and the latter on *falü* (法律) or 'positive law'. Such difficulties are common in many other jurisdictions around the world. However, given the importance of CCP control of the legal system, it is perhaps better to see China as possessing a 'political-legal' culture rather than a legal culture. The continuing traditional influence of strong government, and the dominant position of the Chinese Communist Party in the administration of justice mean that law and the legal system have strongly political and administrative dimensions (see Palmer, 2011, for a characterisation of 'legal culture' in the PRC). Despite the reform attempt to limit the leading position of the CCP in the 1982 Constitution, this foundational document has been infused with core CCP values, and in later years, the Party has continued to strengthen its control of what is called the 'political-legal system' (*zhengfa zhidu*: 政法制度) (Palmer, 2010). These encourage the recruitment and promotion of CCP politically supportive personnel for legal work.

This chapter and that by Unger suggest that in both the PRC and in England and Wales substantial reforms have taken place in the past three decades or so and these reforms are driven, in large part, by forces external to university law schools (even though the latter remain to a significant degree key deliverers of legal education) (Unger, this volume). However, as noted above, the system in China remains deeply embedded in a political-legal environment that stresses the importance of commitment to the ideology and leading position of the Chinese Communist Party. Unlike the PRC, in England and Wales, market forces and professional autonomy are important factors diluting – to some extent at least – the importance of university legal education, changes being justified by the rhetoric of enhancing access to justice and delivery of better quality legal services. The reforms of the qualifying exam in the two jurisdictions have revealed different approaches to the selection of future legal practitioners: England and Wales treats undergraduate education more as contributing to an all-round education, and increasingly positions professional legal training at postgraduate level in the hands of private legal institutions; while, as we will see in this chapter, the PRC has laid emphasis on the importance of an undergraduate law degree (which ordinarily is a four-year programme), hoping that this will improve standards of legal professionalism generally.

Indeed, there remains a significant lack of professional legal education in the PRC, this disinterest perhaps best explained as reflecting a view that professional skills are best learned through the direct experience of legal practice. There is less room in the PRC for innovation in undergraduate law degrees, but at the same time there are well-established specialised law degrees – such as international economic law – that give students the chance to acquire substantive knowledge that may well assist them in legal practice in due course. Lawyers in the PRC constitute an undivided (in formal terms) profession and in addition to requiring a law degree, the four main types of legal professional – lawyers, judges, procurators (prosecutors) and notaries – take a common qualifying test, the national judicial examination. Popular criticism of this examination in the PRC is probably as strong as the disapproval shown in many quarters towards the reforms in the Solicitors Qualifying Examination in England and Wales. The tuition fees in public higher education institutions that offer undergraduate degrees in law are much lower in the PRC than those charged in England and Wales, but competition to enter university by the common entrance examination is fierce. As yet in the PRC there are no nationwide, external, formal evaluations of faculty research and teaching performance, but internally there is a robust annual appraisal scheme of staff that enhances control of performance by university leaders. Legal ethics are not an important part of the undergraduate law degree in the PRC, but there is a strong emphasis – including by means of compulsory courses – on political education. The latter includes, for example, correct characterisation of political issues, education in the policies of the CCP, convincing students of the need to adopt and maintain a particular political outlook and student participation in public service projects such as teaching children in impoverished local communities.

The establishment of a unified Judicial Examination (*sifa kaoshi*: 司法考试) in 2002 opened a new chapter in China's legal education. The Judicial Examination, consisting mainly of a one-shot memory test of positive law, is the required ticket for law graduates who seek to enter the legal profession. The near-exclusive requirement of success in the bar exam for entry into the legal professions is a common feature of East Asian legal systems, and China is no exception. As elsewhere in East Asia, the pass rate for the judicial examination in China is rather low, with only 15 to 20% of all examinees actually passing the test each year. Some scholars (for example, Zhou and Qi, 2009, p.93) do indeed argue that the Chinese bar examination offers a well-designed set of questions that effectively test students' qualities and potential for legal practice, and that legal education should continue to be controlled by the Judicial Examination. Other commentators, such as Guo Xiang (2010, pp.62–63), argue that this exam is a failing system that merely tests students' ability to memorise the wording of statutes and to apply the law in hypothetical situations. It does not assess students' ability to analyse and apply law in realistic circumstances, and the exam questions (many of which are multiple choice) are disconnected from the realities of legal practice. Reform is needed and, in particular, legal education in law schools improved, so that students' ability to understand, analyse and apply law is enhanced significantly.

Continuing reform of the Judicial Examination has also triggered a more general debate on what should be the goals of China's legal education: whether undergraduate law schools should serve the purpose of 'nurturing' all-round legal talent (by providing education in 'academic law') or be aimed at preparing students who can pass the Judicial Examination and then practise law (by providing a rigorous education in 'positive law'). Another view is that undergraduate legal education should focus on a student's all-around development, or perhaps a more general education in legal studies (Ge, 2016).

In addition to these discussions on the domestic purposes of legal education, changes are taking place at international and regional levels, with enhanced collaboration in legal education programmes with agencies outside China and also some overseas law schools establishing a foothold in the PRC itself. These changes will likely encourage multilingual, international legal practitioners who can serve the increasing need for dealing with cross-border transactions, disputes and civil matters.

Historical continuities and political context

After Liberation in 1949, and encouraged by the Soviet Union, some efforts were made to develop a 'socialist' system of legal practice, and in the mid-1950s, a lawyers' system emerged to provide criminal defence. However, lawyers were soon negatively characterised as representing defendants who were anti-social and politically suspects (Zheng, 1988, p.475). They and other law specialists came under political attack during the CCP's anti-rightest movement (*fan youpai yundong*: 反右派運動) of 1957–1959 and, subsequently, law and legal development were given little attention – especially during the Cultural Revolution (1966–1976) (Zheng, 1988, pp.475–476). Following CCP leadership changes, the late 1970s saw a revival of China's 'political-legal' system. Law reform was encouraged, so as to promote social stability (in the wake of the Cultural Revolution), to advance 'socialist legality' and to foster economic growth through encouraging inward foreign investment – a policy shift that was even reflected in constitutional law, so that Article 18 of the 1982 Constitution declares, in a manner comparatively rare in constitutional documents, that foreign investment is welcome and protected in law.

But it was not for another 20 years or so that liberal-democratic values, such as the idea of 'rule of law' and the 'protection of human rights', were introduced (in the 1999 and 2004 amendments to the PRC Constitution). These limited developments encouraged a number of commentators both within and outside China to conclude that law schools might become centres for promoting greater constitutionalism and legal reform in China. The latest revisions to the PRC Constitution (2018) have, moreover, attempted to change the meaning of the rule of law idea in China – dropping the term that is often translated as 'rule by law' (*fazhi*: 法制) in favour of a more robust 'rule of law' (*fazhi*: 法治) in the Preamble. Article 32 of the amendment provides that, in the seventh paragraph of the Preamble to the Constitution, the phrase 'improve the socialist legal system' (which is effectively rule *by* law, one could argue) is replaced by 'improve the socialist rule of law'.

However, it is also true that over the past decade these progressive values have experienced an uncertain history, and many observers now speak of the 'delegalisation' of China (see, for example, Minzner, 2011). The Chinese leadership's concern with social stability has been at the expense of legal development. This concern with social stability and attendant CCP control is manifested in the latest revision to the country's Constitution (a translated version is available at https://npcobserver.com/2018/03/11/translation-2018-amendment-to-the-p-r-c-constitution/ (accessed 8 January 2019)). In the 2018 amendments, Articles 124 and 125 have been revised to create a new anti-corruption agency, the National Supervisory Commission (*Guojia Jiancha Weiyuanhui*: 国家监察委员会), which replaces a system known as *shuanggui*. ('Shuanggui' (双规) is an internal Party disciplinary process that allows the Commission to summon CCP members to account for apparent corrupt conduct or other alleged disciplinary violations 'at a designated location at a designated time'). Although intended to make anti-graft work more legalised, the Commission's anti-corruption functions are integrated with the CCP's own anti-graft work. This relationship between the National Supervision Commission and the CCP will likely make difficult efforts to promote law-based governance.

The Constitution also tightens Communist Party control in other ways, for example, Article 1 of the Constitution has been revised by adding that the 'Communist Party's leadership is the most essential feature of socialism with

Chinese characteristics' (see Article 36 of the 2018 amendments). Moreover, the CCP continues to be able to dominate appointments to key roles by practising a nomenklatura system, to blur policy and law, and to encourage personalised leadership – for example, to allow the conduct of meetings in an exhortatory rather than decision-making style, so that there is very little meaningful discussion, let alone criticism, of leaders' decisions and so on (observations based on authors' personal experiences).

Today, the unhappy experience of the 1950s' experiment with criminal defence still casts a shadow over legal practice. Lawyers, in particular, nowadays prefer to concentrate on commercial matters and to be corporate client focused rather than individual client orientated. Human rights-type lawyers have emerged, but are under constant political pressure (Fu and Zhu, 2018). There are many reasons for the slow progress – or even regression – and difficulties are sometimes quite pronounced when several such influences combine to reinforce one another. Historical legacies and cultural values clearly constitute significant barriers, even though for a pre-urban, pre-industrial society imperial China had a relatively sophisticated system of 'courts, codes and constables'. The dominant position of the CCP in the 'political-legal system' is also, as we have noted already, crucial.

The legal system is still clearly a political-legal (*zhengfa*: 政法) system and we need to bear in mind that for a long time law schools in the political-legal types of institution were mostly concerned with producing graduates who would then work in legal administrative positions, become lawyers and so on. This 'administrative ethos' in legal education has been strengthened by in-house professional training programmes set up by the court and procuracy systems themselves.

PRC legal education

Even today, one of China's top law schools, the Chinese University of Politics and Law (Zhongguo Zhengfa Daxue: 中国政法大学), which has some 16,000 students and 1,000 law teachers and since the early 1950s has been training more than 100,000 students, plays a major role in preparing students to serve as personnel in the *zhengfa* system – as law enforcement officers, and private practitioners who know how to handle the system. It was one of the six political-legal institutes run by the Ministry of Justice that were important in the revival and development of legal education after the decision to pursue a policy of socialist-legality in the late 1970s.

In due course, leadership of this institution and a number of regional political-legal 'colleges' shifted to the Ministry of Education system in the year 2000. Overall, the Ministry of Education is now responsible for the more than 600 law schools located in tertiary educational institutions (with a law student population in excess of 300,000). As a result of the shift in control, in the 1990s, many of the law schools that were originally called schools of *zhengfa* (politics and law) were separated into 'Law Schools' and 'Schools of Public Administration'. But over the past decade, this change appears to have been reversed to some extent and so the term *zhengfa* is reappearing in the names of some newly established law schools, which sometimes also offer degrees in public administration. These provide, as noted earlier, four-year LLB programmes and two- and three-year law masters. More specifically, there are three-year 'academic' LLM degrees (*faxue shuoshi*: 法学硕士) or a two- or three-year 'professional' JM degrees (*falü zhuanye shuoshi*: 法律专业硕士) (mainly for non-law graduates, similar to the JD in the US). Those high-flyers who take the academic LLM will perhaps attempt a PhD programme lasting three years or more, perhaps even to be followed by a post-doctoral scheme. As a result, many law school teachers are in their early 30s before they get their first teaching appointment. Despite some changes in recent years, the former political-legal institutions continue to prepare graduates for legal practice as procurators, judges, notaries and government legal administrators, as well as lawyers, but following their transfer to the leadership of the Ministry of Education in 2000, their programmes have become very close to those of other law schools (Huang, 2012, p.2).

The university law schools remain focused on academic law studies, preparing law students for teaching and research, but also for service in the government and careers in business. Because of their traditionally closer association with legal practice, and the economic reform policy of 'opening up' to the global economy, the political-legal institutions have been more able to 'internationalize' – for example, by creating joint programme with international partners – despite their close association with the PRC's 'political-legal' system.

In many law schools in the PRC today, the transformation from a 'rule of man' (*renzhi*: 人治) system to a more genuinely 'rule of law' approach has been slow, so that the basic classroom spirit often remains that of the teacher as leader (*lingdao*: 领导), an omnipotent disseminator of knowledge, and neither learning outcomes nor student feedback are given enough emphasis. This infuses the whole system, so that many teachers characterise themselves and their closest associates in terms of being the student of a particular 'PhD' supervisor. Indeed, the latter may well form the centre of a network of personal connections (*guanxi*: 关系) used to promote self-interest. This is also one reason why a significant numbers of judges, procurators and others working in the administration of justice study for a doctorate in law. More senior teachers will likely also list as one of their achievements that they have been recognised by the government's Education Department as a qualified 'PhD supervisor' and therefore something of a 'leader'. Indeed, their appointment as full professors may well have been made by the relevant provincial government Education Department rather than by their own university, so that in a sense they are a 'leader' outside the scope of the university at which they are employed.

Undergraduate degrees offer both compulsory subjects, which have relevance for legal practice, and optional subjects, which are often grouped into 'subject groupings' or 'directions' (*fangxiang*: 方向). Optional subjects tend to attract low credits.

In order to graduate within four years, an UG student will typically take eight or more courses each semester, especially in the second or third year. This encourages a rather superficial approach to learning. There is also a pressure to cram much academic legal education into the middle two years – Years 2 and 3 – which comes from, on the one hand, the requirement to take certain non-law courses in the first year and, on the other, a desire to leave the final year as free as possible for work placements and the search for employment. In most law schools, the teaching concentrates on *faxue* (法学) rather than *falü* (法律), so that, for example, whereas constitutional law is a key subject of study in law schools, the 1982 Constitution is itself not justiciable in the Chinese courts. Also, until recently, only a few law schools specifically prepare their law students for participation in the national Judicial Examination required, as noted above, for entry into the ranks of legal practice as a lawyer, judge or prosecutor.

As just observed, a significant period of the fourth (that is, final) undergraduate year is spent in professional placements or internships in a law firm or a court, or an arbitration commission and so on. This is a period of professional 'on-the-job' training but not one that is monitored closely by the student's own law school. Sometimes the placements are good learning experiences and at other times less so. As one law student explained to the authors: '[W]hat I mainly learned was how to present cigarettes to, and prepare cups of tea for, the judges.'

Legal clinics are attached to a number of law schools, giving free legal assistance and some of these have been directly assisted in their establishment and funding by foreign legal assistance (see Baskir, Ma and Li, 2015; Zheng Zhen 2002). Students are encouraged to apply for CCP membership before they graduate and their decision to join it is often less for ideological reasons and rather more to help them to enhance employment prospects and to please their parents. Graduates' employment rates are a success indicator within a university and it is the responsibility of law schools to try to ensure that graduates find employment post-graduation. Within the law school, the Party Secretary (*shuji*: 书记) bears a heavy responsibility for helping law graduates with the early stages of their career, whether it be in the legal profession or elsewhere. But it is often only in this sense that most law schools effectively prepare graduates for legal practice. Moreover, because courts, procuracies and many law firms in recent years have been downsizing, as a result of official policies and market pressures, law graduates are finding it increasingly difficult to secure employment after graduation. This is one of the pressures encouraging curriculum reform so that law graduates have a broader academic profile and therefore enhanced future employability.

The legal education system is directed from the Ministry of Education in Beijing, since Chinese governance continues in the main to be a process that the historian of Roman law revival in Europe, Walter Ullman, has firmly characterised as 'descending' (Ullmann, 1965, pp.12–14). This perhaps explains the fact that in many respects there is a dominance of the system by the major law schools of northern China. Thus, for example, only a restricted number of journals issued by southern Chinese law schools are allowed to carry the CSSCI (China Social Science Citation Index) mark, which gives authors prestige when they publish. The top-down approach is also found in the manner in which law schools are assessed and funded and the ways in which law schools conduct themselves. Rather blunt 'success indicators', reminiscent of state planning philosophy, are used both to rank and to encourage competition between law schools – these include admissions requirements (the scores for the university entrance examination), quality of buildings, number of prestigious professors and so on. Research often seems to lack depth. This reflects not only a paucity of understanding of research standards found in other parts of the world, but also the impact of relatively unsophisticated measures of research publication output. Journal and book publication often require monetary payments of one sort or another to publishing staff before there is agreement to publish a submission. Also, the Party–state keeps university teachers' salaries relatively low, while increasingly opening up possibilities of government research funding, thereby discouraging political non-conformity in research endeavours. The relevance of academic legal education for professional legal practice is an issue that the central government has only recently started to consider.

Legal education: popular and professional

Popular legal education (*pufa*: 普法) – the 'legal literacy campaign' (*falü puji yundong*: 法律普及运动) – is a distinctive aspect of the Chinese legal education system. In a society such as that of the PRC, with its record of ambivalent official attitudes to formal law and legal institutions (often characterised officially as 'blind to the law' (*famang*: 法盲) and general lack of legal consciousness, the legal literacy campaign has been seen as critically important to enhance awareness of the value of law. Accordingly, the Party–state launched an ambitious national movement in 1985 aimed at disseminating information in society about important laws and new legislation (Meng, 2014, p.43). One feature of this campaign has been regular newspaper and television reports on the value of law and the need for citizens to observe the law. These often provide spicy accounts of examples and cases in which problems have arisen because the people or officials have 'overlooked' the law. Such publications attract a broad audience and reinforce the leadership's message that there are now laws and that these laws are to be obeyed. It has also encouraged the growth of the 'netizen', with internet exposures and pressures sometimes acting as a forum for undoing injustices.

In addition, until recent years many judges and prosecutors in the PRC have lacked relevant legal qualifications, being recruited for 'legal work' (*falü gongzuo*: 法律工作) on the basis that, as demobilised soldierss they knew how to give and take orders. Accordingly, systems of education and training on the job through 'professional' colleges within the main legal institutions developed – for example, the National Judges College (*Guojia Faguan Xueyuan*: 国家法官学院) and the *zhengfa* or 'politics and law' education bodies – have provided a range of part-time and distance learning courses for people who want to work in the legal sector.

The Ministry of Justice administers the national Judicial Examination and thereby controls entry to the legal professions. The Ministry of Justice also dominates the All-China Lawyers' Association – the PRC's bar associations – and local branches of the Ministry have strong powers in issuing business licenses to lawyers. This is very much a Party–state-dominated system. Law schools, as noted earlier, have been increasingly willing to organise a preparatory programme for students who wish to sit for the Judicial Examination. Typically, until recent changes to the law (see later), the juniors have prepared for the examination, with the aid of a special course offered by private providers, over the summer vacation of their third year in law school, taken the examination in September and received results early in their final year (so that a quite common situation is that final year students find themselves being taught by law teachers who have themselves failed the Judicial Examination several times). In the more successful of these initiatives, the pass rate is two to three times higher than it is in other law schools. Another approach has been to suspend regular classes in September, so that students can focus on preparation for the bar exam at the end of the month when they enter their fourth (final) year. Other law schools see the Judicial Examination as a private matter for their students and so do not offer such opportunities.

The current Judicial Examination began as the 'Test for Lawyers' in 1986. At that time, the 'Test for Lawyers' only aimed at examining and selecting personnel for qualification as lawyers. Judges and prosecutors were selected according to schemes provided for in the 'Judges Law' and the 'Procurators Law', both of which were promulgated in 1995. The three forms of exam differed in terms of questions set, areas of law covered and the performance standards for qualification. Unlike the 'Test for Lawyers', the selection schemes for judges and prosecutors were criticised as being too 'enclosed' (*fengbi*: 封闭) – that is, too easy to pass and too 'casual' in spirit (Xue and Luo, 2017, p.24). Also, in the 1980s and 1990s, a large proportion of judges and prosecutors consisted of retired military officials and cadres from other administrative departments. These were selected without having been tested. As a result, the professional quality of lawyers was often significantly higher than that of most of the judges and prosecutors – who, indeed, might not have received any legal education at all before commencing service.

In 2001, the Supreme People's Court, the Supreme People's Procuratorate and the Ministry of Justice published a joint notice on 'Measures for the Implementation of the National Judicial Examination (for Trial Implementation)' (a translated version of the document is available at http://english.legalinfo.gov.cn/2015-05/29/content_30089409.htm (accessed 8 January 2019)). This, very significantly, merged the exams for the main types of legal practitioner – judges, prosecutors, notaries and lawyers. In the following year, 2002, the unified Judicial Examination was held for the first time, with around

360,000 candidates, of whom some 24,000 passed (Jiang, 2018, p.25). Prior to the establishment of the new scheme, early in 2001, the 'Judges' Law' and 'Prosecutors' Law' were modified so as to include the requirement that aspiring judges and prosecutors now had to pass the national Judicial Examination. The unified Judicial Examination remains an essential qualification for entry into the legal profession, whether that be as a judge, a prosecutor, a lawyer or a notary.

After 2008, the Judicial Examination regulations allowed law undergraduates to be examinees. However, some scholars are unhappy at this development, arguing that pre-graduation preparation for Judicial Examination has distracted students from studying law for academic purposes (Wang, 2014, p.120). Students tend to choose within their degree programme courses that are relevant to the Judicial Examination and largely ignore those that are less relevant, such as general jurisprudence, western legal theory, criminology, international law and so on.

In 2015, the General Office of the CPC Central Committee and the General Office of the State Council jointly issued the 'Opinions on Perfecting the Legal System of National Unified Legal Profession' ('the Opinions'). The Opinions proposed the introduction of a 'National Unified Legal Profession Qualification Examination' (*Guojia Tongyi Falü Zhiye Zige Kaoshi*: 国家统一法律职业资格考试). This would replace the old national Judicial Examination. In April 2018, detailed 'Implementation Measures for the National Unified Legal Profession Qualification Examination' ('the Implementation Measures') were published in accordance with the reforms suggested by the Opinions. Article 2 of the Implementation Measures has expanded the criteria for selecting legal practitioners, so that besides lawyers, judges and notaries, they now include a wider range of legal service providers such as arbitrators and civil servants handling legal matters. Also, Article 9 of the Implementation Measures has tightened the eligibility criteria for examinees, who must be law degree holders or hold a degree and possess three years' legal work experience (subject to certain transitional measures provided for in Article 22).

In contrast to the 2008 requirements, junior-year students at university are no longer eligible to take the new judicial exam (that is, after the transitional phase has been completed). Obviously, the new exam makes it more difficult to enter the legal profession, emphasising that intending legal practitioners should possess a law degree, or a non-law degree plus relevant extensive legal experience.

But the changes in the examination system have also placed enormous emphasis on encouraging legal practitioners who uphold socialist legal values and the 'legal' philosophy of state President and CCP Secretary General, Xi Jinping. The part of the examination based on multiple choice (which asks relatively objective 'black-letter' type questions) has been reduced in importance, whereas essay questions (which tend to raise issues that encourage subjective, ideologically correct answers) are expanded in the new exam (Stern, 2016). While in the old scheme, the test for essay questions occupied only one of the four exam papers taken over two days, under the new version of the examination, candidates must first pass the 'objective' questions test in an initial examination, and then subsequently take the more 'subjective' questions test only if they have passed the preliminary test (see Article 13 of the Implementation Measures for the National Unified Legal Qualification Examination, Order No.140 of the Ministry of Justice, promulgated on 28 April 2018). Under the Implementation Measures, the new exam scheme took effect in late 2018.

International and regional collaboration

With Deng Xiaoping's inspiration and support, and in contrast to the former Soviet Union, since the early 1980s the PRC has placed a distinctive emphasis on the value of legal education experience abroad. This value has included the experience of living in a community outside mainland China for an extended period of time and working side by side with seasoned legal professionals from a different legal system. In the case of the United Kingdom, motivated in part by the issue of the return of Hong Kong to Chinese sovereignty in 1997, three training programmes stand out: the Lord Chancellor's Training Scheme for Young Chinese Lawyers (1988–2010), the Lord Chancellor's Training Scheme for Young Chinese Judges (1997–2011) and (as one party to) the EU–China Legal and Judicial Training Programme (2000–2006). In the United States, there have been similar schemes – for example, at Temple University. Nowadays gaining an LLM, MCL (masters in common law) or JD overseas or in Hong Kong at a high-reputation law school is one way that a Chinese student may secure training place at one of China's large law firms – and, in this way, they are in effect giving themselves a form of 'trans-systemic legal education' (Glenn, 2005).

It is clear that there are still only limited connections between university legal education and legal practice, even though many university law students receiving an academic law education also aspire to a legal professional career. There continues to be little creative thinking about how these two dimensions of the legal education system might be more effectively related. There have been discussions between the Ministry of Justice and overseas professional legal training providers about introducing specialised programmes of professional legal training, but these seem to have floundered. As a result, there remains a major gap in the provision of legal education, namely, dedicated professional legal training.

Instead, the China 'market' is now encouraging the establishment of foreign law school presence in China, at least in the sense of law schools such as that of NYU offering semester abroad programmes for its home JD students in its Shanghai campus. More importantly, however, is the obvious growing dependence of law schools in North America and Europe on LLM students from China. Within China, something of a response to this may be seen in a small number of top Chinese law schools offering LLMs taught in English for students from overseas. At one of the leading law schools in China – Xiamen University Law School – the doctoral programme even accepts students who have no command of the Chinese language and who write their dissertations in English. Other elite law schools such as the East China University of Politics and Law offer summer schools in language and law or English-language one- or two-year LLM programmes. Peking University has established a School of International and Global Law in Shenzhen with a three-year US-style JD programme (although this seems unable to secure ABA recognition).

Conclusions

In the PRC, despite some efforts at reform, there remains a significant gap between academic law, as taught in universities by law teachers, and positive law, as understood and applied by those operating in the political-legal system. Changes to the judicial examination-based system of professional qualification have done little to change the position. A system of professional legal education, particularly one with a skills-focused orientation, remains undeveloped, apart from in-house training offered by official agencies such as the courts and the procuracy and by law firms to trainee lawyers. Complicating efforts at reform is the fact that legal specialists have to operate within, or in the shadow of, a 'political-legal' system, with strong CCP dominance rather than a legal system infused with a strong sense of the rule of law as understood in many other jurisdictions around the world. This is an authoritarian context that makes it inherently difficult to assess what might be the most appropriate or effective 'professional' skills to be learned. It also makes it difficult for the PRC to grasp the nettle of legal profession autonomy as understood more generally and as requiring meaningful commitment to rigorous standards of the rule of law and good governance (including at the local level).

We can see that general globalisation is impacting on legal education in China, and that a more globalised legal education is emerging in China in various ways. The real import of these developments remains uncertain, however, and while there has been some progress in education reform, there has also been much resistance. Here we should add that the generational divide in China is serious, reflecting the very rapid pace of social changes in China. Many of older law teachers are committed to CCP values, and continue to resist the implications for legal education of both globalisation and the role of legal practice. As in all legal systems, there is a strong argument for prioritising the learning of 'domestic' law because that is how a student becomes a legal professional and there are China cultural identity issues that also infuse resistance to change. The growth of the internet has made the generational divide even more severe.

As a result, there remains a need to give much greater attention to issues of the nature and quality of legal education in China if such education is to meet international standards and to assist the legal professions in the PRC. Our personal experience is that there should be much greater attention given to 'sustainable learning' policies and practices. More 'realistic', less 'theoretical' (often meaning 'ideological') law teaching is an urgently required reform. And more innovative approaches to course assessment are needed too. Greater attention needs to be given to relating academic and professional training to each other, including in areas such as rule of law and human rights. Nevertheless, knowledge of foreign law is becoming ever more important for successful legal practice and legal education in China needs to enable law students to engage more effectively and meaningfully with foreign law. This need has been recognised on China from the beginning of the reforms in the early 1980s, but at the local level there is often opposition to teaching foreign law, especially outside the field of commercial and economic law. The example of legal education reforms in other East Asian jurisdictions is now seen as pointing one way forward for China's own much needed improvements, although for reasons of space we have not been able to include them here.

Note

1 The authors are members of the Chinese Law Programme at the Hong Kong Institute of Asia-Pacific Studies at the Chinese University of Hong Kong, and have recent direct personal experience of education in mainland Chinese law schools.

References

Baskir, C. E., Ma Liqun and Li Ao (2015). Chinese clinical legal education globalizing and localizing. In Sarker, S.P. (ed.). *Clinical Legal Education in Asia: Accessing Justice for the Underprivileged*. New York, Palgrave Macmillan.

Dai Long (2008). Quanqiuhua shidai de riben faxue jiaoyu yu fazhan [Japanese legal education and its development in the era of globalisation]. *Nanjing Hangkong Hangtian Daxue Xuebao [Journal of Nanjing University of Aeronautics/Astronautics]*, 10(2), 58–62, 100.

Dicks, A. (1989). The Chinese legal system: reforms in the balance. *China Quarterly*, 119, 540–576.

Ding Xiangshun (2009). Bijiaofa shiyexia de dongya falü rencai yangcheng zhidu gaige [Reform of the system for cultivating legal talent in East Asia from a comparative law perspective]. *Faxuejia [Jurist]*, 2009(6), 9–19.

Fu Hualing and Zhu Han (2018). After the July 9(709) crackdown: the future of human rights lawyering. *Fordham International Law Journal*, 5(41), 1135–1164.

Ge Xianyuan (2016). Falü zhiye zige kaoshi Beijing xia benke faxue jiaoyu gaige yanjiu [Analysis of the reform of undergraduate law education against the background of the legal profession examination].*Dongbei Nongye Daxue Xuebao [Journal of Northeast Agricultural University]*, 14(2), 68–73.

Glenn, P. (2005). Doin' the transystemic: legal systems and legal traditions. *McGill Law Journal*, 50, 863–898.

Guo Xiang (2010). Lun sifa kaoshi yu faxue jiaoyu de guanxi – jian yu Zhou Xiang, Qi Wenyuan liangwei xiansheng shangque [On the Relationship between the Judicial

Examination and Legal Education: Discussion with Zhou Xiang and Qi Wenyuan]. *Faxue* [*Law Science*], 2010(2), 62–68.

Huang Jin (2012). Zizi yiqiu, fazhi tianxia [Diligently strive for a rule of law around the world] *Jiancha Ribao* [*Procuratorial Daily*]. 10 May 2012, 003, Xueshu [Academics].

Jiang Haishun (2009). Hanguo faxue jiaoyu de zhuanzhe – lun fake zhuanmen daxueyuan de sheli fang'an [The turn of ROK's legal education – on the plan for the establishment of special law schools], *Dongjiang Xuekan* [*Dongjiang Journal*] 26, 96–100.

Jiang Haitao (2018). Goujian guojia tongyi falü zhiye zige zhidu ruogan sikao [Thoughts on establishing the unified national legal qualification examination]. *Zhongguo Sifa* [*Justice of China*], 217(1), 23–32.

Lubman, S. (1969). Form and function in the Chinese criminal process. *Columbia Law Review*, 69(4) 535–575.

MacCormack, G. (1996). *The Spirit of Traditional Chinese Law*. Athens, GA, University of Georgia Press.

Meng Tao (2014). Zhongguo dalu fazhi pinggu yundong de huigu, shuping yu qianzhan [Reflections, comments and prospects on the movement of rule of law assessment in mainland China]. *Renmin University Law Review*, 2014(2), 43–70.

Minzner, C. F (2011). China's turn against law. *American Journal of Comparative Law*, 59(4), 935–984.

Nader, L. (1990). *Harmony Ideology: Justice and Control in a Zapotec Mountain Village*. Stanford, CA, Stanford University Press.

Oh Soogeun (2016). A reflection on practical training in legal education in South Korea. *Asian Journal of Law and Society*, 3(2), 227–236.

Palmer, M. (2010). Rethinking children's rights and interests? Economic reform, social protection and legal culture in post-Mao China. *Journal of Comparative Law*, 5(2), 260–280 (republished in Nelken, D. (ed.) (2012). *Using Legal Culture*. London, Wildy, Simmonds & Hill, pp. 251–277).

Qiu Fanggui and Tang Xinhua (2011). Zhong-ri faxue jiaoyu zhi moshi bijiao yanjiu [Comparative research on Chinese and Japanese modes of legal education]. *Jingji yu Shehui Fazhan* [*Economic and Social Development*], 9(3), 142–145.

Sato Nobuyuki (2016). The state of legal education in Japan: problems and 're'-renovations in JD law schools. *Asian Journal of Law and Society*, 3(2), 213–225.

Stern, R. E. (2016). Political reliability and the Chinese bar exam. *Journal of Law and Society*, 43, 506–533.

Tao Binzhi (2011). Xin zhidu jingjixue shijiaoxia zhong-ri faxue jiaoyu moshi bijiao yanjiu [Comparative research on the Japanese and Chinese modes of legal education (from the perspective of) the new institutional economics]. *Xuelilun* [*Theory Research*], 2011(3), 262–264.

Ullmann, W. (1965). *A History of Political Thought: The Middle Ages*. Harmondsworth, Penguin Books.

Wang Aiqun (2014). Cong riben fake daxue yuan kan woguo sifa kaoshi yu faxue jiaoyu zhi guanxi [Interpreting the relation between China's judicial exam and legal education from the perspective of Japan law school]. *Dalian Daxue Xuebao* [*Journal of Dalian University*], 35(1), 119–121.

Xue Zhisheng and Luo Guannan (2017). Falü zhiye zige kaoshi zhidu bianqian yu tfaxue benke jiaoyu zZhuanxing iaozheng [Changes in the legal qualification examination system and the adjustment of transformation of undergraduate education in law]. *Journal of Tianjin Academy of Educational Science*, 2017(4), 23–26.

Zheng, H. R. (1988). The evolving role of lawyers and legal practice in China. *American Journal of Comparative Law*, 36(3), 473–524.

Zheng Zhen (2002). *Zhengsuo Falü Jiaoyu zai Zhongguo* [*Clinical Legal Education in China*]. Beijing: Law Press China.

Zhou Xiang and Qi Wenyuan (2009). Faxue jiaoyu yi sifa kaoshi wei daoxiang de heli xing – yi sifa kaoshi xingfa juan weili [The reasonableness of directing legal education with [the aid of] the judicial examination – an example of the criminal law paper of the judicial examination]. *Faxue* [*Law Science*], 2009(4), 93–102.

Part 2

Legal education, interdisciplinary approaches and collaboration

The following two chapters focus on the ways in which legal education interacts and works with other academic disciplines. In Chapter 3, Burton and Watkins consider the UK context, with a particular emphasis on the evolution of socio-legal approaches to legal study. Such approaches commonly combine insights from both law and the social sciences to provide a contextual framework for the understanding and evaluation of legal issues. In Chapter 4, de Vries focuses specifically on the use of socio-legal studies in the Netherlands, drawing on case studies to consider both the opportunities for, and challenges to, its use in preparing students for the future of law. Both chapters share a common view of the importance and value of socio-legal approaches within the law school, despite the potential impact of market and other forces, placing it firmly at the heart of legal education.

Chapter 3

Interdisciplinary approaches and collaboration in legal education in England and Wales

Mandy Burton and Dawn Watkins

Introduction

In this chapter, we reflect on the development of the law school curriculum in England and Wales, the market pressures that have shaped it in the past and will continue to shape it in the future, and we consider the implications that this has for interdisciplinary approaches and collaboration. Like de Vries in the following chapter, we focus our discussion on socio-legal approaches and we emphasise the significance of these approaches in providing law students with an '*external* perspective'; through engagement with non-law disciplines and theories emanating from these disciplines, law students are provided with multiple lenses through which they can consider and critique law and legal practice.

Law has been taught in universities since the 1800s, but the approach to teaching law has not been consistent over that time. By contrast, one thing that has been consistent is the tension between law as an intellectual pursuit and legal education as preparation for a vocation as a practicing lawyer (Boon and Webb, 2008, pp.85–86). This has had implications for how law is taught; including the space that is given to interdisciplinary approaches and collaborations within the law school curriculum. Interdisciplinary approaches have been on the rise in recent years but, as we shall observe, they are not always valued outside the law school. Recent reviews of legal education, such as the Legal Education and Training Review (LTER) (Webb et al., 2013), might suggest that there will be less space for interdisciplinary approaches in the future. However, we argue that, in fact, the reverse is true. Drawing on our own and others' work, in this chapter, we argue that an interdisciplinary approach is vital to legal education, be that viewed as an academic or a vocational discipline.

The historical perspective

Law first emerged as a discipline to be taught in universities in the nineteenth century, but it has grown exponentially over the last half century or so (Boon and Webb, 2008). Now in the UK over 100 universities, including private universities, offer law degrees. The competition for places tends to be fierce, particularly among the more highly ranked universities. Part of the explanation for this is that potential law students see a law degree as a gateway to the legal profession and a well-paid career as a practising lawyer. Although many law students go on to have careers outside the legal profession (Bradney, 2018), there is no doubt that in the minds of many (potential) students there is a strong link between the desire to study law and an ambition to become part of the legal profession (Hardee, 2012, 2016).

As a consequence, university law schools have designed their undergraduate law degree courses in line with the training requirements of the regulatory bodies for solicitors and barristers, the Solicitors Regulation Authority (SRA) and the Bar Standards Board (BSB), respectively. Students who intend or might intend to join either of these professions are, at the time of writing, required to have a qualifying law degree (QLD). This must include the 'foundations of legal knowledge' in seven areas of law: contract, criminal law, tort, property, equity, public law and EU law (Joint Statement, 1999). In principle, law schools have quite a large element of freedom in designing their courses and approaches in these seven core subjects, as they are required to teach 'key elements and general principles', rather than following any detailed curriculum. However, in the early days of university legal education, there was a focus on black-letter law and the so-called doctrinal approach predominated (Cownie and Bradney, 2017).

In more recent years, it has been suggested that doctrinalism has been fading into the background as law degrees become more interdisciplinary or socio-legal in content and approach (Bradney, 1998). This seems in part to be supported by shifts in the composition of legal academics (Cownie, 2004). In the 1970s and 1980s, it was not uncommon for those entering law schools as teachers to be practising lawyers. It was relatively rare for legal academics to have PhDs and publications. These days, however, a PhD is virtually an entry requirement. We consider the training and background of PhD entrants into legal academia may have positive implications for the continued or further integration of interdisciplinary approaches in the curriculum of law schools. Rather than taking it for granted as the 'default' position, postgraduate research students now need to explain and justify a decision to take a purely doctrinal approach to their research and they have a wide range of methodological approaches to consider (Watkins and Burton, 2017). Some research questions cannot be answered by a purely doctrinal approach. An in-depth study of the legal rules provides little or no understanding of how these rules are applied in practice (Burton, 2017). Any PhD student will need to reflect on this and consider whether socio-legal, interdisciplinary approaches are required to address their research question instead of or in addition to a purely doctrinal approach (Cownie and Bradney, 2017).

Interdisciplinary approaches in UK law schools

While individual law schools have freedom, within the confines of a QLD, to teach undergraduate law students what they want and how they want, many have interpreted the QLD requirements as prescribing a doctrinal approach to core subjects. While the Joint Statement (1999) does not prescribe doctrinal approaches to teaching, it has been observed that it may be used as a reason or 'excuse' for adopting a doctrinal approach to teaching law (O'Brien, 2012).

Despite this, interdisciplinary approaches to teaching law can be found in the curricula of many law schools. It is hard to find comprehensive data on the prevalence of interdisciplinary approaches in teaching in law schools, however, as a starting point, we can look at evidence relating to the integration of socio-legal studies and socio-legal approaches. In her edited collection on this topic, Caroline Hunter (2012) begins by noting that the definition of socio-legal studies is, in itself, controversial. On a narrow interpretation, it might be confined to empirical research (using quantitative or qualitative social science methods) to examine the law and legal practices. The Nuffield Inquiry on Empirical Legal Research (Nuffield Inquiry, 2006) was specifically designed to investigate the capacity for empirical legal research in law, leaving aside criminal justice and criminology. The underlying premise of the Inquiry was that strategies were needed to support empirical studies in law at all levels, including undergraduate education. The Inquiry found that the incorporation of empirical approaches within the law school curriculum were limited, although the methods of the inquiry itself did not allow it to robustly assess the prevalence of empirical studies. It is quite likely that few law undergraduates are taught social science methods, in most cases, at best their exposure to empirical legal studies will be as consumers of empirical research conducted by others. While it can be argued that the lack of training in social science methods is a limitation on law students' education, a definition of interdisciplinary or socio-legal approaches which focuses on empirical research is arguably too narrow.

Hunter (2012) and others have argued for a broader definition of socio-legal studies that encompasses theoretical and empirical analysis of law as a social phenomenon (the Economic and Social Research Council definition) or 'Where law meets the social sciences and humanities' (the Socio-legal Studies Association strapline) (Hunter, 2012, p.3). The chapters in Hunter's book make the case for integrating socio-legal perspectives in this broader sense. Halliday (2012) has shown how empirical approaches can shape and enrich the study of public law, for example revealing how public bodies operate. He concludes that socio-legal 'is an umbrella term which embraces a multiplicity of disciplinary and theoretical approaches' (p.153). Thus, while empirical approaches might be part of socio-legal approaches, it does not necessarily have to be the case. Legal academics may define themselves as doctrinal because they interpret socio-legal as meaning empirical, while at the same time acknowledging that they do teach law in context not just black-letter law (Cownie, 2004). On the other hand, it has also been argued, some doctrinal academic lawyers will describe their work as socio-legal when really it is not (Sanders, 2015). This is another facet of the difficulty in establishing how far interdisciplinary approaches are adopted. While establishing the prevalence of interdisciplinary approaches is problematic, it is much easier to find examples of good practices in incorporating interdisciplinary approaches and collaborations.

Hunter's (2012) collection provides an overview of examples from different universities of how modules and assessments can be designed to integrate socio-legal approaches both into the core subjects of a QLD and optional modules. She observes that there are few standalone modules on socio-legal studies but the book provides a range of examples to demonstrate how interdisciplinary approaches can be incorporated into core subjects of property law (Auchmuty), contract (Mulcahy and Wheeler), tort (Devine), public law (Halliday), criminal law (Weait) and EU law (O'Brien). It is important that socio-legal approaches are incorporated into the foundation subjects for many reasons, but one compelling reason is that these tend to dominate the first year of study when students expectations of what it means to study law may 'become fixed' (Hunter, 2012, p.7). If we do not start how we mean to go on then the opportunity may be missed.

Further examples of interdisciplinary approaches in optional modules can be found in the work of Bankowski, Del Mar and Maharg (2013). Bankowski et al. have sought to 'contribute to the reinvigoration of legal education' (p.1) through their exploration of non-textual approaches, practised in experiential workshops and published subsequently in their edited collection. Here, Andreas Philippopoulos-Mihalopoulos describes his interdisciplinary approach to teaching law of the environment, where students are each encouraged to take a long walk, while reflecting on themselves, their movement and their surroundings. This activity is designed to increase students' awareness of the relationship between law and space (see, further, Philippopoulos-Mihalopoulos, 2015). Gary Watt also focuses on movement, as he describes the walk that he and his students take at the commencement of his Law and Literature module. Here Watt (p.135) points out that law and education are themselves discrete disciplines, and proposes the 'special problem' of legal education is that 'the fundamental ideas of law are predominantly stationary or tending to the static, while the essential ideas of education are predominantly moving or tending to motion.' The interdisciplinary nature of law and education per se is something that Paul Maharg (2007, p. 23) alerts us to, too, as he considers the potential role of interdisciplinarity in transforming legal education in the twenty-first century.

The changing legal landscape

In the following chapter, de Vries describes how the legal landscape is changing dramatically in the Netherlands. The same can certainly be said in England and Wales. Indeed, it has been argued by Sommerlad et al. (2015) that: 'We are currently witnessing an unprecedented transformation in the legal profession and legal education.' Two key legislative developments have changed the legal landscape to produce this 'tipping point' in legal practice: the first is the Legal Services Act 2007 and the second, the Legal Aid, Sentencing and Punishment of Offenders Act (LASPO) 2012. These two pieces of legislation have dramatically altered the way in which the legal profession is structured, removing the distinctiveness of legal services and drastically cutting public funding for certain types of legal work, particularly family and criminal justice. Sommerlad et al. argue that these radical changes to the profession have profound implications for law graduates and, consequently, law schools are presented with the challenge of how to respond. As Sommerlad et al. observe, not everyone will agree on the best way to respond to the challenges and opportunities that are presented. While some may make the case for a more doctrinal or skills-based approach to legal education, others will argue that socio-legal approaches are more important than ever. We are in the latter camp.

Within legal education itself, proposals for change that are currently being pursued by the SRA have been described as 'possibly the most significant shake-up of legal education since the early 1970s' (Davies, 2018, p.102). The SRA proposals are rooted in the Legal Education and Training Review (LETR), authored by Webb et al. and commissioned by the SRA, the Bar Standards Board (BSB) and the Institute of Legal Executives Professional Standards (the regulatory body that oversee the professional training requirements for legal executives). The LETR was intended to be a wide-ranging and substantial review, with the primary objective of ensuring that the system of legal education and training in England and Wales is in line with the objectives set out in the Legal Services Act 2007. Once the report was published, it was up to the regulators who commissioned it to determine how to respond.

The LETR was published in 2013 and, as Hardee (2014, p.69) describes, in general it 'came out to underwhelmed response: nothing radical; nothing to be overly alarmed about'. However, for some legal academics, and especially those dedicated to pursuing an interdisciplinary approach, some aspects of the report gave cause for concern. For example, Guth and Ashford (2014, p.8) expressed disquiet over the LETR's recommendation that the foundations of legal knowledge should be 'reviewed' and they also expressed uneasiness about the apparent shift to an outcomes-based approach. This concern was later echoed by Sanders, who pointed out that although the LETR focused in most detail on the vocational stages of training, rather than on the undergraduate law degree, it nevertheless included all of these stages in its suggested move to an outcomes-based approach to learning, 'working back' from the knowledge, skills and attributes required by a legal professional (Sanders 2015, p.140). The concern is, of course, that this emphasis on vocational outcomes potentially diminishes the scope for the study of law as an intellectual pursuit in itself.

A further, more specific concern relates to the LETR's treatment of socio-legal approaches. In a table reporting the views of practitioners, the report identifies 'Socio-legal Studies' as the least important area of knowledge among a selection of 16 subjects. Guth and Ashford (2014, p.10) observe that a cursory look at this table 'would suggest that socio-legal studies as a subject has no place at all within a new world of legal education for legal services'. However, they go on to point out that this categorisation of 'socio-legal studies' as a discrete subject is mistaken. In line with the views we express elsewhere in this chapter, Guth and Ashford argue that each of the subject areas set out in the table 'could, and indeed often are, subject to socio-legal inquiry, research, teaching and learning' and the top-scoring subject, legal and professional ethics, 'arguably necessitates a socio-legal analysis' (Guth and Ashford, 2014, p.10). Sanders supports this view, arguing that the value of the socio-legal approach to any subject area is 'incontestable' (Sanders, 2015, p.152).

Sanders is highly critical of the approach taken by the LETR. From a methodological point of view, he argues that the table reporting the views of practitioners on the importance of socio-legal studies is flawed. There was no random sampling and the numbers in each category were small. This critique is particularly poignant and somewhat ironic, demonstrating clearly that we all need to be critical consumers of empirical studies, including those making recommendations for changes in legal education. However, an equally important critique is the flawed assumption that we should be led by what practising lawyers think is the most important content or approach to studying law. As Sanders observes, the opinion poll with a huge sampling error made no attempt to analyse whether what lawyers said was necessary or desirable (p.152). He convincingly argues that it does not matter how many lawyers want a particular subject or approach if there is no justification for it. Going back to the regulatory objectives of the LSA 2007, Sanders demonstrates how the LETR failed to take into account three key objectives: access to justice, promoting the public interest and encouraging an independent, strong and effective legal profession, which are best served by a liberal intellectual education.

How can a student study criminal law effectively without an understanding of the context in which it operates? Most criminal law courses do focus on the principles of criminal law, such as *actus reus* and *mens rea*, and specific offences such as murder, assault and rape (Weait, 2012, p.162) Despite the pragmatic arguments for this approach, if we teach law in a purely doctrinal way, students will complete their course 'without engaging in the way in which the law plays out in practice in the trial courts. This means their understanding of the law is limited' (ibid.). This is not only 'regrettable', but neglectful, because students need an understanding of law in the real world. Weait demonstrates how they can achieve this through an example of analysing the transcript of a trial on assault and transmission of HIV. Sanders develops the example of *mens rea*, showing how students who are taught the subjective *mens rea* of intention and recklessness will have a significant gap in their understanding if there is no discussion of how these concepts are interpreted by magistrates and juries in practice, even if that discussion centres on the fact that we do not have empirical studies that give us clear insights into this topic. The examples are potentially endless, but a few more will suffice. It is not enough for students studying rape and sexual assault to learn the Sexual Offences Act 2003 and associated case law. Students also need to understand how juries may reach their decisions in these cases (Munro, 2017) and also the role that legal professionals play, for example barristers' attitudes to the presumptions relating to lack of consent and lack of reasonable belief in consent in the Sexual Offences Act (Carline and Gunby, 2016). As well as providing studies with a more comprehensive understanding of how law is made and applied, incorporating these studies into the teaching of criminal law brings exposure to different ways of looking at the world, feminist legal approaches, for instance. It also provides the opportunity to educate students to be critical consumers of empirical research, analysing the strengths and weaknesses of mock juror research, for example.

Thus we agree with Sanders' (2015) conclusion that socio-legal, interdisciplinary approaches are needed to develop truly 'professional' lawyers. Lawyers, he argues, are not plumbers, adopting Twining's (1967) timeless observation on the value of a liberal education. While it is implicit in Sanders' discussion, we argue here explicitly that his comments can be applied to all law students, and not just those intending to practise law in the future. So, in our provision of education for all law students, despite the increasing marketisation of legal services and higher education, we should be resisting the pressures to focus on employability skills and 'commercial awareness'. 'An academic education is supposed to challenge the status quo, not simply equip students with the skills to leech off it' (Sanders, 2015, p.154). Again, regarding all law students, we further agree with Sanders' conclusion that 'social awareness' is just as important as commercial awareness and that understanding 'poor people's law' from a socio-legal perspective is fundamental, as well as having the potential to be transformative. There is little point teaching family law students the remedies available to victims of domestic abuse under the Family Law Act 1997, without also educating them on the complex nature of domestic abuse and the barriers to accessing justice, including the lack of awareness among solicitors offering advice about what they are actually dealing with (Burton, 2010). As one possible means of 'cultivating humanity' (Nussbaum, 2003) among law students, Watkins argues that students need to be made aware of the significant role that human actors play in legal proceedings and she adopts a range of narrative approaches to facilitate this, in the context of equity and trusts, one of the seven foundational subjects (Watkins, 2011, 2013, 2014).

The concerns about a shift towards a vocational, outcomes-based approach and a lack of regard for the benefits of a socio-legal approach have proved to be well-founded. At the time of writing, the SRA is intending to introduce from 2021 a new scheme of assessment for any person intending to qualify as a solicitor in England and Wales. The Solicitors Qualifying Examination (SQE) or 'super exam' (Walters, 2018) will be set centrally, and will be taken in two stages; SQE 1 focusing on legal knowledge across six subject areas and SQE 2 testing practical legal skills. The six subject areas for SQE1 (SRA, 2016) are:

- principles of professional conduct, public and administrative law and the legal systems of England and Wales
- dispute resolution in contract or tort
- property law and practice
- commercial and corporate law and practice
- wills and the administration of estates and trusts
- criminal law and practice.

As Guth (2017) points out, this selection of subjects reads rather like 'a syllabus of "rich man's law"' as it excludes the unglamorous, day-to-day legal problems that fall within the remit of family law, employment law, social welfare law and immigration law. Further, she argues:

> It does not include contextual understanding of how law operates in society, it does not include an understanding of different approaches, such as feminist or queer approaches to law, or how they might shape our understanding of law and legal problems. It does not, it seems, require any context at all. If law schools are to incorporate preparation for the SQE, which will examine this knowledge by way of multiple choice questions, into their degree programmes in some way, there is a real risk that socio-legal approaches and socio-legal modules or courses will be pushed out.

Significantly, under the SRA's new scheme of assessment, the QLD and the graduate diploma in law (GDL – a conversion course for non-law graduates) will no longer be required. This means that law schools will no longer be required (at least from the SRA's point of view) to cover the seven foundational subjects that presently make up the QLD. An added complication is that the SRA's approach stands in contrast to that adopted by the BSB, for which the QLD or GDL will continue to satisfy the academic stage of training (BSB, 2017).

This major shift in approach potentially frees law schools to radically revise their curricula, ignoring the requirements of the SQE. But as Davies (2018, p.102) points out, these changes will also oblige law schools 'to face the prospect of balancing their future academic preferences with market predictions'. So, apart from this, there are a number of possible courses of action that law schools can take. These range from embracing the status quo (so continuing to offer the QLD with no opportunity for SQE preparation) to a part or whole curriculum redesign that embraces a more vocational approach (so building preparation for SQE 1 into the undergraduate programme). Bradney argues convincingly for maintaining the status quo. Drawing on statistics published by the Law Society, (Bradney, 2018, pp.4, 9) he points out that 'only a minority of law graduates go on to become solicitors or barristers' and that thus far law schools have achieved considerable success 'by not tying themselves to a particular employment sector'. In his discussion of some of the possible implications for law schools, Davies (2018, p.124) also envisages that some law schools may choose to reject the more vocational approach that the SQE requires. However, at the opposite extreme to Bradney, he suggests that the SRA's proposed reforms present law schools with an opportunity to radically redesign their curricula, embracing a much more interdisciplinary approach.

Making (and keeping) space for interdisciplinary approaches

We argue that, whatever approach to the SRA reforms is taken by law schools, an interdisciplinary approach remains both possible and necessary. Dealing first with law schools that either partly or fully embrace an 'SQE preparation' model, we suggest that the vocational, outcomes-based demands of the SQE require a robust engagement with the environment or context that legal professionals are and will be working in. In other words, we argue that even where the focus of legal education is on equipping students with the knowledge, skills and attributes required by a legal professional both now and in the future, then this necessarily includes equipping students to think and work from an interdisciplinary perspective.

As long ago as 1897, Oliver Wendell Holmes maintained that 'the rational study of law is still to a large extent the study of history. History must be a part of the study, because without it we cannot know the precise scope of rules which it is our business to know. It is a part of the rational study, because it is the first step toward an enlightened scepticism, that is, towards a deliberate reconsideration of the worth of those rules.' In line with the views of Guth and Ashford (2014) cited earlier in this chapter, we suggest that for the legal professional, this call to context and to a critical approach to the study of law, are intrinsic aspects of the first of the core subjects for SQE 1 (principles of professional conduct, public and administrative law, and the legal systems of England and Wales).

Webb (2015) has pointed out that the increasing dominance of market forces has resulted in the unbundling of legal services and routinisation of many legal tasks. There has been a rise in hybrid legal/managerial workers with commercial awareness and managerial skills, however, the dominance of market forces means that there is a need for ethics to be part of the legal education and professional training. Competition is assumed to be the best protector of both the consumer of legal services and the public interest. Ethics will be part of the SQE. At the moment, ethics is not generally part of the law school curriculum in a specific sense, in that we do not teach informed consent and avoidance of harm etc. University research ethics committees have had a 'chilling effect' on students undertaking empirical research as part of their law dissertation options; it is difficult to get approval, particularly for sensitive research topics involving potentially vulnerable research subjects. So there is limited explicit exposure to the principles of carrying out ethical research, which may also be valuable to further reflection on ethical work practices and life more generally.

From a practical, vocational point of view, Schäfke, Díaz-Asensio and Stagelund Hvidt (2018, p.274) point out that an interdisciplinary approach can help students to develop 'boundary crossing competencies' that equip practising lawyers to work effectively with graduates from other disciplines on interdisciplinary teams; as well as facilitating 'a more comprehensive understanding of legal phenomena that are inextricably linked to society'. In a similar vein, Dingwall (2017) maintains that 'an understanding of society, institutions and interaction matters' is required because legal professionals will need to draw on these understandings when giving advice to clients, rather than simply (or even at all) merely applying the law to the facts. Further, he argues that in order to become successful in their working lives, legal professionals need to be given opportunities to develop the ability 'to deal with a diverse society, and a diverse world' that is constantly changing and uncertain.

If we confine the interdisciplinarity/socio-legal approach to just empirical studies (using or at least being able to understand and critique quantitative or qualitative social science methods (Hunter, 2012)) then the argument becomes even stronger. We live, teach and learn in the 'big data' era, where skill in data analysis (and especially quantitative analysis) is becoming increasingly important, together with a clear but critical appreciation of the growing role of technology in the legal services sector. The success of 'Legal Geek' and its associated activities is evidence of this, its most recent conference attracting over 2,000 participants from more than 40 countries (Legal Geek, 2018). Citing Oliver Wendell Holmes once more, we suggest that his prediction was correct: 'For the rational study of the law the blackletter man may be the man of the present, but the man of the future is the man of statistics and the master of economics.' The arguments that we make with regard to the need to understand data analyses can, of course, be applied equally to students pursuing the study of law primarily or entirely as an intellectual pursuit; be that through a continued, traditional QLD approach or through a radically 'freed up' curriculum. And in the context of a non-vocational, or 'not-just-vocational' law degree, the argument for a maintained or increased interdisciplinary approach can be easily made out.

Conclusion

In this chapter, we have argued that interdisciplinary approaches to the academic study of law have been gaining ground over the past few decades within law schools, at least from the perspective of academic researchers. However some would question how far socio-legalism has penetrated the teaching as opposed to the research of legal academics, as perhaps is evident from the doctrinal focus of many textbooks on law school courses (Collier, 2004). We have provided examples of the adoption of a socio-legal approach, situated mainly within the confines of discrete modules that are part of the qualifying law degree. The broader, programme level examples provided by de Vries in the following chapter provide an interesting contrast to these. It remains to be seen how far law schools will move towards this broader approach if and when the SRA proposals are implemented and – in principle at least – the opportunity for radical curriculum redesign arises. Whatever the outcome of the SRA proposals, we conclude by arguing that it is critical that interdisciplinary approaches are adopted within any law school curriculum. This is necessary not only from the perspective of providing a liberal education, but also from the pragmatic perspective of preparing students for the real world where they will be increasingly called on to engage with issues and data that only an interdisciplinary approach can effectively equip them to do.

Bibliography

Auchmuty, R. (2012). Land law and equity and trusts. In Hunter, C. (ed.). *Integrating Socio-legal Studies into the Law curriculum.* London, Palgrave Macmillan, pp. 69–103.

Bankowski, Z., Del Mar, M. and Maharg, P. (2013). *The Arts and the Legal Academy.* Farnham, Ashgate.

Bar Standards Board (2017). Policy statement on bar training.

Boon, A. and Webb, J. (2008). Legal education and training in England and Wales: Back to the future? *Journal of Legal Education*, 58(1), 79–121.

Bradney, A. (2018). The success of university law schools in England and Wales: or how to fail. *The Law Teacher*, 52(4), 490–498.

Bradney, A. (1998). Law as a parasitic discipline. *Journal of Law and Society*, 25(1), 71–84.

Burton, M. (2017). Doing empirical research: exploring the decision making of magistrates and juries. In Watkins, D. and Burton, M. (eds.). *Research Methods in Law*, Abingdon, Routledge, pp. 66–85.

Burton, M. (2010). Civil law remedies for domestic violence: why are applications for non-molestation orders declining? *Journal of Social Welfare and Family Law*, 101–120.

Carline, A. and Gunby, C. (2016). Rape politics, policies and practice: exploring the tensions and unanticipated consequences of well intentioned victim-focused measures. *Howard Journal of Criminal Justice*, 56(1), 34–52.

Collier, R. (2004). We're all socio-legal now – legal education, scholarship and the global knowledge economy – reflections on the UK experience. *Sydney Law Review*, 26, 503–536.

Cownie, F. (2004). *Legal Academics Culture and Identities.* Oxford, Hart Publishing.

Cownie, F. and Bradney, A. (2017). Socio-legal studies: a challenge to the doctrinal approach. In Watkins, D. and Burton, M. (eds.). *Research Methods in Law.* Abingdon, Routledge, pp. 40–65.

Davies, M. (2018). Changes to the training of English and Welsh lawyers: implications for the future of university law schools. *The Law Teacher*, 52(1), 100–125.

Devine, K. (2012). Tort law: how should tort law be taught? Utilizing expertise and telling tales in an innovative law curriculum. In Hunter, C. (ed.). *Integrating Socio-legal Studies into the Law Curriculum.* London, Palgrave Macmillan, pp. 121–140.

Dingwall, R. (2017). *Responding to Guth, J. on behalf of the SLSA Executive Committee, the SQE, Law Degrees and Socio-Legal Studies, SLSA Blog*, 8 May, http://slsablog.co.uk/blog/blog-posts/the-sqe-law-degrees-and-socio-legal-studies/ (accessed 6 February 2019).

Guth, J. (2017). *On Behalf of the SLSA Executive Committee, The SQE, Law Degrees and Socio-Legal Studies, SLSA Blog*, http://slsablog.co.uk/blog/blog-posts/the-sqe-law-degrees-and-socio-legal-studies/ (accessed 6 February 2019).

Guth, J. and Ashford, C. (2014). The Legal Education and Training Review: regulating socio-legal and liberal legal education? *The Law Teacher*, 48(1), 5–19.

Halliday, S. (2012). Public law. In Hunter, C. (ed.). *Integrating Socio-legal Studies into the Law Curriculum*. London, Palgrave Macmillan, pp. 141–160.

Hardee, M. (2016). *The Cohort Study Of the Career Expectations of Students on Qualifying Law Degrees in England and Wales*, https://ials.sas.ac.uk/about/leadership-and-collaboration/legal-education-research-network-lern/grants (accessed 28 February 2019).

Hardee, M. (2014). To prescribe or not to prescribe? That is the question. *The Law Teacher*, 48(1), 69–78.

Hardee, M. (2012). *Career Expectations of Students on Qualifying Law Degrees in England and Wales*. London, Higher Education Authority.

Hunter, C. (ed.) (2012). *Integrating Socio-legal Studies into the Law Curriculum*. London, Palgrave Macmillan.

Law Society and the General Council of the Bar (1999). *Joint Statement on the Academic Stage of Training*. London, Law Society.

Legal Geek (2018). *A Year's Networking In a Day*, https://www.legalgeek.co/conference/ (accessed 6 February 2019).

Maharg, P. (2007) *Transforming Legal Education: Learning and Teaching the Law in the Early Twenty-First Century*. Farnham, Ashgate.

Munro, V. (2017). The masters tools? A feminist approach to legal and lay decision making. In Watkins, D. and Burton, M. (eds.). *Research Methods in Law*. Abingdon, Routledge, pp. 194–210.

Mulcahy, L. and Wheeler, S. (2012). Contract law: socio-legal accounts of the lived world of contract. In Hunter, C. (ed.). *Integrating Socio-legal Studies into the Law Curriculum*. London, Palgrave Macmillan, pp. 104–120.

Nuffield Inquiry on Empirical Legal Research (2006). *Law in the Real World: Improving our Understanding of How Law Works*. London, Nuffield Foundation.

Nussbaum, M. (2003). Cultivating humanity in legal education. *University of Chicago Law Review*, 70(1), 265.

O'Brien, C. (2012). European Union law. In Hunter, C. (ed.). *Integrating Socio-legal Studies into the Law Curriculum*. London, Palgrave Macmillan, pp. 184–202.

Philippopoulos-Mihalopoulos, A. (2015). *Space, Materiality and the Normative*. Abingdon, Routledge.

Sanders, A. (2015). Poor thinking. Poor outcome? The future of the law degree after the Legal Education and Training Review and the case of socio-legalism. In Sommerlad, H., Harris-Short, S., Vaughan, S. and Young, R. (eds.). *The Futures of Legal Education and the Legal Profession*. London, Hart, pp. 139–168.

Schäfke, W., Mayoral Díaz-Asensio, J. and Stagelund Hvidt, M. (2018). Socialisation to interdisciplinary legal education: an empirical assessment. *The Law Teacher*, 52(3), 273–294.

Solicitors Regulation Authority (2016). *A new route to qualification: the Solicitors Qualifying Examination. A consultation summary*. London, SRA.

Sommerlad, H., Harris-Short, S., Vaughan, S. and Young, R. (eds.). *The Futures of Legal Education and the Legal Profession*. London, Hart.

Walters, M. (2018). LSB approves 'super-exam' application. *Law Society Gazette*, 9 April, 2(1).

Watkins, D. (2014). The shaping and misshaping of identity through legal practice and process: (re)discovering Mr Kernott. *Law and Humanities*, 8(2), 192–216.

Watkins, D. (2013). Recovering the lost human stories of law: finding Mrs Burns. *Law and Humanities*, 7(1), 68–90.

Watkins, D. (2011). The role of narratives in legal education. *Liverpool Law Review*, 32, 113–133.

Watkins, D. and Burton, M. (2017). *Research Methods in Law*. Abingdon, Routledge.

Webb, J. (2015). The LETRS (still) in the post: the legal education and training review and the reform of legal services education and training – a personal (re)view. In Sommerlad, H., Harris-Short, S., Vaughan, S. and Young, R. (eds.). *The Futures of Legal Education and the Legal Profession*. London, Hart, pp. 97–138.

Webb, J., Ching, J., Maharg, P. and Sherr, A. (2013). *Setting Standards: The Future of Legal Services Education and Training Regulation in England and Wales*. London, Legal Education and Training Review.

Wendell Holmes, O. (1897). The path of the law. *Harvard Law Review*, 10, 457.

Weait, M. (2012). Criminal law: thinking about criminal law from a trial perspective. In Hunter, C. (ed.). *Integrating Socio-legal Studies into the Law Curriculum*. London, Palgrave Macmillan, pp. 161–183.

Werner Schäfke, W., Mayoral Díaz-Asensio, J. A., and Stagelund Hvidt, M. (2018). Socialisation to interdisciplinary legal education: an empirical assessment. *The Law Teacher*, 52(3), 273–294.

Chapter 4

Law in context – towards a reflexive approach in (Dutch) legal education

Ubaldus de Vries

Introduction

Socio-legal studies have a long tradition within the curriculums of law schools across Europe and beyond. Although they might differ in substance, what they share is their *external* perspective on law. Such a perspective enriches the experiences of law students, as it confronts them with different types of question and, hence, different answers about how to look at law and how to understand law. It familiarises students with different approaches towards law and can be considered as a stepping stone towards interdisciplinary learning and cooperation.

Nevertheless, socio-legal studies (including jurisprudence and legal theory, I would add) similar to Hunter's argument (Hunter, 2012), as outlined in the previous chapter, seem to be a standalone strand within legal curriculums. They have to show their *raison d'être*, at least in the Netherlands. This ties in to the tension between law as an academic pursuit or a vocational training; something Stolker (2014) also points to in his broad study on the future of law schools. As former dean of Leiden Law School his comments echo the discussion about the tension between the academic and vocational approach towards legal education, as referred to in the previous chapter.

At the same time, the legal landscape is also changing. Susskind (2013, p. xv), for example, predicts a 'discontinuity [forcing lawyers] to dispense with much of our current cottage industry and re-invent the way in which legal services are delivered'. He refers to three forces directing this change. The first is financial and relates to the fee-based structure of legal services. The current structure can no longer be maintained, where clients start asking more for less. The second one relates to information technology, which leads, among other things, to the commodification of services. The third one concerns the liberalisation of the legal services market with new categories of legal service providers entering the market, breaking down the lawyers' monopoly. This breaking down will be accelerated, I would add, if lawyers are insufficiently able to cooperate with professionals from other disciplines.

The changing landscape calls for a different legal professional. Martijn Snoep (2014), former managing partner of De Brauw, Blackstone Westbroek, as well as Van der Zwaan (2017, p.156), former Rector of Utrecht University, argues that the market needs so-called T-shaped professionals, including T-shaped lawyers – lawyers who, with an in-depth knowledge of law (the leg) and knowledge of other disciplines (the beam), are much better able to cooperate in an interdisciplinary team of professionals. I would argue that this is not merely true in commercial legal practice but also in the public sector, particularly in the development and execution of governmental policy and regulation.

This new unfolding landscape asks lawyers to be able to connect with other disciplines. What strikes me is that in reaction to this changing landscape, the vocational aspect of legal education is overemphasised, at the cost of legal learning as an academic pursuit. I argue that the above-mentioned 'connect' should go beyond the T-shaped professional and the instrumentalisation of legal education. We need lawyers who are able to do and *be* more than 'technicians'. This is a recurrent debate as to the role of lawyers and their ethical consciousness when acting in the interests of their clients; see, for example, the research by Vaughan and Oakley (2016).

We need lawyers (law students) who are able to think about the law and its worth *in the context* of other disciplines, embedded in modern-day society. Critical thinking strengthens their capability of judgment, ethical integrity and problem-solving potential as well as the ability for cross-disciplinary professional cooperation. I seek to stress the academic nature and purpose of legal education to train such lawyers. Socio-legal studies (understood in the broad sense) can fill in the gap and strengthen law students' curriculum to prepare them for the future of law, as it will be they who can change the law of the future.

Socio-legal studies can function as a bridge towards other relevant disciplines, depending on the professional context. In the Netherlands, such a repositioning of socio-legal studies vis-à-vis traditional law courses and the professional context is slowly taking place. It has led to new initiatives in law programmes at various law schools, transforming or supplementing the traditional law curriculum. At the same time, there is a shift from a more normative and dogmatic embedded legal education (and research) towards empirical legal studies. Although empirical legal studies contribute to a better understanding of law, in the end the normative foundation of law remains too important to be ignored. To this end, the normative base must also be made more explicit in legal education and can benefit from more interdisciplinarity.

This contribution starts descriptively. Rather than taking a historical perspective (as done elsewhere in this volume) it seeks to sketch an overview of interdisciplinary initiatives that are currently been developed, at undergraduate level, in a number of Dutch law schools. This contribution is (in the descriptive part) limited to developments at undergraduate (bachelor) level. In sketching such an overview of interdisciplinary initiatives, this contribution also addresses the shift towards empirical legal studies in the Netherlands. These initiatives are categorised in terms of integrative, collaborative and innovative initiatives. It zooms in on four specific programmes to illustrate the recent developments. After this descriptive analysis, the chapter is more evaluative. It focuses on the worth of interdisciplinary approaches in the context of socio-legal studies, that seek to strengthen the academic nature of legal studies, rather than the vocational aspect. This part introduces the importance of reflexivity (in the normative sense) as an academic attitude. As law's social context (its environment) is changing fundamentally, the ability to understand law (and its purpose and function) demands an understanding of society and societal developments to enable a reconsideration of law's fundamentals. This evaluation cannot escape criticising the concept of the T-shaped lawyer that seems to serve as a vocational emblem for the initiatives. The T-shaped professional falls short of what is really needed.

First, however, the chapter seeks to create some definitional boundaries in respect of terminology.

Definitional boundaries and 'disciplinarity'

Inter-, cross-, trans- and multidisciplinarity are part of our terminology when talking about changes in university education and research (Karanika-Murray and Wiesemes, 2009). We usually entertain an implied understanding of these terms and sometimes this leads to miscommunication. *For the purposes of this contribution*, I propose a definitional boundary in respect of the terms interdisciplinarity and multidisciplinarity, taking a student-centred perspective.

Multidisciplinarity in (legal) education means that students study one or more disciplines alongside law within a curriculum of which the knowledge base is useful to the student as a future legal professional. It may well be that the students connect the dots, so to speak, between the disciplines but correlating or integrating the disciplines is not necessarily the aim of such a curriculum. An example is when a student, majoring in law, chooses to do a minor in another discipline, such as economics or child psychology (for example, at Utrecht University, 30 credits of the 180-credit bachelor programme is optional, in which students can choose to do a minor of four 7.5 credit courses). Another example are the so-called 'double-degree' programmes. At Utrecht University, for example, students can do a bachelor in liberal arts and science and opt to sit an entrance exam in law towards the end of their second year and register for the bachelor of law programme as well. On successful completion, within four years, students gain a BA and an LLB (https://www.uu.nl/en/organisation/university-college-utrecht/academic/curriculum-planning/curricular-options/double-degree-in-law-and-liberal-arts-sciences (accessed 8 December 2018)).

Interdisciplinarity is more integrative by nature. Here, students are taught to study and, ultimately, are expected to understand the different disciplines as an integrative whole, albeit from a legal perspective. The emphasis here is to what extent other disciplines bear on law and legal practice. in the case studies described below, each takes a different view as to achieving this aim. The bottom line here is how students can understand the other disciplines in the context of the legal discipline. In other words, the other disciplines can be seen as instrumental to understand law differently, allowing for a reflexive stance. (This will be further elaborated on below in the evaluative part of this contribution.)

Curriculum development: towards interdisciplinarity

This paragraph provides a sketch of collaborative, innovative and integrative initiatives that are being or have been developed in a number of Dutch law schools. Four examples function as case studies: the so-called PPLE programme at the University of Amsterdam, presented here as a collaborative initiative. Examples of innovative initiatives consist of the newly established Global Law Programme at Tilburg University and the programme Law in Society at the Free University Amsterdam, which launched in September 2019. The integrative initiative is illustrated by Utrecht University Law School, which seeks to integrate external perspectives within traditional law courses, in its bachelor programme, to challenge students to think differently about law.

The sketch is based on the various programme and course descriptions available online and the official reports of the Accreditation Organisation of the Netherlands and Flanders (NVAO). This organisation is responsible for accrediting new programmes of study and re-accrediting existing ones. (All the reports are available on the website of the NVAO, https://www.nvao.com (accessed 14 December 2018).)

Note: one obstacle in designing new initiatives in respect of legal education in the Netherlands is how law programmes must meet certain requirements laid down in a covenant, agreed on by the schools of law and legal practice – the Dutch Bar Association, the Council for the Judiciary and the Netherlands Public Prosecution Service. This 'Convenant Civiel Effect' (2016) stipulates, for example, the amount of European credits a law programme must have and how these credits are differentiated among the traditional legal sub-disciplines. (The covenant seems similar to standards sought in England and Wales, as described in the previous chapter.) The problem with the covenant is that it leaves little room for non-legal disciplines to be incorporated in a bachelor curriculum that gives direct access to a master in law, necessary to enter legal practice (Laemers, 2017). A way around it, as will be referred to below, is that in the new initiatives, 'minors', bridge years or pre-master programmes are offered for students who seek to enter legal practice. I look with some degree of envy, in this regard, at developments in the UK, where the QLD and the graduate diploma in law (GDL) will no longer be required, as explained in the previous chapter.

Collaborative (PPLE)

PPLE programmes are blossoming across Europe and are programmes that combine politics, psychology or philosophy, law and economics into one curriculum. The PPLE programme of the University of Amsterdam is presented as a three-year bachelor degree course, taught in English, that combines politics, psychology, law and economics (NVAO report, 2014). It is a selective degree course, which means that students have to apply and be accepted, based on certain selection criteria. The programme taps into the idea that contemporary society, with its complexity requires professionals who can integrate 'different fields of knowledge into new solutions' (http://coursecatalogue.uva.nl/xmlpages/page/2018-2019-en/search-programme/programme/4888 (accessed 14 December 2018)). The four classic socioeconomic disciplines are considered to be the combined sources in which answers can be found to comprehend contemporary questions. The NVAO report (2014, p.3) affirms that the relevance of these disciplines is recognised by the professional field.

The programme is designed along disciplinary, interdisciplinary and thematic lines. The emphasis is on a broad disciplinary knowledge of the four disciplines after which students chose (in the third semester) in which discipline they want to 'major'. During the three years, students also engage each semester in interdisciplinary courses and what are called 'integrative seminars', as well as course in research skills. In the interdisciplinary courses, for example 'politics, power and governance', students seek to understand how the manifestations of politics and power relate to the four disciplines. In the integrative seminars, students learn to identify connections and disparities between the different disciplinary perspectives in respect of a particular societal phenomenon. For example, in the integrative seminar 'human rights', students learn to understand the basic concepts, problems and methods concerning human rights and their relationship with politics and governance. In the integrative seminar 'solidarity', students learn to understand instances and problems of solidarity from different theoretical approaches such as psychology and economics. The thesis is a capstone experience, in which students show their interdisciplinary ability in respect of a particular societal problem. The didactic approach is that of research-based learning where the learning content of courses is fed by academic research and student research projects (NVAO report, 2014, p.15).

This initiative is presented in this chapter as 'collaborative' because it condenses four traditional disciplines into an integrative whole through collaboration between monodisciplinary lecturers. In this sense, it goes a step further than existing liberal arts and sciences programmes, which usually miss such a particular interdisciplinary structure. The collaborative aspect is also reflected in the organisational structure in which each discipline is represented by a head of study and a team of lecturers. Collaboration in teaching and learning is subsequently found in the interdisciplinary courses and the integrative seminars, providing for the interdisciplinary perspective in respect of societal themes, such as human rights, solidarity, security and societal challenges.

The programme stands out in the sense that it is not a law programme per se, although students can major in law. Students majoring in law who wish to go into practice have to finish a pre-master programme of one year in order to be able to register for a law masters that gives them 'civiel effect'. In this sense, the programme meets the requirements of how we could perceive the T-shaped professional to be, where students gain a more in-depth knowledge in one of the four disciplines and a broader knowledge of the other three. The programme goes a step further in the sense that student also learn to understand how the four disciplines are interrelated when it comes to addressing societal themes and problems.

Innovative (Global Law Programme and Law in Society)

Both the Global Law Programme at Tilburg University and Law in Society at the Free University Amsterdam depart from the traditional legal curriculum, albeit in different ways. The traditional curriculum is usually embedded within the national jurisdiction and organised along the lines of the important sub-disciplines of law: private law, administrative and constitutional law, criminal law, international and European law, and usually some reflexive courses ('reflexive courses' is the term I use for courses within the scope of legal theory and socio-legal studies). It starts with introductory courses in the first year, covering the legal landscape and is followed in subsequent years with more in-depth courses and the possibility of taking a number of elective courses. The degree is completed with a thesis. Academic and legal skills are either integrated in the courses and/or are trained in separate courses.

The Global Law Programme does not focus on a particular legal system, such as the Dutch system, but integrates insights from different legal systems. In doing so, the programme challenges students to consider problems from multiple points of view, preparing them as a 'linking pin in international organisations' (https://www.tilburguniversity.edu/educa-tion/bachelors-programs/global-law (accessed 14 January 2019)). The curriculum is organised along traditional lines, with courses in private and public law, but the themes addressed in these courses are taken from multiple jurisdictional perspectives. It allows, or so it seems, students to study legal doctrine at a more conceptual and transcendental level, for example the meaning of legality, liability or good faith. Reflexive courses on the philosophy of global law are also mandatory. Skills courses on methodology in social science and argumentation are taught separately. In the third year, there is room for going on an exchange, taking a 'minor' in business and law or doing a bridge semester to qualify for a Dutch legal master (to gain 'civiel effect').

The background to (developing) the programme seems to lie in research on the whole notion of global law in the context of processes of globalisation that is carried out at Tilburg University. Here, global law can be understood as (Backer, 2012, p.177):

> [T]he systematization of anarchy, as the management of a loosely intertwined universe of autonomous governance frameworks operating dynamically across borders and grounded in functional differentiation among governance communities. More conventionally, global law can be defined as the law of non-state governance systems.

Others (Augenstein, 2016; Augenstein and Kinley, 2015), for example, develop new approaches to understand law in the global context, for example human rights law and its position vis-à-vis the international order, where processes of internationalisation coincide with processes of globalisation. These research approaches are visible in the programme, something that was recognised by the NVAO (2012, p.3). It makes the programme unique, at least in the Netherlands, in respect of both its conceptual *and* normative approach to studying law.

Law in Society

The Law in Society Programme at the Free University Amsterdam takes an entirely different approach, introducing a large social science component into a thematically structured curriculum. It prepares students 'to gain relevant insights in the role and effects of law in the context of current societal challenges and through the use of the "mixed classroom" concept' (NVAO, 2018, p.3). In doing so, these insights, if applicable, are 'based on and substantiated by social scientific observations or insights' (NVAO, 2018, p.7).

It is, like the Global Law Programme and the PPLE Programme, an English-language programme for selected students. The aim is to create and apply the concept of the 'mixed classroom', in which students from different nationalities and cultural backgrounds form a community of learning. It provides 'an effective learning environment to develop competences in intercultural interaction and negotiation' (NVAO, 2018, p.7). The innovative aspect, for the purposes of this contribution, is how the curriculum is structured, departing from the traditional curriculum. The focus of the programme is not on the traditional areas of law. Rather, it focuses on real societal problems studied from different legal perspectives simultaneously. Students employ research-based learning, in an international/intercultural setting, using a multidimensional approach with a strong component of social scientific methodology (https://bachelors.vu.nl/nl/opleidingen/law-in-society/index.aspx (accessed 26 January 2019)). The programme distinguishes four societal themes, which are studied at the 'local' and 'global' level across the first four semesters: security, globalisation of markets, migration and sustainability.

These themes are studied in four parallel learning trajectories: law and legal skills, empirical research skills, social science and general academic development. Law, in the end, is thematically studied. Thus, for example, when addressing the theme of security (in one semester), legal issues in respect of criminal law and private law (libel, blasphemy and assault) are studied in the context of empirical research and methodology as well as philosophy of law, and diversity. In their third year, law students (who speak Dutch) can opt to do a minor in Dutch law in order to gain access to a Dutch masters and obtain 'civiel effect'. The programme is concluded with a thesis in which students demonstrate mastery of the four learning trajectories (https://bachelors.vu.nl/nl/opleidingen/law-in-society/index.aspx (accessed 26 January 2019)).

Integrative (Law in Context)

The law programme at Utrecht University law school is, in contrast to the other examples described above, traditional in its structure and is taught in Dutch. The bachelor curriculum was revised four years ago and is structured along three learning trajectories: the legal knowledge trajectory, the skills trajectory and the context and method trajectory. These trajectories are integrated in the mandatory courses of the programme, covering 150 of the 180 credits. The knowledge trajectory is geared towards an understanding of the major legal sub-disciplines: private law, administrative and constitutional law, criminal law and international and European law. It starts with introductory courses in the first year, deepening the knowledge base in the second and third year. The skills trajectory prepares students to master the relevant legal, professional and academic skills spread over the mandatory courses of the programme in a structured way, enabling students to track their development in respect of the different skills. Innovative and integrative is the so-called context and methodology trajectory.

This trajectory introduces a multidimensional approach towards positive law (based on an internal report (Projectgroep Context en Methoden, 2014), available on request). This approach implies that students study law in a theoretical as well as a societal context. The theoretical context employs approaches that challenge students to look beyond the law in general and beyond the different areas of law. It places the study of law in the context of other non-legal disciplines, such as sociology, economics and governance. Each course on positive law has integrated such a contextual component. For example, in a course on criminal law, developments in this field are placed in the context of risk society theory (Beck, 1992), introducing a social theoretical perspective. In a course on the law of obligations, the tort of negligence is studied also from an economic perspective to determine how loss could be distributed. At the same time, the courses introduce a societal context, incorporating societal questions and dilemmas that arise as a result of developments such as globalisation, climate change and individualisation. Thus, in tort law, the tort of negligence is studied in the context of the so-called *Urgenda* case, where the district court ruled, upheld by the Court of Appeal, the state to be negligent in not meeting the CO_2 emission targets (see ECLI:NL: GHDHA: 2018: 2591 (the original judgment in Dutch); the English version: ECLI: NL: GHDHA: 2018: 2610).

In respect of methodology, the trajectory teaches students the relevance of the different types of question one can ask when studying law within a given context. These questions can be either descriptive (conceptual and empirical) or normative (legal interpretative and 'pure' normative). (This distinction between four types of question is based on a non-published text, available for students (Majoor, Kiewiet, and Quist, 2017), available on request.) Knowing which question to ask is instructive as to what methodology to employ to seek answers to the questions. In the end, students realise that law and the study of law is not only an 'interpretative' exercise but also based on empirical and conceptual knowledge, as well as a normative position. This trajectory allows students to develop a critical mind and strengthens the academic character of the law programme at Utrecht University.

Concluding remarks

This descriptive sketch sought to illustrate how the landscape of legal education is changing, moving away from a traditional and doctrinal inspired curriculum towards an education that introduces interdisciplinary perspectives with an emphasis on empirical studies, theory and methodology. This shift can be explained, for a large part, by a growing need of a different type of lawyer, who meets the requirements of the so-called T-shaped professional. Similar to what Watson argues in the previous chapter (referring to Schäfke, Mayoral Diaz-Asensio and Stagelund Hvidt (2018, 274), the idea is that an 'interdisciplinary approach can help students to develop "boundary-crossing competencies" that equip practicing lawyers to work effectively with graduates from other disciplines on interdisciplinary teams'.

The examples above tap into this concept, be it explicit or implicit.

Overall, the changing landscape challenges students to study law in a different way. Students will be better able to shift between a more doctrinal approach and a more empirical approach, based on observations and insights from the various social sciences (NVAO, 2018). This shift – the legal discipline moving away from a more humanities-based home towards a social science-based home – coincides with or can be explained in itself by the growing attention paid to stimulating empirical legal research in the Netherlands, and seems to suggest an emphasis on the vocational aspect of legal education, providing students with the relevant professional skills set.

Before moving towards the evaluative part of this chapter, criticising this vocational emphasis, a brief examination of the field of empirical legal studies is warranted.

Empirical legal studies

A recent report emphasised the importance of empirical legal studies and its scientific and societal contribution (Elbers, 2018). The report echoes in many respects the Nuffield enquiry (Genn, Partington and Wheeler, 2006), mentioned in the previous chapter. Scientifically, empirical legal studies fill the void of the more normative and doctrinal approaches. These approaches often employ implied assumptions as to the function of law, legal subjects and the effectiveness of rules and regulations. Without making these assumptions explicit, they are not subject to research and, if necessary, reconsideration. In addition, lawyers tend to take facts for granted without the facts of a case having been researched. Indeed, Vranken (2006, p.41) complains about the absence of a solid factual basis where arguments and judicial decisions are based on speculation rather than relevant data. Empirical legal research can fill this void. Its societal relevance is that empirical legal studies can provide legal practice and executive bodies with relevant information as to the effectiveness of law. Empirical research can generate insights and contribute to what Van Gestel and Van Dijck (2011) call 'evidence-based legislation'. What works and how it works is often filled in by assumptions of behaviour rather than by solid empirical research and, if they are available, they tend to be ignored (Elbers, 2018, pp.8–9). It is interesting to note that empirical legal studies is embraced in the Netherlands as a way forward. There is a less conservative stance to it, contrary, or so it seems, to the situation in England. (Twining's 'timeless observation' on the worth of liberal education would resonate well in the Netherlands, as mentioned in the previous chapter.)

Empirical legal studies and legal education

There is certainly merit in the observation that empirical legal studies can fill the 'factual void' and can serve to substantiate the normative claims we can make about law, its function and impact. To this end, empirical legal studies should and could be integrated in legal education. Indeed, looking at the examples, we can observe an increasing attention to this. At the same time, this is a difficult task. Legal education in the context of empirical legal studies is different than merely teaching 'some' sociology and psychology or economics. It demands input from sociology and psychology or economics itself. It calls for a move towards interdisciplinary cooperation between legal scholars and social scientists for the benefit of legal education. The Law in Society Programme, as described above, is unique in that it caters for this approach in a structural way. An important obstacle to overcome is that of miscommunication – the inability of different disciplinary groups to understand one another's language (Elbers, 2018, citing Smit, 2016). Overcoming this and other obstacles starts with changes in legal education without, as will be argued in the evaluative part, considering empirical interdisciplinarity as the holy grail of the future of legal education. Indeed, Smits (2014) reminds us of the 'inevitable normativity of legal studies'. This will be explored in the next paragraph.

Interdisciplinarity

The programmes described above have in common that they emphasise a broadening of academic legal education (at undergraduate level), branching out towards other disciplinary knowledge, introducing a broad skill set. Indeed, it is a welcome development. Nevertheless, it should not blur our vision on the 'inevitable normativity of legal studies'.

With Van Klink and Bleeker (2017), I plead for studying law in a broader social, moral and theoretical context. A broader legal education enables students to contextualise law, preparing students to think about scientific and social challenges of the future and to formulate (legal) solutions for problems these challenges will bring about. In doing so, they contribute to the social evolution of law. It also stimulates students to develop a critical attitude. It strengthens their capability of judgement, ethical integrity and problem-solving potential. It also enhances cross-disciplinary cooperation. Indeed, it allows for awareness of the fact that legal practice is both an empirical and normative activity. I also agree with Mak (2017, p.19) that our future lawyers must 'develop an ethical frame of reference in order to prepare for personal choices of conduct in challenging moral circumstances. (To educate students who are more than legal technicians, as mentioned already above in the introduction to this chapter.)

Why the model of the T-shaped approach falls short

It is clear that the unfolding legal landscape asks future lawyers to be able to 'connect' with other disciplines (but for a different reason). It asks us to reconsider 'legal professionalism' (Mak, 2017). Transferrable skills are obviously necessary but not sufficient. The same goes for a broader knowledge base – although necessary it is not sufficient either. This is why I think that the current notion of the T-shaped lawyer (Smathers, 2014) falls short for two reasons, both relating to the overemphasis on the vocational aspect of legal education.

The first refers to what other disciplinary knowledge is necessary for future lawyers. The beam will look quite different when seeking a career in commercial legal practice than when a student aspires to a career as a litigation lawyer in, for example, criminal law or family law. The beam is too contingent for undergraduate students and often too instrumentally viewed when discussing its content. Indeed, a quick Google scan shows that the beam very much depends on the needs of different legal practices, with many 'hits' referring to broadening the knowledge base of lawyers *after* they have entered legal practice and are confronted with different roles in their professional function, for example as an in-house lawyer (see Peter Connor's blog, https://www.legalbusinessworld.com/single-post/2017/12/22/The-T-Shaped-Lawyer (accessed 29 January 2019). The beam is also on the vocational aspect of legal education (see, for example, this blog by Irene Mo, https://abaforlawstudents.com/2017/

11/02/the-t-shaped-lawyer-disciplines-beyond-law/(accessed 29 January 2019). It raises the question of whether it is the task of law schools, such as in the Netherlands, to provide for this instrumental knowledge, considering the academic nature of legal education rather than its vocational nature, such as in the US. To this end, the T-shaped model is more befitting for lifelong learning and postgraduate professional development than it is for academic development.

This ties in with the second reason, which relates to how the legal and other disciplines are interconnected within a curriculum or programme of study. The T-shaped model seems to be more multidisciplinary than interdisciplinary (as defined above). Thus, the T-shaped model assumes that students study one or more disciplines alongside law within a curriculum of which the knowledge base is useful to the student as a future legal professional. It may well be that the students connect the dots, but integrating the disciplines is not necessarily the aim. Thus, non-legal disciplinary knowledge is presented as supplementary and instrumental. Students may have economic knowledge, for example about the Pareto principle and opportunity costs, but the question remains if this necessarily leads to a better understanding of contact law, as these economic concepts are not studied *in the context of* a contract law course.

Towards disciplinary integration – examples

The examples above illustrate a move towards this interdisciplinarity. Thus, in the Global Law Programme, as already referred to above, the interdisciplinary courses, for example, politics, power and governance, allow for students learning to understand how the manifestations of politics and power relate to the four disciplines. In the integrative seminars, students learn to identify connections and disparities between the different disciplinary perspectives in respect of a particular societal phenomenon.

Likewise, the Law in Society Programme aims at integrated knowledge, where, for example, tort law is studied in the context of the broader, cross-disciplinary, theme of security and commercial law is taught within the context of the cross-disciplinary theme of the globalisation of markets. The programme's strength is how it integrates different legal vocabularies, social science and legal cultures in each course. Thus, in respect of the broader theme of security, students are taught different legal vocabularies (for example about libel) to define a social problem (hate speech) in the context of security and how this social problem can be framed differently in terms of cultural traditions. Based on the concept of the 'mixed classroom', students bring in and engage with one another's experiences (this description is based on the initial accreditation application, in the possession of the author.).

Another example of disciplinary integration is a course on environmental law at Utrecht University on energy transition and its technical challenges (I thank Sanne Akerboom (assistant professor in law and political science) for allowing me to 'borrow' her approach to illustrate a way of disciplinary integration.) It is a course for law students and geography students, engaging both groups of students in how geographical, technical and legal questions are interrelated. Thus, when exploring possible new technologies to enable the energy transition, geography students become aware of the legal questions that need to be dealt with while law students become aware to what extent the law needs to be reconsidered in order to allow for a regulatory framework that enables the energy transition rather than obstructing it. Both sets of students become aware of what is technically and legally possible and/or impossible. This approach makes students aware that there is more than their prospective discipline and that both approaches are essential for stimulating sustainable development. It is aimed at mutual understanding of problems and barriers; without a proper understanding of technology a lawyer cannot legislate properly and without an understanding of institutional barriers an engineer is not prepared for a successful implementation of new technology.

These are merely a few examples of many initiatives in respect of interdisciplinary teaching and learning. What I aim at in my own teaching and what I envisage is to go a step further in this process of disciplinary integration in that this integration should or could take place at a higher cognitive level, beyond pure (conceptual) knowledge.

Law in context – interdisciplinary integration

What I aim at is a contextual understanding of cross-disciplinary knowledge, allowing for a reflexive academic approach. In this last paragraph, I seek to sketch the contours of such an understanding, distinguishing four steps. In doing so, I take a different approach then is sketched in the previous chapter where the emphasis is put on teaching and learning law in the context of a real-world perspective. My approach is more theoretical.

A contextual understanding, taking law as a point of departure, consists first of a firm disciplinary grounding. This grounding exists not only of knowledge of the law, its system and concepts. It goes further than that and refers also to its vantage points or theoretical anchors, the types of research question that are asked and the methodology to be used in order to answer these. This has a normative as well as an empirical component. It asks for a proper theoretical foundation of law and its meaning, teasing out the binary position of lawful and unlawful, of what is law and what is not law, and how law relates to other rule-based systems, such computer code, social conventions, etc. A firm disciplinary grounding allows students to take perspective. Here they discover the limits of the discipline – law – and realise that other perspectives are necessary to understand societal problems, for example the social consequences of climate change. (This is the approach taken in the environmental law course, mentioned above.) Students learn to identify other relevant disciplinary knowledge allowing for a different lens to look at social/legal problems. This allows in its turn for finding common ground. Students learn to recognise the differences and similarities of the different disciplinary perspectives. Here, they discover, for example that law is organised on the basis of the position lawful and unlawful, whereas economics is organised along different anchors, such as supply and demand, efficiency, cost benefit or profit maximalisation. Thus, the economist looks at the market as one of supply and demand, whereas a lawyer regards it as one of offer and acceptance and transfer of property rights. This mutual recognition may lead to disciplinary integration and the ability for fruitful cooperation, for example, teasing out how to regulate a market. This is what I mean by studying law in the context of other disciplinary knowledge and, obviously, it demands a radical new way of teaching and learning law.

The value of reflexivity

Furthermore, being able to study law in the context of other disciplinary knowledge opens up the possibility for a reflexive approach, which I worked out in *Academic Learning in Law* (Van Klink and De Vries, 2016). Reflexivity provides a way to think about law in a critical way. Reflexivity refers to the learning process of a student as well as to the contemporary social context in which legal learning takes place. Social theory is a discipline that provides knowledge of such a context. Instructive is the work of, for example Ulrich Beck (Beck, Giddens and Lash, 1994, p.2), who argues that '"reflexive modernisation" means the possibility of a creative (self)destruction for an entire epoch: that of industrial society' and it entails 'first the disembedding and second the re-embedding of industrial social forms by another modernity'.

Taking an understanding of reflexive modernisation seriously implies a task, Beck argues. It is a task to modernise modernity and to deal with all kinds of side effect, such as the social consequences of climate change or digitalisation. To be able to address these side effects, the ramifications must be known and problematised, taking different disciplinary perspectives. Reflexivity as a task is, subsequently, a means of self-confrontation: 'to lay bare and deal with the uncertainties produced by the successes of modernity through a reconfiguration of its foundations' (De Vries, 2016, p.285). It starts with processing information into disciplinary knowledge and insight, with the aim to uncover the self-evident assumptions that usually direct the way we observe the world. This opens up the possibility to view the world in alternative ways. It helps reconsidering self-evident foundations in law to establish a new normative field for choices and decisions, over and beyond empirical knowledge (as suggested by Vranken (2006)). This uncertainty is threatening but creates also possibilities insofar as one has the courage to embrace this academic uncertainty. Cross-disciplinary learning, cooperation and communication are means to achieve this task.

One example: poetry and authoritarianism

One example may perhaps illustrate this way of teaching and learning. In one course I teach, I seek to problematise the idea of the rule of law, as a means to control (arbitrary) power and facilitate freedom and equality. At the same time, we can observe a move towards authoritarian leadership and how this threatens our modern ideals. When I then confront students with the work of Thomas Hobbes (*Leviathan*), students quickly understand the essence of Hobbes' theory on absolute rule, but they find it difficult to *think* about the text differently, more critically, and analyse its relevance to contemporary problems in (world) politics and law, to discover their own position – their sovereign voice.

To challenge them to discover their own voice (to formulate a particular position on the problem of authoritarianism and the rule of law), I asked them to write a poem about the essence of Hobbes' theory in the context of today's society. The result was a volume of about 25 poems that we read and discussed in class. Students indicated that, while gaining a better understanding of Hobbes, they also felt they had developed an original train of thought, sharpening their *own* view on the problem of authoritarianism and the rule of law.

It helped students to imagine law's social context and that our understanding of society is not self-evident but the result of reasoning about society (or the societal context of a legal problem). As I observed in my article that reports in detail on this intervention (De Vries, 2019, p.8):

> Such understanding and reasoning strengthen our thought processes when dealing with legal problems and dilemmas, opening different avenues for explanation, meaning and solution. It comes with theoretical and methodological rigour. It is the stuff of jurisprudence, legal theory, political philosophy and social theory.

Conclusion

Talking about interdisciplinarity means the extent in which students learn the law and are enabled to think about the law. The study of law is more than vocational training (at least in the continental tradition). To think about the law (what is it, why is it as it is and could it be different, how it relates to social developments, etc.) is, essentially, a normative activity, empirically informed. Fundamental texts, such as in the field of jurisprudence, legal and social theory as well as other disciplines provide a frame of reference for this activity. Indeed, as Stolker (2014, p.218) points out, law remains a normative activity in which a single right answer, based on the case study method, is not sufficient to grasp law – it demands different additional perspectives.

It is obvious that social developments impact on academic legal education. The traditional and monodisciplinary approach can no longer be maintained to prepare law students for real-world problems. Disciplines that for long have been differentiated, each covering its own field, move towards one another, as we understand societal problems in a more integrated way. It leads to a new way of studying law *and* understanding law (as well as studying and understanding other disciplines). This new way cannot but be interdisciplinary inspired. For this to be realised, we have to work out a new or different didactic and pedagogy. The programmes described above have made a first step towards this new way of teaching and learning.

In the end, interdisciplinarity is not an aim itself but serves to contribute to a sense of self-awareness, allowing law students to discover their own voice in law and legal debate and to discover the normative position. Andreas Philippopoulos-Mihalopoulos (2015) does this by walking with students in the environment, when studying environmental law. I use poetry as a means for students to discover their voice (De Vries, 2019). In other words, following Biesta (2013, p.4), law students have to 'come into the world', mastering the act of freedom and responsibility, as (potential) legal professionals and as human beings.

Bibliography

Augenstein, D. (2016). Paradise lost: sovereign state interest, global resource exploitation and the politics of human rights. *European Journal of International Law*, 27(3), 669–691.

Augenstein, D. and Kinley, D. (2015). Beyond the 100 acre wood: in which international human rights law finds new ways to tame global corporate power. *International Journal of Human Rights*, 828–848.

Backer, L. C. (2012). The structural characteristics of global law for the 21st century: fracture, fluidity, permeability, and polycencricity. *Tilburg Law Review*, 17, 177–199.

Beck, U. (1992). *Risk Society. Towards a New Modernity*. (M. Ritter, Trans.). London: Sage.

Beck, U., Giddens, A. andLash, S. (1994). *Reflexive Modernisation. Politics, Tradition and Aesthetics in the Modern Social Order*. Cambridge, Polity.

Biesta, G. J. (2013). *The Beautiful Risk of Education*. London, Paradigm Publishers.

Convenant Civiel Effect (2016, March 22). Utrecht.

De Vries, B. (2019, Jan–Mar). Law, imagination and poetry. Using poetry as a means of learning. Special issue on active learning and teaching in legal education. *Law & Method*, http://www.lawandmethod.nl/tijdschrift/lawandmethod/2019/1/lawandmethod-D-18-00011.

De Vries, U. (2016). Law and lounge. An experiment on student self-organisation and critique as skeptical reflexivity. In Van Klink, B. andDe Vries, U. *Academic Learning in Law Theoretical Positions, Teaching Experiments and Learning Experiences*. Cheltenham, Edward Elgar, pp. 267–287.

Elbers, N. E. (2018). *Rapport Nationale Stimuleringsactie Empirical Legal Studies*. The Hague, NSCR.

Genn, H., Partington, M. and Wheeler, S. (2006). *Law in the Real World: Improving Our Understanding of How Law Works*. London, Nuffield Foundation.

Hunter, C. (2012). *Integrating Socio-Legal Studies in the Law Curriculum*. New York, Palgrave Macmillan.

Karanika-Murray, M. and Wiesemes, R. (eds.) (2009). *Exploring Avenues to Interdisciplinary Research: From Cross- to Multi- to Interdisciplinarity*. Nottingham, Nottingham University Press.

Laemers, M. (2017). Het convenant civiel effect 2016: leidt meer uniformiteit tot meer academische kwaliteit? *Ars Aequi* (February), 155–161.

Majoor, M., Kiewiet, J. and Quist, C. (2017). *Typen van Vragen: Een Landkaartje*. Utrecht, University of Utrecht Press.

Mak, E. (2017). *The T-Shaped Lawyer and Beyond. Rethinking Legal Professionalism and Legal Education for Contemporary Societies*. The Hague, Eleven International Publishers.

NVAO (2018). *Panel Advice WO-Bachelor Law in Society Vrije Universiteit Amsterdam*. The Hague, NVAO.

NVAO (2014). *Panel Advice WO-Bachelor Politics, Psychology, Law and Economics, Universiteit van Amsterdam*. The Hague, NVAO.

NVAO (2012). *Besluit Strekkende tot een Positieve Beoordeling van een Aanvraag om Accreditatie van de Opleiidng WO-Bachelor Internationaal en Europees Recht van de Universiteit van Tilburg*. The Hague, NVAO.

Philippopoulos-Mihalopoulos, A. (2015). *Spatial Justice: Body, Lawscape, Atmosphere*, Abingdon, Routledge.

Projectgroep Context en Methoden (2014). *Naar een nieuwe academische Verdieping: Vervlechting van Context en Methoden in het Curriculum*. Utrecht, University of Utrecht Press.

Schäfke, W., Mayoral Diaz-Asensio, J. and Stagelund Hvidt, M. (2018). Socialisation to interdisciplinary legal education: an empirical assessment. *The Law Teacher*, 52(3), 273–294.

Smathers, R. A. (2014). The 21st-century t-shaped lawyer. *Law Practice Magazine*, 40(4), 33–37.

Smit, M. (2016). Interdisciplinaire samenwerking: complicaties en kansen. *Empirical Legal Studies: Heden en Horizon*. The Hague, NSCR.

Smits, J. (2014). Law and interdisciplinarity: on the inevitable normativity of legal studies. *Critical Analysis of Law*, 1(1), 75–86.

Snoep, M. (2014, Mar 17). Opleiding jurist Moet Breder. *NRC Handelsblad*.

Stolker, C. (2014). *Rethinking the Law School. Education, Research, Outreach and Governance*. Cambridge, Cambridge University Press.

Susskind, R. (2013). *Tomorrow's Lawyers*. Oxford, Oxford University Press.

Van der Zwaan, B. (2017). *Higher Education in 2040. A Global Perspective*. (V. Collingwood, Trans.). Amsterdam, Amsterdam University Press.

Van Gestel, R. and Van Dijck, G. (2011). Better regulation through experimental legislation. *European Public Law*, 17(3), 539–553.

Van Klink, B. and De Vries, U. (2016). *Academic Learning in Law Theoretical Positions, Teaching Experiments and Learning Experiences*. Cheltenham, Edward Elgar.

Van Klink, B., De Vries, B. and Bleeker, T. (2017). Recht in context Naar een brede academische vorming van juristen. *Nederlands Juristenblad* (14), 1–10.

Vaughan, S. and Oakley, E. (2016). 'Gorilla exceptions'and the ethically apathetic corporate lawyer. *Legal Ethics*, 19(1), 50–75.

Vranken, J. B. (2006). *Exploring the Jurist's Frame of Mind*. Deventer, Kluwer Law International.

Part 3

Legal education and technology

The following two chapters explore how developments in technology and its use and application are impacting on legal education. In Chapter 5, Ryan and McFaul consider its growing influence on UK law schools and the legal profession, using The Open University's Open Justice Centre as a case study to demonstrate the potential challenges and opportunities. In Chapter 6, Halder reflects on the role of technology within Indian society, drawing on examples from legal education and a series of important court judgments. Both chapters emphasise the importance of developing law students' engagement with, and understanding of, technology, with Halder's suggesting the use of therapeutic jurisprudence as an appropriate lens.

Chapter 5

Innovative technologies in UK legal education

Francine Ryan and Hugh McFaul

Introduction

Technological innovation has begun to change the delivery and accessibility of professional legal services and has opened up new ways of accessing legal information, support and advice. How should law schools respond to this changing legal landscape? This chapter will assess the impact of digital transformation on the legal profession and administration of justice to consider whether practice-ready law graduates need more than a traditional legal skills base to navigate their way through a changing legal landscape. It will then explore how pedagogical innovations can enhance the teaching of law and consider the extent to which technological literacy should be integrated into the curriculum. It will draw on two case studies to illustrate how law schools have begun to respond by developing pedagogies that equip law students to deal with the protean nature of technological change. It will also consider the differences between the UK and Indian perspectives on this issue, drawing on the discussion in Halder's companion chapter.

How technology has impacted on legal services

The market for legal services is changing rapidly; technological innovation and globalisation are disrupting traditional models of delivery. The internet is revolutionising all aspects of legal practice, including the way in which legal professionals interact with colleagues and clients, how they conduct legal research and how legal practices are managed (Law Society, 2019). Adoption of technology impacts not only on working methods but also on how disputes are resolved; there has been significant growth of online dispute resolution (ODR) providing an alternative method of resolving legal problems. One example is the European Commission ODR platform (launched in 2016), which allows consumers to address issues with goods or services purchased online. Consumers and traders in the EU, Iceland, Norway and Liechtenstein can use the service and thereby reduce the need for expensive litigation. Technology provides an opportunity to re-examine how we resolve disputes, employing new processes that potentially enhance access to justice (Katsch and Rabinovich-Einy, 2017). Improvements in mobile and online communication tools are likely to lead to further developments and growth in ODR.

Digitalisation is also reshaping the administration of justice. In April 2016, the higher criminal courts in England and Wales moved to fully digitalised evidence files, and the introduction of virtual hearings (Ministry of Justice, 2018). But most significant is the £1 billion Her Majesty's Courts and Tribunal Service (HMCTS) reform programme, which aims to integrate technology into the justice system (HM Courts & Tribunal Service, 2018). There are 50 projects in the programme including a digital divorce service, online plea and allocation in criminal cases and a common platform accessible by all participants in the criminal justice system. In terms of the modernisation programme, perhaps the most ambitious element is the adoption of the proposal of Lord Justice Briggs to create an online civil court to resolve money cases up to £25,000 (Briggs, 2016). Implementation and testing are ongoing, so it is too early to judge how far the court will transform our justice system, but, along with ODR, it has the potential to increase access to justice and further transform the legal landscape.

Advancements in technology are not confined to the administration of justice; the practice of law is changing through a shift towards delivering legal services via internet-based technology. Law firms are integrating technology within their practices to enhance the way they operate, responding to demands from clients to provide more efficient and cost-effective services. Advances in mobile technologies have seen the emergence of virtual law firms. Adoption of new technologies that increase productivity are likely to result in less demand for lawyers over the coming years, with the Law Society estimating that the adoption of new technologies and changes in ways of working will lead to 20 percent fewer legal services jobs by 2038 (Law Society, England and Wales, 2018a). Technologies such as artificial intelligence, online data rooms and machine learning are becoming an increasingly important aspect of lawyering. As well as impacting on existing areas of law, such as contract, intellectual property and commercial law, advances in technology also give rise to new areas of law, including robotics law, which offer new employment opportunities both in the practice of law and in the development of new careers for lawyers (Susskind, 2017).

The emergence of legal tech start-ups is significant; investment in new legal technology businesses is now at £16 million (Steer and Vestbirk, 2018). It is still a fragmented market with a wide variety of technological applications being developed but encouragingly lawyers are the CEOs and founders of 45 percent of the legal tech start-ups (Steer and Vestbirk, 2018). Examples include Crowd Justice, a crowdfunding platform for legal actions, and Juro, a contract management platform that uses an AI enabled workflow. Coupled with this is the development of the rise of alternative legal providers such as Legal Zoom, which offers a document creation service and fixed price legal plans for access to lawyers. New entrants into the market are innovating using technology to redesign legal services with the potential to create affordable solutions for those who lack the means to pay privately for a lawyer and address the access to justice gap.

Technology within law schools

Generation Z, those born between 1995 and 2012 and coming of age from 2013 to 2020, are now entering law school as digital natives, born into the mobile revolution and having grown up exposed to high levels of technology (Koulopoulos, 2015). Understanding the motivations and skills of this generation is important in understanding how far legal education should respond to digital transformation. It is difficult to get an accurate picture of how far technology is being incorporated within legal education in the UK. Some law schools offer theory-based law and technology modules but very few incorporate practice-based law-tech courses. Manchester University now offers final-year law students the opportunity to collaborate with lawyers, business and computer academics to design law-tech applications that support access to justice (Steer and Vestbirk, 2018). Law students need core legal skills, but also digital skills as an essential requirement to respond to technological change. Digital skills are defined as:

> Digital competence involves the confident, critical and responsible use of, and engagement with, digital technologies for learning, at work, and for participation in society. It includes information and data literacy, communication and collaboration, digital content creation (including programming), safety (including digital well-being and competences related to cybersecurity), and problem solving. (European Commission, 2019 p.1)

The need for these digital skills raises important question regarding how law schools can prepare their graduates for a changed, and changing, legal landscape. Susskind (2017) argues that we need to consider what we are training lawyers for and his concern is that we are not training them to be twenty-first-century lawyers but twentieth-century ones:

> The technology changes triggered by the economic shock (recession of 2008) have changed the tools lawyers used to deliver legal services. New lawyers entering the profession must be ready to practice in today's more efficient and more technology-driven workplace. For the most law schools, are not currently equipped to teach these new skills and technologies. (Staudt and Medeiros, 2013, p.697)

But to what extent should technological literacy be integrated into the curriculum? What knowledge and skills do law students need and how should these be incorporated into the curriculum to deliver a flexible and integrated response to the rapid pace of technological change? Jackson (2016) argues that legal education has been slow to respond to changes in technology and adapt its curriculums. However, it is increasingly clear that law students need technological acumen and proficiency that goes beyond everyday tech skills. The proposition is not that we teach law students to code, although this happens on a number of law technology courses, but instead give them an understanding of how technology works to effectively engage with the legal issues. Technological applications give rise to a host of legal and ethical issues, from privacy online to how new technology is used. Due to the evolving nature of technology, there will be new ethical and legal implications that lawyers will need to respond to. Technological competence is also required to respond to technological innovation. Evolving technologies are permeating all aspects of legal practice and this requires law students to operate in a new legal paradigm. For example, several large UK-based law firms now offer seats (or training contracts) in legal technology. The law school should engender a commitment to continuous learning to ensure students recognise the value of embracing new technological applications. Developing pedagogies to allow students to understand how law relates to broader society and to recognise the potential of harnessing technology to fill the access to justice gap should underpin the curriculum. The pervasive nature of technology requires it to be embedded in new curricula designs. Affording law students opportunities to prepare for a technologically changing world is becoming an increasingly pressing demand on contemporary legal education.

How are law schools responding to technological change?

Law schools have already begun to respond by developing new pedagogies that equip law students to deal with the protean nature of technological change. The integration of online legal research databases are now commonplace among law schools in the UK and beyond (including, as Halder indicates, in India). By virtue of its place within an increasingly digitised higher education sector, the delivery of legal education has embraced technologies such as lecture capture, virtual learning environments and the integration of social media into the curriculum. However, it is the contention of this chapter that the pedagogy and practice of the clinical legal education movement has a distinct role to play in responding the influence of technology and the practice of law and legal education. Clinical legal education (CLE) is a uniquely fertile environment in which to develop pedagogies that develop the capacity for students to thrive in a technologically transformed and transforming legal landscape. This can be illustrated by reference to three key features of CLE practice: its interdisciplinary origins and outlook, the focus on the practical application of legal principles and, finally, its use of reflective pedagogy. Each will be discussed in turn below.

As discussed by Grimes and Arthurs in their chapters in this volume, the development of CLE over the latter half of the twentieth century demonstrates it to be a countercultural movement within mainstream legal education, and one which has embraced pedagogical innovation and interdisciplinarity. This is illustrated by the origins of the modern CLE movement, which are commonly traced back to Frank (1933). Here, the argument was made that the law schools should move away from the academic- based case law approach, which remains the orthodoxy in common law jurisdictions, and move towards a practical model inspired by medical school clinical teaching. Giddings (2013) highlights that *clinic* is derived from the Greek *klinikos*, which can be translated as 'from the bed'. He argues that this shows the inspiration that legal clinical education has taken from medical education, which emphasises the importance of applying theoretical knowledge in a practical setting, usually for a real or simulated client.

The interdisciplinary origins of CLE illustrate the capacity of this approach to legal education to look beyond disciplinary boundaries, a tendency that is also evident in the common practice of working with partners beyond the university. Externship placements and partnership work to provide students with practical legal experience is commonplace in the UK CLE community, as evidence by the most recent survey of clinical practice (Carney et al., 2014). The focus on providing students with opportunities to experience practical, client-facing applications of legal principles is an integral feature of CLE pedagogy. It is also one that has led to an entrepreneurial and experimental approach to legal education evidenced by the flourishing of a large repertoire of activities that shelter beneath the umbrella of CLE (Drummond and McKeever, 2015; Kemp, 2016). It is the concern to keep the curriculum grounded in practical activities that exposes CLE academics and students to the effects of technological change on legal services and makes them well-placed to pioneer the law school response to it.

Third, CLE emphasises the value of experiential learning, where students are active in the learning process and have the opportunity to reflect and learn from experience. In doing so, it goes beyond skills training and calls on students to engage with the law as an open-ended subject and to scrutinise wide ranging social and legal issues that facilitate professional ethical development in a practical context. (Drummond and McKeever, 2015, p.12). In this way, students are given a framework in which to both experience and reflect on the influence of technology on legal practice.

Thus, CLE provides an environment that can act as a testbed to develop pedagogical responses to the increasing influence of technology on professional legal practice and access to justice. It has already developed a pedagogy that exposes law students to the issues that arise from the practical application of legal principles, whether in simulated or real-world settings. It is entrepreneurial in developing new and varied ways in which to provide students with practical activities, very often with partners in the legal sector. CLE often forms the bridge between the practical and the theoretical aspects of legal education and is therefore well placed to prepare students to engage with the impact of technology on the legal profession as the following two case studies illustrate.

Case study 1. Online law clinic

The creation of an online clinic provides students with opportunities to engage with technology and develop core competencies. Arguably, what we teach in law school needs to reflect changes we are seeing in the delivery of legal services (Susskind, 2017) thus ensuring students are better prepared for the realities of legal practice (Donnelly, 2013).The Open University (OU) in the UK created the Open Justice Centre in 2016 to build a bridge both between the OU law school and the wider community and between law students and the legal profession. It has pioneered the use of experiential learning in distance legal education – it provides opportunities that have a tangible impact on students' employability by combining the provision of real-world professional experience with the development of transferable skills. The defining feature of its pedagogy is the innovative use of experiential learning. The Open Justice Centre has worked to develop pro bono opportunities to allow students to apply their legal knowledge and skills in practical settings to develop transferable professional skills. The challenge was to develop activities that combine experiential learning in a distance law degree – professional pro bono activities require close supervision, carefully managed group work and strong relationships with the legal community. All these present challenges for a distance learning institution.

Our solution was to create an innovative virtual law clinic allowing students to deliver legal services online and serve clients who may not have the opportunity to access a face-to-face law clinic, the Open Justice Law Clinic. A 'virtual law practice' enables the delivery of legal services online through a secure web portal where communication is encrypted and protected (Granat and Kimbro, 2017). The clinic supports students in using technology to advise clients under the supervision of qualified solicitors using a leading industry legal case and practice management system, Clio. Familiarity with practice management software is important because it is what lawyers use to manage day-to-day case work and the operations of their practice. The software allows the clinic to manage the cases, contacts, calendars, documents, tasks, time recording and client communications via one platform.

The students work with clients online to support them with their legal problems and provide advice and information to help them resolve their issues. One of the defining features of the clinic is that it is accessible to anyone with an internet connection – utilising technology to reach clients across the UK. Students interview clients online via Adobe Connect, appointments are offered flexibly including evenings and weekends. All other interaction between clients, students and supervisors takes place within the practice management system via secure messaging. The clinic replicates practice by working electronically and sharing documents via a secure portal. The clinic uses an automated document assembly; all case and contact information is stored within Clio enabling the creation of documents prepared from templates. Students are encouraged to time record not only as important practice-ready skill but for the clinic to track the value of the pro bono work. Working in the clinic affords students the opportunity to gain an understanding of the legal process but also practical experience of using technology to facilitate access to justice.

Case study 2. Utilising smartphone applications in CLE

The exponential growth in the computing power of smartphones has resulted in an equally rapid growth in the use and ownership of these devices. The forecast for the number of smartphone users by 2022 is predicted to be 53.96 million (Statista, n.d.). The near ubiquity of smartphone ownership in the UK has already begun to have an influence on the way legal services have been developed and accessed (Law Society, 2018b). This has led to law schools incorporating this smartphone technology into their clinical curricula. One example of this development is projects that allow law students to develop smartphone apps able to disseminate legal information. For example, the University of Manchester, London Southbank University and the University of Birmingham have all begun to experiment with challenging their students to engage with this form of technology to test out new ways of disseminating legal knowledge and thereby improving access to justice (Legal Cheek, 2018).

The Open Justice Centre at the OU Law School has developed a similar interdisciplinary project in conjunction with computer science academics, which gives law students the chance to develop a smartphone app that will provide legal information. This could potentially be applied to a number of legal topic areas, but the initial phase of the project will design an app to support litigants in person in understanding procedures relevant to discrimination and employment law. Students conduct legal research on the topic area and work with computing specialists to translate this information into a form that would be suitable for inclusion into a smartphone app format and sufficiently accessible to be useful to member of the public with little or no prior legal knowledge. Students are expected to reflect on their experience of participating in the context of overarching themes of social justice, legal ethics and professional identity. In doing so, they are given practical exposure to the way legal services are being transformed by digital technologies.

The Open Justice Centre has also experimented with incorporating smartphone-based virtual reality into the clinical curriculum to support the development of legal communication skills in a distance learning module. The challenges involved in teaching presentation skills in a distance learning setting is recognised in the literature (Rogerson-Revell, 2015; McDougall and Holden, 2017). To help meet these challenges students were provided with communication and presentation skills training to enhance their ability to engage in their clinical work. A smartphone-based virtual reality (VR) application was developed as a bespoke experiential learning application to provide learners with an immersive simulated environment in which to practise their presentation skills, receive automated feedback and increase their confidence and effectiveness in delivering presentations. It provides three virtual worlds: those of a prison, a community centre and a secondary school classroom, each populated with avatars that respond to the presentation with pre-recorded questions. There is also a prototype courtroom virtual world. Students can upload presentation slides to the virtual world, record their presentation and watch themselves deliver the presentation from the point of view of an audience member. The VR app also scores the presenter's eye contact with the audience and where a presenter fails to make eye contact, the audience avatars begin to behave restlessly. It is designed to be used on a smartphone in conjunction with a basic handheld VR headset that was provided to students. The VR app is freely available for both IOS and Android devices and can be found by searching for 'Open Justice VR'.

The incorporation of smartphone-based virtual reality into legal education is a recent development and, as a result, there is little research literature on its effectiveness in this context. However, there is evidence that it has the potential to deliver positive outcomes in higher education settings (Merchant et al., 2014) and its ability to provide an immersive sense of presence in a virtual environment has clear potential in clinical settings where the ability to practise legal skills in a simulated setting is of great value (Dede, Jacobson and Richards, 2017; Maharg, 2017; Sanchez-Vives and Slater, 2005; Slater, 2017). Nwaneri (2016, p.107) alludes to this potential by suggesting that: 'Virtual worlds offer particular promise for those seeking innovative and cost-effective ways to integrate more professional training and skills development into the law school curriculum.'

However, in common with the adoption of many types of novel educational technologies, there are considerable challenges to be faced in successfully incorporating smartphone technologies into the clinical curriculum, challenges that are also encountered elsewhere within the higher education setting. A review from Fitzgerald et al. (2013) of the start of Mobile Augmented Reality Technology in education makes the point that there is a danger in allowing the technology to drive the pedagogy, as this can lead to the failure of technologies to make their anticipated impact in educational settings. This insight seems equally applicable to the development and transfer of smartphone apps into the clinical curriculum.

The Indian context

Educating law students about the impact of technology on the delivery of legal services and legal education extends across jurisdictions. Professor Halder's chapter addresses some of the interesting technological developments happening in India, many of which resonate with our experiences in the UK. Similarities exist between jurisdictions as information technology is also driving change in the administration of justice in India, with the introduction of the e-court system and digital case management systems. India is grappling with the challenges of digitisation and how best to prepare law graduates for a rapidly changing legal environment, as is the UK. Although the kind of work lawyers of the future will do is changing, this change will happen on a global scale and will pay no respect to jurisdictional boundaries. As such, the extent and manner in which legal education responds to the realities of emerging practices will determine how prepared law students are for the changes happening within the legal market place. The market for legal services is becoming increasingly more competitive, expert legal knowledge is being commodified and this has significant implications for lawyers of the future (Deloitte, 2016). The risk is that if legal educators fail to adequately prepare law students for these changes, they will be unable to take advantages of the opportunities that exist from technology (Goodenough and Lauritsen, 2012).

India has also recognised the importance of equipping Indian lawyers with the skills and capabilities required in a globalised and technological arena; CLE is a feature of Indian legal education with legal aid clinics becoming an increasingly significant aspect of the activities that take place within Indian universities. Organisation of clinical projects in India varies from institution to institution as it does in the UK and experimenting with the incorporation of technology into the curriculum appears limited to only a handful of universities, which is symptomatic of resource and infrastructure challenges that can also present obstacles to innovation in the UK context. What is clear is that new and innovative models of CLE are starting to emerge across all jurisdictions, which offer an effective way to teach the skills and attitudes required to enable law students to respond imaginatively to the changes and opportunities that technology can bring.

Clinical programmes have the potential to provide a wide range of learning opportunities that integrate technology into the law curriculum. Those experiences not only develop the skills and competencies required for professional practice, but as students engage with technology, it provides a richer understanding of the possibilities technology can offer to enhance the legal process (Goodenough and Lauritsen, 2012). To achieve this, both the UK and India can draw on some of the experiences of American universities in developing technology education into their curriculums. Jackson (2016) identified 18 American law schools that had law and technology as core part of their mission. In these programmes, students are part of legal innovation labs using a variety of technological tools including document assembly, development of mobile technologies and designing legal templates to provide technological solutions to legal problems. Jackson (2016) predicts that by 2020, most American law schools will offer some form of technology and legal education. Law schools in other jurisdictions therefore need to bridge the gap between providing a traditional legal education and one that includes some form of technology instruction; failure to integrate the two may result in law students becoming increasingly disadvantaged in a globalised legal marketplace.

The incorporation of technology into legal education extends beyond giving students an understanding of how technology can be harnessed to provide innovative solutions to legal problems; technology raises serious ethical challenges that students need opportunities to recognise and explore. The next chapter raises the issues of data protection and privacy within the Indian jurisdiction. Emerging technologies pose new opportunities and threats; how the law responds to and regulates technological innovation are issues that should feature in the legal curriculum (Land and Aronson, 2018). Students need opportunities to critically examine the relationship between law and technology to evaluate whether developments in technology have the potential to undermine the interests and values the law serves to protect (Cockfield, 2003). Integrating and blending technology into legal education has the potential to enrich the legal curriculum; opportunities exist to develop interdisciplinary partnerships to encourage the facilitation of technology within legal education (Goodenough and Lauritsen, 2012).

Law schools in India and the UK need to consider their responsibilities to educate their students to deal successfully with a rapidly changing legal workplace (Pitstone, 2014). CLE has the potential to develop pedagogical responses that offer new models of teaching and learning that can meet the needs of law students and respond to the increasing influence of technology on professional legal practice and access to justice. Now is the time for law schools to re-evaluate the place of technology in their curricula and consider whether they should be teaching students about the legal and ethical implications of technological disruption. Technology has the power to transform the delivery of legal services and the administration of justice (Susskind, 2017); the argument for law schools to actively engage students in the debate around the role of technology within law is therefore a compelling one.

Conclusion

Technological innovation is disrupting the delivery and accessibility of professional legal services and there are new ways to access legal information, support and advice. The extent of the impact of digital transformation of the legal profession and administration of justice can be felt across jurisdictions, including in the UK and India. Law schools need to respond by considering the skills and capabilities law graduates now require to navigate their way through a changing legal landscape. This chapter has argued that the CLE movement provides a rich seam of pedagogical innovation that can be utilised to help law schools respond with imagination and flexibility. Law schools have the opportunity to enhance the teaching of law by integrating technological literacy into the curriculum. If this opportunity is taken, they can succeed in developing pedagogies that equip their students to deal with the protean nature of technological change and flourish within the emerging legal paradigm.

Bibliography

Briggs, M. (2016). *Civil Courts Structure Review*, https://www.judiciary.uk/civil-courts-structure-review/civil-courts-structure-review-ccsr-final-report-published/ (accessed 6 November 2018).

Carney, D., Dignan, F., Grimes, R., Kelly, G. and Parker, R. (2014). *The LawWorks Law School Pro Bono and Clinics Report 2014*, London, LawWorks, https://www.lawworks.org.uk/sites/default/files/LawWorks-student-pro-bono-report%202014.pdf (accessed 6 November 2018).

Cockfield, A. (2003). Towards a law and technology theory. *Manitoba Law Journal*, 30, 383–416.

Dede, C., Jacobson, J. and Richards, J. (2017). Introduction: Virtual, Augmented, and Mixed Realities in Education. In Liu, D., Dede, C., Huang, R. and Richards, J. (eds.). *Virtual, Augmented, and Mixed Realities in Education*. Singapore, Springer.

Deloitte (2016). *From Brawn to Brains: The Impact of Technology on Jobs in the UK*, https://www2.deloitte.com/content/dam/Deloitte/uk/Documents/Growth/deloitte-uk-insights-from-brawns-to-brain.pdf (accessed 12 April 2019).

Donnelly, B. (2013). If only we knew what we know, *Chicago-Kent Law Review*, 88, 729.

Drummond, O. and McKeever, G. (2015). *Access to Justice through University Law Clinics*, Ulster University Law School, https://www.ulster.ac.uk/__data/assets/pdf_file/0003/132654/Access-to-Justice-through-Uni-Law-Clinics-November-2015.pdf (accessed 6 November 2018).

European Commission (2019). *Digital Competence and Technology in Education*, https://ec.europa.eu/esf/transnationality/TPI-2246 (accessed 11 May 2019).

Fitzgerald, E., Ferguson, R., Adams, A., Gaved, M., Mor, Y. and Thomas, R. (2013). Augmented reality and mobile learning: the state of the art. *International Journal of Mobile and Blended Learning (IJMBL)*, 5(4), 43–58.

Frank, J. (1933). Why not a clinical lawyer-school? *University of Pennsylvania Law Review*, 81(8), 907.

Giddings, J. (2013). *Promoting Justice through Clinical Legal Education*. Melbourne, Justice Press.

Goodenough, O. and Lauritsen, M. (2012). *Educating the Digital Lawyer*. New York, LexisNexis.

Granat, R. and Kimbro, S. (2017). The future of virtual law practice. In Haskins, P. *The Relevant Lawyer Re-imaging the Future of the Legal Profession*. Chicago, ABA Standing Committee on Professionalism Center for Professional Responsibility.

H M Courts & Tribunal Service (2018). *HMCTS Reform Programme Projects Explained*, https://www.gov.uk/guidance/hmcts-reform-programme-projects-explained (accessed 6 March 2019).

Katsch, E. and Rabinovich-Einy, O. (2017). *Digital Justice*. Oxford, Oxford University Press.

Kemp, V., Munk T. and Gower, S. (2016). *Clinical Legal Education and Experiential Learning: Looking to the Future*. Manchester, University of Manchester Law School.

Koulopoulos, T. (2015). *Gen Z and Predicting the Future of Behaviour and Technology*, https://www.youtube.com/watch?v=znggH2k7Y6Y (accessed 6 November 2018).

Jackson, D. (2016). Human-centred legal tech: integrating design in legal education. *The Law Teacher*, 50(1),82–97.

Land, M. and Aronson, J. (2018). *New Technologies for Human Rights Law and Practice*. Cambridge, Cambridge University Press.

Law Society (2019) *Lawtech Adoption Research*, https://www.lawsociety.org.uk/support-services/research-trends/lawtech-adoption-report/ (accessed 26 February 2019).

Law Society (2018a). *Legal Tech in 2018: Threats and Opportunities*, https://www.lawsociety.org.uk/news/blog/legal-tech-2018-threats-and-opportunities/ (accessed 6 November 2018).

Law Society (2018b). *Legal Services Sector Forecast 2017–2025*, https://www.lawsociety.org.uk/support-services/research-trends/legal-services-sector-forecasts/ (accessed 6 November 2018).

Legal Cheek (2018). *Three More Unis Launch Lawtech Modules*, https://www.legalcheek.com/2018/10/three-more-unis-launch-lawtech-modules/ (accessed 6 November 2018).

Maharg, P. (2017). The Periclean plumber: simulation and legal education. In Bergmans, B. (ed.). *Jahrbuch der Rechtsdidaktik 2016/Yearbook of Legal Education 2016*. Berlin, BWV Berliner Wissenschafts-Verlag, pp. 187–212.

Merchant, Z., Goetz, E. T., Cifuentes, L., Keeney-Kennicutt, W. and Davis, T. J. (2014). Effectiveness of virtual reality-based instruction on students' learning outcomes in K-12 and higher education: a meta-analysis. *Computers & Education*, 70, 29–40.

McDougall, J. and Holden, H. (2017). The silence about oral presentation skills in distance and online education: new perspectives from an Australian university preparatory programme. *Journal of Open, Distance and e-Learning*, 32(2), 163–176.

Ministry of Justice (2018). *Judicial Ways of Working – 2022 – Crime*, http://www.transformjustice.org.uk/wp-content/uploads/2018/05/jwow-2022-crime.pdf (accessed 6 March 2019).

Nwaneri, C. (2016). Ready lawyer one: legal issues in the innovation of virtual reality. *Harvard Journal of Law & Technology*, 30, 601.

Pitstone, M. (2014). Law schools and technology: where are we now and where are we heading? *Journal of Legal Education*, 586.

Rogerson-Revell, P. (2015). Constructively aligning technologies with learning and assessment in a distance education master's programme. *Distance Education*, 36(1), 129–147.

Sanchez-Vives, M. V. Slater, M. (2005). From presence to consciousness through virtual reality. *Nature Reviews Neuroscience*, 6, 332–339.

Slater, M. (2017). Implicit learning through embodiment in immersive virtual reality. In Liu, D., Dede, C., Huang, R. and Richards, J. (eds.). *Virtual, Augmented, and Mixed Realities in Education*. Singapore, Springer.

Statista (n.d.). *Forecast of Smartphone User Numbers in the United Kingdom (UK) from 2015 to 2022 (in Million Users)*, https://www.statista.com/statistics/553464/predicted-number-of-smartphone-users-in-the-united-kingdom-uk/ (accessed 6 November 2018).

Staudt, R. and Medeiros, A. (2013). Access to justice and technology clinics: a 4% solution. *Chicago-Kent Law Review*, 88, 695–698.

Steer, S. and Vestbirk, J. (2018). *Movers and Shakers: UK Lawtech Start-ups*, www.info.legalsolutions.thomsonreuters.co.uk/LegalGeek (accessed 6 March 2019).

Susskind, R. (2017). *Tomorrows Lawyers*. Oxford, Oxford University Press.

Vaikutytė-Paškauskė, J., Vaičiukynaitė, J. and Pocius D. (2018). *Research for CULT Committee – Digital Skills in the 21st Century, European Parliament, Policy Department for Structural and Cohesion Policies, Brussels*, http://www.europarl.europa.eu/RegData/etudes/STUD/2018/617486/IPOLSTU(2018)617486_EN.pdf (accessed 17 November 2018).

Chapter 6

Legal education and legal advocacy in the age of digital technology

An Indian perspective

Debarati Halder

Introduction

This chapter will explore the ways in which legal education in India has engaged with the growing role of technology within its legal systems and Indian society as a whole and how it continues to do so. The previous chapter by Ryan and McFaul has demonstrated that, on an international scale, technology now impacts on the way in which legal services are provided, the design and delivery of the court system and myriad other aspects of society and justice. This chapter will briefly sketch the development of legal education within India, with a particular focus on the influence technology has had on this, before moving on to consider a series of seminal judgments that illustrate the importance of raising law students' awareness of this topic. It will also explore the concept of therapeutic jurisprudence as a valuable way in which to ensure students' can critically examine the therapeutic (and anti-therapeutic) consequences of both technology itself and issues around data protection and privacy rights.

The development of legal education in the digital age

In modern India, the legal procedural system, courts and the legal education system are much influenced by the English legal system due to the 200-year-old colonial British rule, which ended in 1947 (Bar Council of India, 2019). The traditional law colleges, which were funded by the government and were parts of the government-funded universities, originally offered law degree courses that spanned three years. Students could join the courses after completing regular graduation or masters courses (Mohan Gopal, 2009, pp.20–21). The subjects that were offered in this course of legal education were designed to cater to the needs of the government and the public who would use the criminal justice system and the civil courts for cases such as crimes against the state, crimes against fellow human beings, civil suits including property matters and corporate-related issues. The English legal system, however, did not override customary law, which has existed in India since the ancient period, tracing its roots in ancient scripts including the Vedas and the Smritis, including Manusmriti, which governed issues such as marriage and succession (Halder and Jaishankar, 2008). Matters such as matrimonial disputes, custody cases and adoption were left in a grey area whereby both customary laws and English laws played their roles for the benefit of the colonial rulers in the pre-independence era (Halder and Jaishankar, 2008). Nonetheless, this system of legal education could not cater to the needs of a welfare state such as India, which experienced a period of "rights explosions" for a long period from the late 1960s until the millennium. The emergency period (1975–1977) in India was a turbulent one, in which rules created by the then prime minister put heavy censorship on several rights, including the right to speech and expression, the right to movement and the right to information (Dutt, 1976, pp.1124–1138). This period is essentially considered as the dawn of a new era of public interest lawyering. As I have observed elsewhere:

> [T]wo judges of the Supreme Court of India, Justices Krishna Iyer and P. N. Bhagawati, started a silent revolution of free legal aid by way of extending the principles of locus standi, ushering in the modern functional concept of free legal aid (Dutt, 1976). Bhagwati was India's first judge who, while heading the Gujarat State legal aid committee, developed a comprehensive meaning of legal aid in 1971. In his words: legal aid means providing an arrangement in the society so that the missionary of administration of justice becomes easily accessible and is not out of reach of those who have to resort to it for enforcement of its given to them by law, the poor and illiterate should be able to approach the courts and their ignorance and poverty should not be an impediment in the way of their obtaining justice from the courts. Legal aid should be available to the poor and illiterate, who don't have access to courts. One need not be a litigant to seek aid by means of legal aid. (Halder, 2019)

As a result of this growing emphasis on public interest lawyering and increasing focus on legal aid and protection of the most vulnerable in society, legal education in India went through a sea change in the 1980s and 1990s. The doyen of modern legal education in India, Professor Madhava Menon, introduced the concept of national law universities, which are autonomous law schools that are governed by the laws of the state. Slowly the concept of a fully fledged, five-year-long, technical legal education system, like that used in the study of the medical sciences in India, was introduced. This was with the massive support from the Bar Council of India, which is the governing body of the legal profession in India. Professor Menon placed more emphasis on clinical legal education rather than theory-based legal education (Mohan Gopal, 2009, pp.117–121). He observed that the advocacy system in India was becoming outdated compared to that of the West, mainly because Indian courts and lawyers were not equipped with modern information communication technology (ICT) and digital communication technology (DCT); the court case management system was not supported by ICT and DCT and there was no IT-enabled database for legal research.

The use of backdated, paper-based communication methods delayed the justice delivery system, which further affected the system of legal advocacy, pro bono advocacy, public interest lawyering and the provision of free legal aid. Professor Menon therefore heavily advocated for including a modern ICT- and DCT-based legal education system that would influence the court management system as a whole (Mohan Gopal, 2009, p.118). With this vision, several national law universities were created by the government with Professor Menon as the main protagonist. These universities offered traditional topics as well as new legal subjects that catered to the needs of a modern internet-era society. These included traditional topics such as procedural law, constitution, jurisprudence, tort law, contract law and international laws, on the one hand, but also modern subjects such as theories of criminology, victimology and penology, intellectual property law, environmental law, animal protection law, sports law and cyber law, on the other. The creation of several private law schools swiftly emerged in India, which followed a similar pedagogy. These were also influential in creating ICT- and DCT-based smart classroom-enabled teaching methods. Using these methods, teachers can deliver lectures using ICT, guide students to access several legal literature databases and connect students to faculties from different jurisdictions through Skype or other similar video chatting systems. The national law universities and the private law schools also revamped their libraries to offer digital databases. This enabled students and faculty members to accesses study materials, legal research papers and digitised books from across the globe.

In spite of this progress, however, it needs to be mentioned that the pedagogy for subjects such as victimology, criminology and cyber law is still developing. These subjects have not yet been introduced by many law schools due to lack of trained faculty members and infrastructure. Only a handful of national law universities, including the National Law School of India University, Bangalore, and the National Academy of Legal Studies and Research, Hyderabad, and private universities, including Karnavati University, are providing credit courses on victimology and optional courses on cyber law. Those that do include courses on cyber law cover topics such as cyber law, cyber criminology, cybercrimes against women and children, cyber security-related issues, data privacy and law-related issues.

Although such pedagogy and offering are still at an emergent stage, the internet and digital technology (including artificial intelligence technology) wave in the legal education sector in India has already impacted on the Indian court management system. The importance of providing digitised information about free legal aid, case status, judgments and orders by the lower and higher judiciary could not be ignored by the Justice Department, Law Commission of India and the Bar Council of India. It was only in 2005 that an e-court system was introduced in India on the basis of the 'National Policy and Action Plan for Implementation of Information and Communication Technology (ICT) in the Indian Judiciary – 2005' (see http://ecourts.gov.in/ecourts_home/static/about-us.php (accessed 1 March 2019)).

One of the drivers for this development of an e-court system and digital case management system is the way India is now embracing a new era of privacy jurisprudence. Ironically, even though the Constitution of India came into existence in 1949, the right to privacy was not recognised as an independent fundamental right until 2018 when the apex court observed, in the case of *Justice Puttaswamy vs Union of India & others*, Writ Petition © no.494 of 2012, that the right to privacy should be given the status of a fundamental right. Incidentally, the case of *Puttaswamy* dealt with various privacy aspects ranging from the rights to both physical and virtual privacy, to a right against government surveillance through the Adhaar platform. This resulted from the government's making it mandatory for every citizen to register their biometrics, birth data and residential data through digital technology, which would be connected with the personal banking system and mobile phone facilities. This increasing emphasis on privacy jurisprudence, and digital privacy, has, in turn, meant that key stakeholders in legal education in India are now trying to place more emphasis on knowledge and understanding of privacy rights, including topics such as data security and data privacy. This is likely once again to encourage national law universities and private law schools to continue to develop their offering and pedagogy in relation to ICT and DCT.

The wider impact of ICT, DCT and privacy jurisprudence in the Indian courts and further society

While modern legal education in India has begun to embrace smart teaching pedagogy and include subjects that may enable lawyers to defend their clients on issues of digital privacy rights, laws addressing these issues are still not developed in India. The government is yet to frame strong laws and policies in India to address online criminal activities, patterns of cybercrimes targeting data and new types of online harassment of private individuals. In relation to the court system in particular, there is a huge data flow on issues that should, arguably, be considered as confidential. The laws regarding responsibilities of data managers, including individual data creators and webpages that may be used to broadcast data in regard to legal cases, are still developing and this means that law students, lawyers and the general public at large are getting access to the confidential information of litigating parties (including women and children and victims of abuse, including sexual abuse), government departments, government officials, judges, patients, teachers, students, tourists and others. There has been wide-ranging discussions on petitions, victims, defendants and offenders on social media and law students are encouraged to do research on the issues before the actual judgments are passed. As a result, the names, personal information and the case details of the parties to the cases may remain available on the internet for a long time, making the victims and offenders more vulnerable to criticism, harassment and privacy breaches. Parties to both criminal and civil suits may be exposed unwantedly to a worldwide audience. While the courts are beginning to interpret rules and regulations to broaden jurisprudence on digital privacy, parties in criminal cases or civil suits are still not yet fully appraised of their right to be forgotten or their right to confidentiality, which may be pleaded in the courts. The consequences of this could include people losing trust in the confidentiality management system of the lawyers, courts and different stakeholders who are responsible for protecting the confidentiality of data.

While there are several pieces of research on privacy jurisprudence in India (Bali, 2007; Basu, 2010) not much academic research has been done on the use of ICT and DCT within the court system and the legal education sector or on the right to privacy. This is an important area for law schools to engage with in future to ensure that the development of the laws in this area, and the resulting court processes and procedures are able to withstand the various challenges that they face.

As well as these issues relating specifically to the Indian court system, it is important for national law universities and private law schools to be aware of the wider impact of technology within Indian society and the broader ways in which ICT and DCT are interacting with justice. In particular, there are four important judgments that created landmarks in the right jurisprudence in India that national law universities and private law schools need to engage with to ensure both that their students are well-informed and that appropriate research and discussion takes place. These four important judgments of the Supreme Court of India had been influenced by ICT- and DCT-based campaigns about rights awareness in India. During July to October 2018, India witnessed a series of judgments that broke the age-old social customs and perspectives targeting women and members of the lesbian, gay, bisexual, transgender and queer (LGBTQ) community. First to be mentioned in this series is the judgment in the case of *Navtej Singh Johar & others vs Union of India*, Writ Petition (Criminal) no. 76 of 2016, where the Supreme Court of India decriminalised consensual homosexual activities between two adults. The court in this case struck down a 157-year-old colonial penal law (part of S.377 of the Indian Penal Code) and apologised to the nation for the historic wrongs that have been caused due to the orthodox interpretation of S.377 by the criminal justice machinery (Halder, 2018). The LGBTQ community started gathering the support of human rights lawyers, activists and the general public through social media long before the *Navtej* judgment. Even though members of the LGBTQ community were previously barred from entering into interpersonal relationships such as marriage or even forming associations in real life, online platforms such as Facebook has provided them with a space in which to network with like-minded people and also to seek legal advice from allies and friends. At the same time, this attracted several types of victimisation, including bullying and trolling and the creation of fake avatars. Unfortunately, due to the legal restraints on the LGBTQ community, they could get no solace from the police and criminal justice machinery (Halder and Jaishankar, 2016, pp.47–53).

The second judgment that needs to be mentioned in this series (*Shayara Bano vs Union of India & others*, Writ Petition © no. 118 of 2016) rendered the use of the triple *talaq* (a form of instant divorce achieved by stating the word *talaq* three times) unconstitutional. Following this 2017 judgment, the Indian parliament introduced the Triple Talaq Bill (Muslim Women Protection of Rights on Marriage Bill), which criminalised the pronouncement of *talaq* to nullify a marriage (Halder, 2018). Unlike in the LGBTQ rights issue, the ICT- and DCT-based communication system has brought more negative effects in relation to the triple *talaq* issue. Post-triple *talaq* judgment, many Muslim women have complained about receiving *tin talaq* over the telephone or through ICT- and DCT-based communication media such as WhatsApp, for example, in the case of a woman from the northern part of India who was given triple *talaq* over the telephone for arriving home late (Outlook Magazine, 2019). It becomes a Herculean task for such women to take such matters to the courts in spite of the *Shayara Bano* judgment, either because they may not be able to reach out to the lawyers or the police due to fear of social taboo or because they may not be aware of the relevant judgments due to lack of information. Noticeably, several district and state legal services authorities in the courts in India have now digitised platforms to reach out to these victims for free legal aid, spreading awareness about rights against domestic violence and domestic abuse. However, many women may still not be aware of such services. The reasons could be various: either they may not be allowed to attend the awareness camps that may be held in the villages that may impart information about such digitised complaint mechanisms or they may not be allowed to possess a smartphone that may enable them to access internet and digital communication facilities.

Third in the line of important judgments was *Indian Young Lawyers Association vs State of Kerala & Others*, Writ petition © no. 373 of 2006. This judgment was regarding the permission of women to enter the Sabarimala Temple, dedicated to Lord Iyappa, situated on the hills of Sabarimala in Kerala. In this, the court came to the conclusion that 'devotion cannot be subjected to gender discrimination'. This judgment broke the tradition of debarring the entry of Hindu women from the age of 10 to 50 (the menstruation age) into the temple devoted to a god who is a *naishtika Brahmachari* (in Indian mythology, Lord Iyappa, the presiding deity of Sabarimala, is considered to be celibate and he may not, therefore, be in the presence of women and girls). The *Sabarimala* judgment is celebrated as a path-breaking judgment for gender equality but also requires a special mention from the perspective of the impact of ICT and DCT on legal policies and court decisions in India. The positive nod of the Supreme Court of India towards women's rights to enter the shrine was spread virally by news media channels, petitioners and other rights activists through social media websites. Two women (one of whom was a law teacher) decided to execute this judgment by visiting the shrine in early January 2019. They had met through Facebook and got huge phenomenal emotional support from several Facebook groups and users. While these two women initially had to face violent protests from groups who were against the Supreme Court judgment, the administration and the police took extra precautionary measures to protect the two women from a violent mob inside and outside the temple (for more information on this, see Shaji, 2019).

The fourth judgment in the series is the *Puttaswamy* case, discussed above, on the constitutional validity of the Aadhar Act 2016, which was challenged by privacy advocates who felt that Aadhar, a unique 12-digit identification number based on biometrics and demographic data, an initiative of the Unique Identification Authority of India (UIDAI) infringed the privacy of individuals who are subject to it. The Supreme Court in the Aadhar decision took a very protective step in maintaining the constitutionality of the Aadhar Act, thereby making it mandatory for all stakeholders to have their Aadhar number, but rejected certain provisions that proposed data infringement by third parties and unnecessary state surveillance. The judgment debarred banks and mobile companies from linking with Aadhar numbers and thereby took steps to prevent privacy infringements (Halder, 2018).

It is important for law students and faculty members to be aware of these cases and to understand the ways in which each one was influenced by, and could in turn also influence, the uses and abuses of ICT and DCT within Indian society. In addition, national law universities and private law schools also need to be aware that such landmark judgments by the court may become meaningless if they are not implemented and executed properly. Law students may be roped in to research on the issue and draft a proper law or amendment to the concerned law under the monitoring of the law teachers and judges (Halder, 2018). Here it needs to be mentioned that ICT- and DCT-enabled research tools and artificial intelligence can help tremendously in this regard. Researchers can create networks to discuss global scenarios that may help in the comparative analysis of laws and policies. Many law school libraries in India are now subscribing to online database services to access research papers, books and government documents from across the globe. Such ICT-enabled academic research can make a huge impact in encouraging judges to consider academic analysis of laws, rules, principles and sociological occurrences.

New approaches to teaching technology in Indian legal education

The discussion above has demonstrated that ICT and DCT have an important role to play in national law universities and private law schools in India. This is relevant to the subjects and topics that are included in legal education, with students being increasingly required to learn the substantive law on areas such as privacy rights and cyber law. It is also of importance because of the impact of ICT and DCT on the Indian court system, particularly in light of the current weaknesses of the system in terms of privacy, data protection and security. As potential future legal advocates, law students need to be aware of these issues and their potential impact on the reputation of the justice system. Studying these in an academic context also allows students (and faculty members) to address these issues in a well-informed and critical manner, enabling them to consider ways in which to combat the challenges being faced and their potential consequences. There is the potential for ICT and DCT to enhance legal research more broadly, through the provision of access to digital databases and international research networks. The four key judgments discussed above also demonstrate the need for law students to appreciate the wider implications of technology within Indian society in areas as diverse as LGBTQ rights, divorce, religious worship and data collection. However, careful thought needs to be given to the ways in which such topics are taught. It is arguable that therapeutic jurisprudence sessions may be of great benefit in this regard. According to David B. Wexler, the co-founder of the therapeutic jurisprudence movement:

> Therapeutic jurisprudence is an interdisciplinary perspective that looks at the law itself as a potential therapeutic agent. It focuses on the impact of the law on emotional life and psychological well-being. The law consists of the law in action, and not merely the law on the books, and law is defined to include legal rules, legal procedures, and the roles of legal actors. One thrust of therapeutic jurisprudence is law reform, but another important dimension is in exploring ways in which the existing law may be more therapeutically applied. The latter aspect of therapeutic jurisprudence enables psychological insights to be effectively employed in judging and in the day-to-day practice of the law. (Wexler, 2000, p.125)

Taking this form of approach and emphasising the need for technology's interaction with society to promote therapeutic outcomes in terms of well-being could go a long way to make law students understand what should be considered as anti-therapeutic and what should be discarded while drafting the law. Interestingly, therapeutic jurisprudence has been introduced in few law schools so far. However, in my classes, I have introduced law students to the concept while teaching public interest lawyering, victimology and cyber law (especially regarding difficulties with the current laws that are intended to address criminalities on cyber space, which can be characterised as anti-therapeutic (Halder, 2013, 2015, 2018; Halder and Jaishankar, 2013, 2016). This again had been possible by interacting and networking with foreign law faculties and therapeutic jurisprudence researchers through ICT and DCT. Smart classrooms have even enabled streaming of lectures on therapeutic jurisprudence by professors from the West to law students in India.

Ryan and McFaul's chapter emphasises the ways in which clinical legal education can be used to facilitate law students' engagement with technology. While their discussion and case studies focus on the utilisation of specific forms of technology within this setting (for example, smartphone and virtual reality apps), clinical legal education also has a potentially important role to play in introducing students to new concepts in lawyering, such as therapeutic jurisprudence. While many law schools in India offer instruction to students on the drafting of petitions, notices and other legal papers and pleadings as part of clinical legal education programmes, not many offer teaching on the drafting of model laws and concepts such as therapeutic counselling, lawyering skills and preventive lawyering skills as part of this clinical legal education work. It is expected that law students will learn this through internships with law firms or senior lawyers. However, as Professor Madhava Menon apprehended, this will make a bunch of lawyers 'who are mere craftsman manipulating advocacy skills in the traditional role of conflict resolution in court' (Menon, 1998, p.50). As Professor Menon opined, a greater depth in terms of legal advocacy and approaches to lawyering can be initiated in the clinical legal education classes within national law universities and private law schools. Almost every law school in India has a free legal aid clinic that can be used as a law laboratory in which to experiment with different approaches. Students can and should observe the problems the beneficiaries come with and use this practical experience in not only developing therapeutic counselling and lawyering skills, but also in developing legal drafting skills. This law-drafting process should also be monitored by faculty members and judges in a way that could increase understanding of concepts such as therapeutic legal jurisprudence, as well as highlighting anomalies in the area of law and ICT and DCT, such as the aforementioned issues within the court system (Halder, 2018). Another potentially interesting use of technology in this context relates to the way in which, at present, almost all lawyers heavily depend on formatted drafts for drafting. However, lawyers also need to add emotion along with the facts and legal points to explain the situation of the parties to the case during pleadings. To do this, several lawyers use computer algorithms and artificial intelligence to research on best pleading and drafting methods from across the globe. Indian courts are also using ICT for video conferencing with offenders detained in prisons, demonstrating other interesting ways in which technology and communication skills can interact.[1]

Conclusion

This chapter shows how ICT and DCT are being used for legal education and in the court case management system. It demonstrates that ICT- and DCT-enabled teaching methods, law libraries and changes to the court system are all contributing to a huge transformation of Indian legal education and the court systems. At the same time, it illustrates that there are lacunas in the court infrastructure and also in the laws, which mean that national law universities and private law schools must ensure their students both understand the impact of technology on the court system and wider Indian society and are equipped to fully critique it and suggest alternative approaches. Introducing law students (and faculty members) to concepts such as therapeutic jurisprudence and using clinical legal education programmes to develop teaching around skills and communications are all potential ways in which students can be equipped to develop this breadth of knowledge and understanding in relation to law and technology.

Ryan and McFaul's preceding discussion demonstrates the international impact of technology on legal education, with a particular emphasis on the UK context. This chapter has focused on the Indian context to argue that, overall, it is necessary for all Indian law schools to engage in more teaching activities and research activities in cyber law, cyber criminology and data security. It is only then that India can have responsible lawyers and judges who may protect the digital, data and offline privacy of individuals.

Note

1 See Centre for Internet and Society, India. Artificial Intelligence in the Governance Sector in India, https://cis-india.org/internet-governance/ai-and-governance-case-study-pdf (accessed 2 March 2018).

References

Bar Council of India (2019). *Brief History of Law*, http://www.barcouncilofindia.org/about/about-the-legal-profession/legal-education-in-the-united-kingdom/ (accessed 12 March 2019).

Basu, S. (2010). Policy making, technology and privacy in India. *Indian Journal of Law & Technology*, 6, 65, https://www.researchgate.net/profile/Subhajit_Basu5/publication/45691547_POLICY-MAKING_TECHNOLOGY_AND_PRIVACY_IN_INDIA/links/549311c20cf286fe31243ea1.pdf (accessed 31 May 2019).

Burgard, A. and Schelmbach, C. (2013). Frames of fraud: a qualitative analysis of the structure and process of victimization on the internet. *International Journal of Cyber Criminology (IJCC)*, 7(2), 112–124, http://www.cybercrimejournal.com/burgardschlembachijcc2013vol7issue2.pdf (accessed 11 December 2015).

Citron, D. (2014). *Hate Crimes in Cyber Space*. Cambridge, MA, Harvard University Press.

Dutt, V. P. (1976). The emergency in India: background and rationale. *Asian Survey*, 16 (12), 1124–1138.

Halder, D. (2019). Free legal aid for women and therapeutic jurisprudence: a critical examination of the Indian model. In Stobbs, N., Bartel , L. and Vols, M. (eds.). *Methodology and Practice of Therapeutic Jurisprudence Research*. Chapel Hill, NC, Carolina Academy Press, pp. 253–273.

Halder, D. (2018). *Child Sexual Abuse and Protection Laws in India*. New Delhi, Sage.

Halder, D. (2017). Corporate liability for data protection in India: a critical analysis of S.43A of the Information Technology Act 2000 (amended in 2008). In Saxena, N. (ed.). *Cyber Crimes in 21st Century*. New Delhi, Manakin Press, pp. 323–340.

Halder, D. (2013). Examining the scope of the Indecent Representation of Women (Prevention) Act 1986, in the light of cyber victimization. *National Law School Journal*, 11, 188–218.

Halder, D. and Jaishankar, K. (2017). Cyber crime victims: responsibilities, reactions and issues of criminal justice social workers. In Chong, M. D. and Francis, A. (eds.). *Demystifying Criminal Justice Social Work in India*. New Delhi, Sage, pp. 244–261.

Halder, D. and Jaishankar, K. (2016). *Cyber Crimes against Women in India*. New Delhi, *Sage*.

Halder, D. and Jaishankar, K. (2015). Irrational coping theory and positive criminology: a framework to protect victims of cyber crime. In Ronel, N. and Segev, D. (eds.). *Positive Criminology*. Abingdon, Routledge, pp. 276–291.

Halder, D. and Jaishankar, K. (2013). Revenge porn by teens in the United States and India: a socio-legal analysis. *International Annals of Criminology*, 51(1–2), 85–111.

Halder, D. and Jaishankar, K. (2008). Cyber crimes against women in India: problems, perspectives and solutions. *TMC Academy Journal Singapore*, 3(1), 48–62.

Menon, N. R. Madhava (1998). Clinical legal education: concept and concerns. In *A Handbook on Clinical Legal Education*. New Delhi, Eastern Book House.

Mohan Gopal, G. (ed.) (2009). *Prof. N.R.Madhava Menon's Reflections on Legal and Judicial Education*. New Delhi, Universal Law Publishing Co.

Outlook Magazine (2019). *UP Woman Given Triple Talaq Over Phone For Reaching Home 10 Minutes Late*, https://www.outlookindia.com/website/story/india-news-up-woman-given-triple-talaq-over-phone-for-reaching-home-10-minutes-late/324549 (accessed 1 March 2019).

Shaji (2019). *How A Facebook Page Helped Two Women Enter The Sabarimala Shrine. Huffington Post*, https://www.huffingtonpost.in/entry/kerala-sabarimala-temple-bindu-kanakadurga_in_5c2e2db1e4b08aaf7a96d9c6 (accessed 1 March 2019).

Wexler, D. B. (2000) Therapeutic jurisprudence: an overview. *Thomas M. Cooley Law Review*, 17, 125–134, https://ssrn.com/abstract=256658 (accessed 10 October 2018).

Part 4

Clinical legal education

The following two chapters focus on aspects of clinical legal education, an experiential approach to learning that now forms a well-established part of legal education. In Chapter 7, Grimes provides an overview of many aspects of clinical legal education, with a particular emphasis on the UK context. He proposes a taxonomy to define how such clinical models can successfully serve a mix of educational and legal service needs. In Chapter 8, Arthurs traces the evolution of clinical legal education in the United States and argues that it has the ability to positively influence the future of both legal education and the legal profession.

Chapter 7

Experiential learning and legal education – the role of the clinic in UK law schools[1]

Richard Grimes

Introduction

Learning through experience and reflection based on that experience is hardly new in terms of education but neither is it rocket science. Hands-on learning opportunities coupled with an analysis and deconstruction of what has occurred has been common in many fields of study from the teaching hospital to the science laboratory (see, for example, the variety of settings discussed in the *Australian Journal of Clinical Education*). Legal educators have, however, been relatively slow in using experiential learning, at least ever since the responsibility for educating lawyers became the primary preserve of universities and other higher education providers. Since this time, however, there has been an uneasy relationship between the aims of a liberal course of study and the demands of a practicing profession and this has impacted on how we approach teaching and learning in law (Boon and Webb, 2008).

Educators have dominated formal legal learning with a curriculum delivered principally through lectures – where students are seen and treated as passive recipients of knowledge . If education in general and legal education in particular is to meet the needs and demands of contemporary society and serve the career aspirations of those concerned then knowledge, skills and values, together, are needed to form a holistic framework for learning.

Much has, of course, been published on both the content and means of delivery of legal education. While the former must be seen in context – undergraduates, for example, may have very different outcomes set for them as compared with those on an overtly vocational course – the latter has a common denominator. This is to do with how students learn and how they can be encouraged to take responsibility for, and make the most of, that. Learning through experience, supported by the means to conduct critical reflection – in this instance often termed clinical legal education (CLE) – is central to this chapter and to the following one by Sean Arthurs. In this chapter, I look at identifying and developing models of 'clinic' where students, under requisite supervision, engage in real or realistic casework in order to comprehend relevant content, be that legal doctrine, lawyering skills and/or professional and ethical considerations. In this process, others may benefit, including clients. This contribution leads, in the following chapter, into a further consideration of 'clinic', putting the exponential growth of 'clinic' in the USA, UK and further afield into context, notably in the light of recent and past legal education reviews and bearing in mind an apparent tension between the study of law as an academic discipline and the call from the legal profession and other potential employers for recruits who have the knowledge, skills and attributes deemed necessary in the modern world.

The conclusions reached here and in the following chapter include the recognition of the importance of clinic (actual and potential) in serving the various agendas held by relevant stakeholders be they students, clients, the legal profession, other potential employers and wider society.

Learning experientially and clinic – definitions, benefits and challenges

Definitions

I take here, as a given, that learning through experience is a positive. To be clear, by experiential learning I mean developing one's understanding through the application (and reapplication) of theory to practice – real or simulated – using reflective techniques. This means of learning is positive in the sense that by its very nature and rationale it is designed to promote and support engagement in the educational process and give context for the learner. It is also positive in that it can provide an opportunity for structured reflection. Whether the impact bears out the promise is not the subject of this contribution, although, as will be seen, anecdotal evidence abounds that it does and some empirical evidence suggests likewise (Kemp, Munk and Gower, 2016). As will be seen below, much has been written on the nature of learning through experience and the perceived consequential value of it. Simply put, if a student is motivated by and interested in his or her study it is highly likely (or at least more likely compared with a student who is less engaged) that he or she will do well, however that might be measured.

A definition of CLE might be helpful to begin with. The relevant literature largely agrees that there must be a practical or applied component through which the student experiences law and the legal process. Over time these attempts to encapsulate what CLE is (and therefore what it does and how it does it) have gone beyond just the doing and have started to include a process that can be summarised as a deconstruction of experience (Amsterdam, 1984). For Amsterdam, this is a technique designed to educate students through systematic exposure to experience. Giddings' definition helpfully includes a wider range of key features or characteristics including intensive small group or solo work, personal (student) responsibility for that activity, collaboration with supervisors, feedback on work done, reflection on the experience, interaction with others in the clinic and a consideration of ethics (Giddings, 2013). A similar definition can be found in earlier (and, for the UK, pioneering) work (Brayne, Duncan and Grimes, 1998). More recently a succinct definition is stated as: 'learning through participation in real or realistic legal interactions coupled with reflection on (the) experience' (Kerrigan and Murray, 2011, p.5).

I suggest that CLE is a methodology that is underpinned by intent and values as well as taking particular forms of activity. It is a process by which students study legal and related knowledge, skills and/or values through exposure to real or realistic legal cases or scenarios and are required to critically reflect on that experience as a structured part of their study.

The definition above, however, hides much complexity. The 'doing' part is perhaps the most overt and clear but is constrained by the nature and extent of what is done – for example, is it simulated, is it live client, is it advice, is it full representation, is it hands-on or is it shadowing, is it in-house or is it on placement? The 'reflection' component is also far more involved than might first appear, for both teacher and learner. The process of reflection is neither intuitive nor straightforward (Grimes, 2016). Dewey rightly identifies that experience in itself does not necessarily lead to reflection and that 'habit' may stifle the reflective process (Dewey, 1933) – 'disturbance' being required to instigate learning through reflection and the effective testing of hypotheses (Miettinen, 2000, pp.61–62). A structure is needed for prompting and capturing reflection. This can be aided by pre-setting key questions (such as: what did you do?; what happened?; and, what might you do differently (and better) next time?), together, perhaps, with a template for the student to record their deliberations and for peers and teachers to comment on, and otherwise engage with, the reflective process.

The main difference in the approach taken here as compared, say, with Dewey's need for the interruption of habit or Kolb's cycle of learning (Kolb, 2015) is that most, if not all, experience has the potential for learning – even if that experience is habitual and/or previously encountered. Experiencing something again in a like or similar way can reinforce understanding as well as develop it. As Havighurst notes, a combination of tutor and student awareness and a system for capturing the 'teachable moment' can give the reflective process relevance, weight and meaning (Havighurst, 1953). Using slightly different terminology, Tripp refers to the use of devices by which critical incidents can be identified and utilised (Tripp, 1993). I suggest, as valuable and relevant as this concept is for optimising learning opportunities, more seemingly basic and often repeated encounters can also be building blocks in the process. What is simple or routine to the experienced practitioner may be perceived and utilised very differently by the novice (in this context, the law student). Teachable moments can therefore arise in a number of different settings – from the new and challenging to the more mundane and repetitious.

With this summary of what 'clinic' is in terms of learning and teaching let us now turn to the perceived benefits and challenges of this approach to education.

Benefits

A number of anecdotal claims have been made for CLE. These are often about the power of the model pedagogically, the impressive performance of students who study through clinic and the positive feedback from the many stakeholders who identify the value of clinic in terms of developing doctrinal understanding, legal and transferable skills and an appreciation of professional and wider ethical issues. Anecdotal material and comment apart, there is, however, sufficient evidence to be found in academic writing, particularly in the field of education more generally, that establishes a solid theoretical framework against which such developments in legal education can be analysed and evaluated. As will become apparent from what follows, the claims for the value of 'clinic' can be based on an assessment of relevant academic works and on the consistent accounts of and reports from a range of interested parties including clients, students, teachers and legal practitioners to examiners, employers, regulators and related critiques.

So what are the perceived benefits of CLE? These can be summarised as follows:

- High levels of engagement and motivation among participants (including students and teachers) – personal experience across many different jurisdictions suggests that most students see clinic as the best thing they did in law school. Many stress how self-confidence and professional commitment are enhanced as well as knowledge and skills being developed.
- An opportunity for a holistic approach to study avoiding the pigeon-holing represented by the more traditional curriculum where law is studied by subject and often in isolation.
- The chance to apply theory to practice and to deconstruct the result with a view to further application and analysis.
- Where live-client clinics are used, a customised, free, service to members of the public.
- The linking, in pedagogic terms, of legal knowledge with lawyering skills and an appreciation of professional responsibility, attributes and values.
- The generation of material for teaching and learning that is based on actual case work – which, subject to preserving client confidentiality, can be used elsewhere.
- Serving the educational institution's mission and/or its approach to corporate/ social responsibility through providing a service to the wider public.
- The production of graduates who have had exposure to real-life experience and may, as a result, be better equipped to secure and retain future employment.
- Serving the needs of employers through the provision of work-ready employees.
- Enhancing the reputation of the legal profession in terms of lawyers who have enhanced skills and values sets.
- Development of more lawyers with a commitment to pro bono and 'legal aid' work.

The claims for the suggested benefits of CLE that are set out above can be found in various publications domestic to the UK and worldwide including Bloch (2010) and Brayne, Duncan and Grimes (1998).

Challenges

Setting up and running clinics can be problematic or has the potential to be so. The issues that must be faced cover both educational and professional practice considerations. For convenience, these too are set out in bullet point form:

- Professional practice rules – in England and Wales (regulation may differ in other jurisdictions) if the clinic is offered to the public as either a solicitor's or barrister's practice relevant professional practice rules must be followed, including avoiding conflicts of interest, protecting client confidentiality and running an office to the required standard. Importantly, this impacts on the levels of supervision (of participating students and staff) that must be in place to ensure compliance with professional standards (Thomas, 2017). Even if the law school clinic is not held out as to be a professional lawyer's practice there are still legal implications and a failure to meet requisite expectations may give rise to civil action.
- Professional indemnity insurance (PII) – one of the requirements, at least in England and Wales, for a legal practice is to have PII. This is potentially problematic on two fronts. First, the extent of the cover and, second, the cost. I suggest that the insurance issue, which is often seen as a significant challenge, is less of a problem than might otherwise appear. The reason for this is that all educational providers, at least in the Western world, will almost certainly (and may be legally required to) take out insurance to cover various risks including public liability. It is highly likely that the coverage will include aspects of professional indemnity. Personal experience suggests that insurance companies will readily extend PII cover to the activities of a law clinic providing the service offered is supervised by a lawyer with an appropriate professional qualification and certification, that no client money is held and that the categories of work are deemed as low (monetary) risk (offering a service, for example, in 'welfare' cases such as housing, employment and social security benefits). A reluctant university insurer might be reminded of the value of the university's insurance provision and that the university could consider moving cover to another provider. I have found that normally focuses any straying minds! Even where high street insurers are slow to offer cover, policies exist that have been specifically designed for not-for-profit legal service suppliers and these are relatively low cost
- Institutional resistance – universities and other providers may see the work of a law clinic as expensive (on this see what is said below under resource implications), potentially risky and being unconventional and, therefore,

worrying. The answer, of course, in addressing such concerns is in itself educational. The institution, or at least higher levels of management, may need to be better informed on what the clinic can and will do, how it will be run and managed and the benefits of doing so. My experience is that university management is quick to pick up on and publicise the clinic when it is up and running. Careful planning is required and discussions need to take place at faculty or departmental level to inform all and to secure the support of relevant committees and powers that be. Alliances can also be very effective including with the local legal profession (more on that below), the student body, teaching and research teams (yes, the clinic can offer a research outlet and may have 'impact' implications in terms of teaching and research league table assessments), local not-for-profit advice organisations and the wider community. A business plan setting out how the clinic will operate including requisite supervision, training and case management details should allay fears on quality control. Finally, under this point, a handbook containing operational rules, an annual report setting out statistics and possible case studies and an advisory board should all help reassure and are likely to build confidence and promote constructive relations.

- Resources – of all the challenges involved in CLE, finding the financial, human and physical wherewithal is perhaps the most pressing and, in real terms, the most significant of all of the barriers. The resource need list can, depending on the type and nature of the clinic, be extensive. At one extreme, a full representation clinic offering advice, assistance and possible court or tribunal work to a large number of students on a full-year basis represents a major expense in terms of premises, supervisory arrangements, teaching time and running costs. The justification for such an outlay is likely to centre on the commitment to public service and the extent to which a student is deemed to benefit from the involvement in the clinic's work. Thus, for example, a clinic that serves the needs of a student undertaking a vocational course (or integrated degree/vocational provision such as found at Northumbria University) may be considered as a price worth paying in terms of output. At the other end of the spectrum, a placement clinic (or to use the term found in the American literature – 'externship') where students undertake legal work under the auspices of another body that takes responsibility for conducting relevant case work will be relatively resource light. The only cost implication here, if the activity is to be clinical (as compared with an internship where the students spends time on placement but does not bring that experience back formally into the law school for deconstruction) is for teaching resources to be dedicated to the placement experience – for example, a weekly seminar to discuss the students' experiences and placement monitoring visits. There are many options in between these two positions – for example a modest law school clinic offering term-time and advice-only services for a limited number of students and clients. A clinic that simulates real legal casework may have many benefits in the sense of exposing students to how the law works in practice but will have none of the implications of actual client care. Where live-client work is carried out supervision could be arranged in conjunction with external lawyers on a pro bono basis with the cost for the law school consequently and significantly reduced. Whichever model is used the resource issue must be addressed if the clinic is to be of requisite quality and be sustainable.

- Managing expectations – I suggest that this is perhaps the least appreciated of the challenges in running a clinic. Whose expectations are we talking about? If the clinic deals with members of the public then client expectation needs to be managed. What can the clinic do for the client? How will the service operate in terms of what is done, by when and by whom? What if the client needs more than the clinic can provide in terms of scope or expertise? The questions do not end there. Student expectation is a serious consideration. As well as having clear operational rules so the students know what is expected of them what about the practicalities? Many clinics operate with students working in small teams. What if members don't pull their weight? What if students are so engrossed in their clinic work that they neglect other aspects of their studies or wider life? What if their clinic work conflicts with other commitments such as at assessment pinch points? How are students to be selected to take part – clinics are often heavily oversubscribed? The institution and its staff may also have expectations – in terms of resource input, evidencing achievement of social mission, delivering on research and publications and doing work pro bono (see below under 'workloads'). There are no simple answers to any of these questions other than to say that all of the clinic's work needs to be documented in terms of what can be done, who is responsible and how it will work. Two devices can help here – first, the clinic handbook (mentioned above). This should contain not only operational rules but copies of expectation management documents such as a student contract and clear summary of supervisory arrangements. Second, there must (if the clinic is professionally regulated in England and Wales) be a client-care letter or leaflet setting out for all clients how the clinic functions, the fact that there is PII in place, what to do if there is a concern or cause for complaint and whom to contact in the event of problems. In addition, the client must receive regular updates on progress and, of course, complete records of case progress must be kept and in a place where confidentiality is maintained. With robust and transparent systems in place expectation can be effectively managed.
- Supervision – it is both a professional requirement (at least in the domestic context) and an educational imperative for effective supervision of all student work (and the work of any other non-qualified and certificated people) to take place. The professional dimension can be relatively easily

done through having all student and other work submitted for the comment, amendment if needs be and, in any event, final approval of the supervising lawyer. Student supervision from an educational viewpoint is perhaps more complex. In CLE, one important mechanism for ensuring that teachable moments are monitored and identified is in the use of 'rounds'. This word originated in the medical world and describes the tour of the hospital ward by a qualified, and often senior, doctor or consultant who, accompanied by medical students, uses a 'round' of the hospital ward to question and discuss the diagnosis and treatment of each patient. Transferred to the world of the law clinic, the round has particular use in facilitating discussion and reflection (Bryant and Milstein, 2007). The use of rounds – or, as I put it, regular, weekly, 'firm' meetings – to discuss case progress and engage in critical reflection, is strongly recommended as a conduit for 'deep' learning. Of course, supervision needs to happen at other points and can be done in a variety of ways including a review of case files, individual meetings with students working on a case and the supervisor just being present to ask and field questions.

- Assessment – CLE provides a powerful and possibly unique environment for providing feedback and assessing student performance. To use the educational jargon, the likely regular and frequent requirement to oversee student work in the clinic gives formative assessment opportunities – assessment designed to explain to students the extent of their understanding and educational progress. Summative assessment – meaning here measuring performance at a designated point – is also possible in the clinic setting and the extent to which this dominates will depend on learning outcomes set and the assessment regime applicable. While clinic may lend itself more to formative assessment than other more traditionally taught modules the often intimate nature of the clinic, where students and teachers interact so often, can compromise the assessment process particularly in terms of any summative requirement. This is examined further elsewhere with specific examples given of how to address possible bias, the extent to which group work can be fairly evaluated and the role of non-traditional forms of assessment including by viva voce (Grimes and Gibbons, 2016).
- The legal profession – other lawyers, notably those in the locality of the clinic, will inevitably find the concept of CLE of interest including the critical, the sceptical and the positively supportive. When establishing a clinic time is well spent in consulting with the profession, perhaps through the local law society/bar association. At the very least this will alert the profession to the work of the clinic and give sufficient information for members to be reassured in terms of quality assurance and non-competition Having the profession on board can reap many benefits including attracting their support – volunteer supervisors, advisory board members and possibly donations.

- Workloads – one final challenge. As all academic and administrative staff will no doubt be acutely aware the demands of working in higher (and other) education in the current world are significant, changing and ever demanding. Introducing innovative teaching and learning practices imposes further burdens. Clinic staff are typically characterised by high levels of enthusiasm and commitment. It is all too easy for that to be exploited by management, even if done innocently. Many clinic and pro bono initiatives rely on dedicated people willing to go the extra mile. Additionally, given the intensive and interactive nature of clinic and, where real clients are involved, professional requirements, clinic teachers and administrators often find that they spend far more time and effort in clinic than they have to do elsewhere in the curriculum. All this, of course, leads back to resources and expectations but, if the clinic is to be sustainable, a realistic account needs to be taken of what it takes to set up and maintain the clinic.

Models – goals, logistics and sustainability

Any discussion of different models of CLE might be expected to start with consideration of the subject matter of the clinic, for example, is it generalist advice or does it specialise in, say, family law, juvenile justice, housing, employment or social security? I suggest that this is of little importance, at least educationally. Of course, it matters to the client and some, perhaps rightly, argue that a clinic should have as its principal goal the advancement of social justice (Bloch, 2010). At the very least, in order not to compete unnecessarily with other legal service providers and to address otherwise unmet legal need, the clinic might focus on those areas where service provision is absent or otherwise insufficient. Depending on the type of case handled by the clinic, there may be regulatory considerations such as restricted rights of audience or the need for authorisation as in debt and immigration work in England and Wales (Thomas, 2017). That said, the clinic's focus on one or more particular type of case is of limited relevance to the advancement of students' education. The essential element in terms of learning is the exposure to real (or, in the case of simulation, realistic) legal problems and issues and reflection on that exposure.

Consideration of a clinic taxonomy that identifies broader aims and objectives and defines who is responsible for the clinic in practical and legal senses may be a more helpful starting point. Law school clinics are, if they involve live clients at least, necessarily a balancing act between education and public service functions. If this basic classification is taken as the two competing (if, as I have argued elsewhere, manageable) extremes of the CLE aims spectrum, existing literature and practice suggests that the point on the line between them will throw up a variety of clinical models that serve specific objectives – be those primarily educationally oriented or more service driven (Grimes, 2010).

In identifying specific models, experts in the field tend to specify four or possibly five clinic types – the in-house law school clinic, the outreach law school clinic, placements or externships, project-based clinics (focusing, for example, on miscarriages of justice, law reform or legal literacy) and simulation (see Brayne, Duncan and Grimes, 1998; Kerrigan and Murray, 2011).

Even though it is true that there are many iterations of the basic clinic model the picture can perhaps be simplified if one takes as a base for a taxonomy not just service vs. education but the concept of accountability and responsibility. There are, with this approach, just two generic models – one run by the law school (whether it is advice, representation, in-house, outreach, legal literacy or whatever) and the other run by non-law school organisations (be it within the legal profession, an agency of the state, a not-for-profit, non-governmental, organisation (NGO) or more generally within the world of the administration of justice, commerce or industry). For reasons of clarity, I will refer to these two generic models simply as the law school and non-law school clinic – indicating that the former is run by the law school, which is legally and practically responsible for the relevant activity whereas accountability in the latter falls on the organisation outside the law school that runs the clinic (albeit with law school input such as providing students and monitoring their work). Some variants on this may be seen to exist – for example, where lawyers from local law firms and/or chambers take responsibility for advice or other help given, with the law school providing students, perhaps premises and even some supervisory and administrative help. I still maintain that the generic models fall either under the law school or non-law school banner as the deciding factor is who assumes responsibility for the service rather than physical location or personal commitment.

The key here, for the purposes of the current discussion on classification, is to determine who is responsible for what. Simply put this involves potential liability for, and of, participants (including staff, students, clients and host organisations), any relevant professional accountability (for example, under applicable codes of conduct such as those of the Solicitors Regulation Authority (2011) and Bar Standards Board (2004)) and rules, policies and protocols imposed through other forms of regulation, be those institutional or legislative. For example, the Quality Assurance Agency for Higher Education (QAA) (2015), *Subject Benchmark Statement, Law,* University regulations will inevitably vary from one institution to another but in the discipline of law will, because of QAA and professional body requirements, frequently be very similar.

It is at this point that the education verses service lineal becomes more complex, with the development of subcategories within the spectrum. It might be helpful to see this in diagrammatic form with four axes – education, service, law school and non-law school with examples, pros and cons for each quadrant (see Figure 7.1).

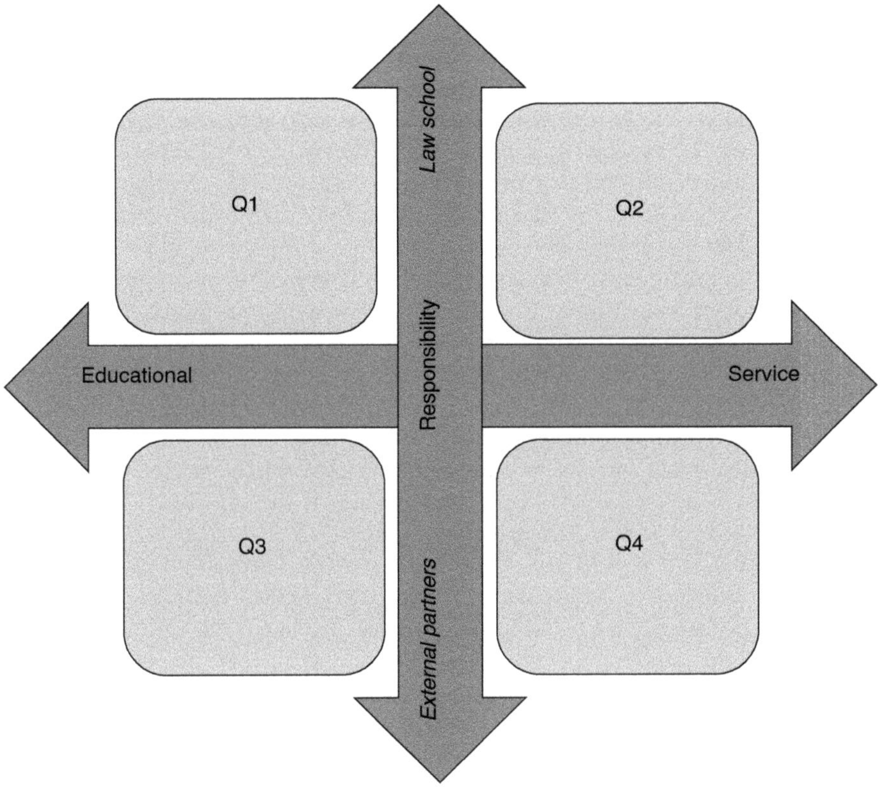

Figure 7.1 The education/service relationship in law school and non-law school clinics

For quadrant 1 (Q1), the priority is the education of the student. Any clinical activity is controlled by the law school either through in-house activities or in outreach sessions (perhaps an advice centre in the community). Whichever, the law school remains responsible for both education and service. The extent of the service offered is determined by educational, rather than client, demands, albeit that professional standards will likely need to be met if the clinic acts for clients. York Law School at the University of York in the UK is a good example of this, with both in-house and outreach services but with help limited to advice only. The relative advantages and disadvantages are clear – the law school is (or should be) in control, the clinic's work can be aligned with the curriculum and the service provided can be tailored to suit resource availability and comply with applicable accountability. On the downside, the students may be restricted in what they can do for the client and the client, in consequence, receives restricted, but predefined, help.

In the second quadrant (Q2), again the law school provides, and is responsible for, the service but client need is more the determining factor than overt educational objectives. Typically unmet legal need will dictate the level of service provided. There are many examples of such law school-run, but service-driven clinics, notably in parts of the world where legal aid and pro bono provision is either non-existent or not widely available (for example, as described by Sarker, 2015). The advantages are a wide and varied experience for students, an often comprehensive form of help for the client and an enhancement of the reputation of the law school in terms of its social mission. The potential problems are likely to include intense resource demands, potential risks from the nature and extent of work undertaken and a possible neglect of students' needs – educational and otherwise.

In either case (Qs 1 or 2), student involvement can be based on simulation that immediately lends itself to learning as the 'case' can be run and rerun to suit educational need and the responsibility, in terms of client care, is removed. For quadrant 2 this, of course, only makes sense if the simulation is used as a training ground for later client-driven services.

Quadrants 3 and 4 (Q3 and Q4), both see the law school as the source of students rather than the provider of the legal service itself. Here, another organisation, typically an NGO, for example, a legal aid centre, runs the service and the student is effectively placed with that body to increase human resource capacity. Given the service provider's mission – helping clients – it is more likely that the assistance offered will be focused on client need rather than student education. This means for the purposes of the classification used above that Q3 is unlikely to feature much, if at all, in terms of CLE unless the law school takes the student experience back into the seminar room for analysis. Q4 will see priority given to clients, not students, with its applicable rationale and service manifestation. That is not to say that students will not gain from the experience in Q3 or Q4 – they may get helpful feedback from the service provider and, if the student placement is an integral part of the law school's agenda, the students may be given an opportunity to reflect on that experience in a more structured way. There are many examples of such placement programmes, many highly sophisticated in terms of pedagogy (for example, as described by Wortham et al., 2016).

The attraction of non-law school clinics is obvious – the resources required to run the service and the responsibility for doing so rests with the organisation concerned – not the law school. The students may encounter a rich and varied diet of casework and experience. The disadvantages are also clear – the law school loses an element of control, cannot ensure consistency of experience and may have to input resources to monitor quality of experience and to enable students to deconstruct that encounter.

A clinic may therefore be simulated or might involve actual advice and/or further representation. It could assist in miscarriage of justice cases or it might involve a public legal education project. The clinic concerned may be a research facility for those wanting to know about new legal proposals or possible aspects ripe for reform. It may place students with other providers where they shadow and/or provide additional help.

I suggest therefore that the two generic models – the law school and the non-law school – may take the form of an in-house or outreach clinic (operating within the providing institution or outside of it), a placement – including the placement of others in law school clinics, a legal literacy initiative, a law reform clinic, a clinic focusing on miscarriages of justice or a research project based on specific requests from community-based groups. The clinic may offer a specialist service (for example, housing or disability law) or might take on a variety of different types of case. It may be extra curricular or credit bearing; it may be optional or compulsory.

In terms of taxonomy, the clinic might have education or service as its priority or may, as many, if not most, do, balance or juggle with the demands of the student and client by managing expectation and defining the scope and extent of the learning and service involved. Each specific clinic then fits at some point along the education–service line reflecting relevant aims and objectives. Similarly, if the taxonomy has an accountability dividing line then the specific model used will be found under either the generic heading of the law school or non-law school clinic.

It might, as I have suggested elsewhere in this chapter, be that the educational dimension includes an ethical component, particularly developing an understanding of one's professional identity as a lawyer and what that means in philosophical, regulatory and practical terms. If so, without a service dimension (real or simulated), that facet of the educational aim cannot be easily addressed. This consideration perhaps contradicts the model taxonomy I have described in the sense that education and service become interdependent rather than polar extremes.

Before leaving the taxonomy of clinic, I would like to add one further dimension and image. If we accept that clinics can be focused on education and service, to some extent at least, how can the management of tensions or conflicts between the two be handled? The word 'balance' was used above and in some ways this is misleading. It implies that both service and education demands bring pressures that must be managed so that both interests are equally served and an equilibrium is achieved – a balancing act.

Let me use another analogy – that of the juggler. Imagine this: a law school clinic is being set up. The forward-thinking dean and his/her staff want to incorporate a clinic into the assessed curriculum. They are aware of local unmet legal need and the university as a whole has a strong commitment to community service. Resources are, however, tight and student recruitment a challenge. One of the academic staff members is a qualified solicitor and keen to supervise casework in a clinic. The law school has a positive relationship with the local legal profession and not-for-profit sector organisations. The dean, or his delegatee (perhaps the academic/solicitor) instantly becomes a juggler with a variety of proverbial balls in the air from day 1 of the clinic's existence, including resources, client care, research, teaching, assessment, external partnerships, insurance and various sets of expectation.

There could be many more balls in the picture – for example, premises, confidentiality, conflicts of interest, timetabling and work allocation, not to mention pressure on students and wider educational objectives such as the integration of experiential learning across the curriculum. So how does the juggler respond and what might the end result be?

Clearly, the biggest challenge here is not dropping anything or at least not in a way or for any period of time that matters. The task may be more than one person can or should be expected to reasonably and competently manage. Even if our juggler is most able, there is the risk of human error. Systems are needed to assist. The starting points are clear, as suggested at various points above including operational rules and an induction to complement that – a handbook and protocols – together with constructively critical reviews of processes and procedures. Students and clients need to be given definitive statements, possibly in the form of client-care letters, student contracts and memoranda with any partner organisations. In this way, expectations can be managed. There is then the need for administrative support, professional or student led, to ensure that procedures are followed, logistics run smoothly and the client interface is handled effectively. On resources more generally, physical space needs to be found where clients can be seen in private, where confidentiality can be preserved, where students can work on cases, where learning can take place and where any attendant risks can be safely managed.

But before all this, the priorities need to be determined. What and who is the clinic for? Here we return to the education/service issue. I suggest again, regardless of whether the students' or clients' needs are allowed to dominate, responsibility lies with the law school to be clear about what comes first. There is no right or wrong (other than if there is a failure to comply with any relevant professional obligations) – just different ways of doing clinic. If live clients are involved the extent of the service offered is the key issue and one that will depend on mission, resources and need. Clinical initiatives need to be piloted, kept small and manageable and possibly run on a simulated basis first – until everyone is confident and competent in what they are expected to do.

Given this grounding in the nature and form of 'clinic' let us now turn to experiential learning in context – in the USA, UK and the wider international setting. What does the clinic have to offer stakeholders today and what this may mean for legal education in the future? In the next chapter, Sean Arthurs outlines the development of clinical legal education in the United States, and explores the challenges it faces in the context of contemporary legal education.

Note

1 This chapter draws, in part, on a submission made for the award of PhD – see Grimes, R., *Learning through experience: developing clinical models for legal education.* A commentary submitted in partial fulfilment of the requirements of the University of Northumbria at Newcastle for the degree of Doctor of Philosophy by Published Work, July 2017, available from the University of Northumbria library.

Bibliography

Amsterdam, A. (1984). Clinical legal education – a 21st century perspective. *Journal of Legal Education*, 34, *612*.

Bar Standards Board Code of Conduct (2004). *Governing Barristers*, 8th edn, https://www.barstandardsboard.org.uk/media/1353125/word_version_of_full_code_of_conductannexes_jan_2012_.pdf (accessed 14 November 2017).

Bloch, F. (ed.) (2010). *The Global Clinical Movement: Educating Lawyers for Social Justice-* New York, Open University Press.

Boon, A. and Webb, J. (2008). Legal education and training: back to the future . *Journal of Legal Education*, 58(1), 79.

Brayne, H., Duncan, N. and Grimes, R. (eds.) (1998). *Clinical Legal Education: Active Learning in Your Law School.* London, Blackstone Press.

Bryant, S. and Milstein, E. (2007). Rounds: a 'signature pedagogy' for clinical legal education. *Clinical Law Review*, 14, 195.

Dewey, J. (1933). *How We Think: A Restatement of the Relation of Reflective Thinking to the Educative Process.* Lexington, DC, Heath & Company.

Giddings, J. (2013). *Promoting Justice through Clinical Legal Education.* Melbourne, Justice Press.

Grimes, R. (2016), Reflection in teaching, learning and practice. In Ashford, C. and Guth, J. *Legal Academic's Handbook.* Basingstoke, Palgrave.

Grimes, R. (2010). Clinical approach. In Robins, J. (ed.). *Pro Bono: Good Enough?* London, Solicitors Journal Justice Gap series, 44.

Grimes, R. and Gibbons, J. (2016). Assessing experiential learning – us, them and the others. *International Journal of Clinical Legal Education*, 23(1), 107.

Havighurst, R. (1953). *Human Development and Education.* London, Longman.

Kemp, V., Munk, T. and Gower, S. (2016). *Clinical Legal Education and Experiential Learning: Looking to the Future*, https://www.researchgate.net/publication/309135248_Clinical_Legal_Education_and_Experiential_Learning_Looking_to_the_Future (accessed 5 June 2019).

Kerrigan, K. and Murray, V. (eds.) (2011). *A Student Guide to Clinical Legal Education and Pro Bono.* Basingstoke, Palgrave.

Kolb, D. (2015). *Experiential Learning: Experience as the Source of Learning and Development*, 2nd edn. New York, Pearson Education.

Lachman, S. (1997). Learning is a process: toward an improved definition of learning. *Journal of Psychology: Interdisciplinary and Applied*, 131(5), 477.

Miettinen, R. (2000). The concept of experiential learning and John Dewey's theory of reflective thought and action. *International Journal of Lifelong Education*, 19(1), 54.

Sarker, S. P. (ed.) (2015). *Clinical Legal Education in Asia.* Chennai, Palgrave Macmillan.

Solicitors Regulation Authority Code of Conduct (2011). *Governing Solicitors*, http://www.sra.org.uk/solicitors/handbook/code/content.page (version 16) (accessed 14 November 2017).

Thomas, L. (2017). Law clinics in England and Wales: a regulatory black hole. *Law Teacher*, 51(4), 469.

Tripp, D. (1993). *Critical Incidents in Teaching: Developing Professional Judgement*. Abingdon, Routledge.

Wortham, L., Brooks, S., Scherr, A. and Maurer, N. (eds.) (2016). *Learning from Practice: A Text for Experiential Legal Education*, 3rd edn. St Paul, MN, West Academic.

Clinics today: the what, why and how

Unsurprisingly, the first modern wave of legal clinics in the 1960s, conceived and delivered during the 'war on poverty' and growing law student commitment to social justice, focused primarily on providing legal services to the nation's indigent population (Grossman, 1974). Law students worked in community aid and public defender offices, supporting the overworked staff attorneys in myriad ways (Grossman, 1974). As the clinical legal education movement developed, however, the growing recognition of the need for a formal educational component and more control over law students' experiences spurred the growth of in-house clinics. These clinics, operated on-site or in relevant communities and supervised by clinical law professors have emerged as the prototypical law school clinic (Bliss and Peters, 2015). Most offer some form of academic credit, require students to produce graded work product, and include both formal skills training and required reflection.

As clinics moved in-house and gained official standing within American law schools, the variety of clinical offerings expanded exponentially (Haydock, 1983). Today, law clinics exist for nearly every possible area of the law (albeit not at the same law school), from domestic violence to prisoners' rights, from landlord–tenant to public benefits and from legislative reform to environmental advocacy. With the proliferation of clinical offerings since the 1970s also came an expansion in articles, suggested best practices and the emergence of both conferences and professional communities supporting and promoting clinical legal education. As the field grew rapidly, so too did an appreciation for the potential benefits of clinical legal education.

Learning how to learn – how, through an intentional combination of experience and reflection, to transfer the learnings from one situation to another, to bring analytical processes and problem-solving skills developed in one specific context to a completely new context – is undoubtedly one of the most important benefits and goals of clinical legal education (Goldfarb, 2012). It is far from the only benefit, however. As discussed in the preceding chapter, many of the benefits of clinical legal education are axiomatic or self-evident: law students get the opportunity to practise being lawyers, to work with real clients with real legal problems, to develop lawyering skills and analytical thinking skills in live situations, to evaluate and consider different legal options and to prepare written and/or oral arguments, all while simultaneously navigating the complex interplay between client expectations, legal realities and the demands and constraints of the legal system. Other potential benefits, development of a professional lawyering identity and ethos, an increased understanding of the legal system and governmental institutions, exposure to social justice issues and skills such as creative problem solving, negotiation, ends–means thinking, collaboration and understanding a problem in context are equally important and realisable through the experiential and reflective components of clinical legal education (Goldfarb, 2012).

To understand the significance of the benefits of clinical legal education, one must understand their value in context. Law schools exist to 'prepare individuals to provide legal and related services' yet law school graduates report 'insufficient development of core competencies that make one an effective lawyer, particularly those relating to representation and service to clients' (American Bar Association, 2014a, p.26). The competencies and skills that do make an effective lawyer, perhaps expressed best in Shultz and Zedeck's 26 lawyering effectiveness factors, are all competencies and skills that law students can practise and hone through clinical legal education (Shultz and Zedeck, 2011). Significantly, many of these competencies and skills are unique to clinical legal education and not exercised or available through doctrinal or case method coursework (Goldfarb, 2012). When students study appellate case law in the case method system, for example, students are presented with a closed universe of settled facts, choose from a narrow range of scripted legal claims and review, post hoc, the reasoning of judges. In clinical work, by contrast, students encounter vast uncertainty; they must first unravel client narratives and are then called on to discern and evaluate facts, claims and legal options in broader contexts with far fewer signposts.

Clinical legal education is not without its deprecations, of course. Chief among these is the perspective that legal education is a zero-sum game; any increased coursework or credits expended on clinical education requires a corresponding decrease in the strictly academic or intellectual study of law. This tension is often reduced to a purported election between law schools as intellectual proving grounds and law schools as trade schools, with proponents of each side labelling the other as failing to construe the true purpose of a legal education (Barry et al., 2000). Clinics are also more costly than doctrinal classes, with clinical courses typically consisting of as few as 10 students for one professor while doctrinal classes can accommodate more than 100. Additionally, despite the proliferation of clinical scholarship in the last half century, the field still lacks consistency in definition, methodology, assessment and structure. Proof of student learning outcomes also remains scant, as does the effect of clinical experiences in preparing better lawyers (Goldfarb, 2012; Sandefur and Selbin, 2009)

Importantly, this is not to suggest that clinical legal education lacks value or fails to realise its aims. First, as Grimes highlights, many of the objectives or goals of clinical legal education are not ends based but instead seek to expose or introduce students to real clients and cases – a process that has value in and of itself. More broadly, the evidence that does exist, primarily from a survey of early career attorneys, indicates that these attorneys credit clinical legal education as better preparation for their legal careers than other law school experiences (Reuter and Ingham, 2015). And the prepare, practice and reflect components of clinical legal education not only make intuitive sense as the best training grounds for practice but are also based on decades of sound research around adult learning theory. Other professional schools such as medicine and teaching have long relied on the internship or clinical model of training despite similar difficulties in assessing hard-to-measure competencies and skills. The challenge facing clinical legal education is that, as the lesser known and lesser valued model seeking to claim a more prominent role in American legal education, the absence of clear proof of efficacy makes the task that much more challenging. Fortunately, efforts to generate more research on the effects of clinical legal education are one of four emerging trends that will shape clinical legal education in the future.

Trends: what role will clinical legal education play in the future of legal education?

Clinical legal education remains a relatively young and still developing field. The extent to which clinical legal education plays a role in the future of American – and global – legal education will turn on how the field and the clinical community continue to evolve and mature. Four trends, in particular, will shape this trajectory: substantive reach, model evolution, standardisation and proof of concept.

The first trend that will shape the relevance and reach of clinical legal education is how well the field accommodates and expands to match the demand for substantive legal services in the twenty-first century. This is a four-part task. First, as the legal profession and the provision of legal services becomes more globalised and interconnected, implicating different legal authorities, complex jurisdictional issues, foreign procedures and remedies and unique client expectations and needs, so too should the offerings of legal clinics adapt. Second, legal clinics need to be developed to respond to the rapidly expanding demands of the digital and technological age. Cybersecurity, artificial intelligence, space law, digital privacy and internet regulation are among a growing list of new practice areas that both appeal to the twenty-first-century law student and offer the chance to develop skills and knowledge of increasing relevance to corporations, governments and employers at every level. Third, clinical legal education offerings need to better attend to the interests and anticipated practice areas of corporate law practitioners, students who are presently both underrepresented in clinical education and least likely to value a clinical experience (Reuter and Ingham, 2015). Fourth, and finally, the reach and relevance of clinical legal education will turn on how well the field continues to develop and expand in the above three substantive areas without sacrificing the quality or breadth of existing offerings in the more traditional criminal and civil arenas.

The second major trend that will shape the role of clinical legal education within the legal education curriculum is the continued development of diverse and flexible clinical models. The traditional model of a one (or two) semester upper level clinical course with mandatory prerequisites, housed at a law school, taught by a law school professor, offered only during the academic year and in constant competition with doctrinal courses, limits both the supply of and demand for clinical courses. This is true for both clinical courses at the individual law school level as well as for clinical legal education across all law schools. As with any educational programme, the more inflexible and condition laden the model, the harder it is to reproduce or scale that model. For clinical legal education to become more widely adopted, it must have not only the ability to adapt and thrive in multiple different law school settings but also the ability to accomplish this without sacrificing the core conditions of success that make clinical legal education such a valuable experience. Law schools, professors and clinical legal education innovators have proposed a range of new models to balance these twin aims, many of which are already in use or being piloted, albeit in only a handful of law schools.

The ends of the spectrum of possible options are easy to define, from doing nothing (or even reducing the amount of existing clinical offerings) to completely eliminating the case method approach and operating a law school that offers only clinical courses. Within those two extremes, there are four broad ways of thinking about the potential role of clinical education within the legal education curriculum: (1) modification/more of the same; (2) integration/complement; (3) conversion/third year; and (4) restructuring/core.

Modifying the existing legal education model to make clinical courses more accessible, less practical and more relevant is a 'more of the same but better' approach. Expanding clinical offerings in new substantive areas, hiring dedicated clinical professors, increasing the number of clinical education credits required for graduation, offering clinical certificates or designations and increasing partnerships with local and community legal groups are examples of such modifications.

A second possible model centres on increased integration of doctrinal and clinical coursework. Although the two puzzlingly remain largely discrete learning tracks within the law school curriculum, as most practising lawyers know, this is a false dichotomy and practitioners need to be able to both analyse case law ('think like a lawyer') and apply practical legal skills and competencies ('act like a lawyer') to resolve real legal issues (Tokarz et al., 2014). Better integrating the theory and practice disciplines could take several forms, including requiring all doctrinal courses to include clinical components such as simulations, mock arguments or other experiential education while also increasing the doctrinal aspects of clinical course work. Eliminating the distinction between the pathways through cross or co-teaching, paired course offerings or designed clinical and doctrinal sequences would also help establish and reinforce the complementary nature of the two fields. Importantly, an intentionally more integrated approach would help prepare better practice-ready lawyers and shift the perception of clinical legal education as an 'add-on' or supplement to traditional legal education.

A third way to rethink the clinical legal education model focuses on converting the third year of law school into a more practical, experiential year with an emphasis on the transition to legal practice. The third year of law school in

America has become a bit of a punchline among students and professors with many, including former law professor President Obama, calling for the elimination of the third year entirely (Krantz and Millemann, 2015). A different way to think about the third year would be as a unique opportunity to help law students better transition into legal practice with clinical courses as the centrepiece of that effort. Through guided learning experiences with real clients and the opportunity to both reflect and gather constructive feedback, third-year clinical courses can provide students with the chance to develop their practical skills and competencies with a heightened sense of immediacy – whether they have a job secured or are still marketing themselves as a ready-to-contribute applicant. This approach, typically called an 'incubator' or 'residency' model, can help develop a range of professional skills and competencies – from the procedural filing steps to the soft skills of client interviewing and from the administration of a legal office to the ethical obligations of the profession (Krantz and Millemann, 2015).

A fourth and final model moves beyond calls for integrating clinical and doctrinal to restructuring legal education so that clinical legal education is the core focus of the law school curriculum. There are different permutations but several key conditions for success. Restructuring legal education around clinical courses and experiential learning requires that student involvement in such experiences is initiated early, progressive and intentional. Law students would be introduced to clinical methodologies, practices and objectives during the first year of law school (Barry et al., 2000). As students progress and gain experience, their responsibilities for case and client management would increase, as would their capacity for problem solving and abilities to handle more complex legal matters. The ultimate objective would be to position and prepare students for live-client representation with minimal supervision (Grose, 2013). Doctrinal courses would still be part of the legal curriculum but the learning objectives of these courses would be reconfigured to support practical application of the law and preparing students for practice.

The challenge with integration, however, as with any of these proposed developments, is not to merely bring one example of a model into practice but rather to develop a model that can become standard – or at least popular – practice. Clinicians seem to have embraced the first step of this process, developing and experimenting with various different concepts and programmes, while largely neglecting the second and third necessary steps of the diffusion process: standardisation and evaluation. Recent attempts to change this narrative constitute our last two major trends in clinical legal education.

Standardisation, the third major trend in modern clinical legal education, will play an important, cross-cutting role in determining both the professionalisation of clinical legal education (and the important derivative value of perception as a professional field) and the ease of adoption by new practitioners and law schools. At present, the only requirements to qualify as a clinic are the recently adopted ABA standards, requiring live-client representation, supervision and student performance, evaluation and a classroom component (ABA, 2017). The ABA does not specify how intense or structured the supervision should be, objectives or methods for the performance, evaluation or feedback requirements or specific guidelines for the depth and extent of the client and case management or required classroom components. And while an emerging group of professional clinical legal organizations, including the Clinical Legal Education Association (CLEA), the Global Alliance for Justice Education (GAJE), and the Alliance for Experiential Learning in Law, continue to develop and promote best practice recommendations, adoption of these practices remains entirely voluntary and there remains tremendous diversity within clinical legal education objectives and desired outcomes, methodology and evaluation.

Additionally, there is scant attention paid to the training of clinical legal education professors. The prevailing wisdom, much like within law schools generally, is that practice experience or subject matter expertise is the only necessary qualification of a clinical educator (Mlyniec, 2012). As any education professional can attest, however, knowing a great deal about a subject does not mean that one is equipped with the skills and competencies required to effectively teach others about that subject. The effects of this lazy misunderstanding are particularly deleterious in the clinical fields where indirect supervision, meaningful and constructive feedback and student-centred learning play an essential role. Efforts to more intentionally attend to the art of clinical pedagogy and the preparation of clinical professors, notably through programmes at Georgetown University Law Center and initiatives spearheaded by professional organisations such as CLEA, unfortunately remain the exception rather than the rule, resulting in a wide diversity of methodologies and pedagogies employed across the clinical legal education field (Mlyniec, 2012).

The advantages of standardisation, of developing more concrete and shared clinical typologies, methodologies and pedagogies include an increased understanding and appreciation for the role and benefits of clinical legal education, a more commonly defined set of expectations and goals for students and faculty and would facilitate the easier adoption, acceptance and spread of clinical legal education, especially within new settings or practice areas. Additionally, continuing to build and promote best practices and standards more uniformly employed across the clinical legal education field would also allow for more comparative analysis and evaluation of clinical legal education's outcomes and efficacy, an area in dire need of additional research and attention. How the inherent tension between the two trends of standardisation and the development of more flexible and diverse clinical education models is balanced and attended to will play an important role in shaping the mainstream appeal and viability of clinical legal education.

The fourth, and final, trend in clinical legal education that will shape the future role of CLE within the legal education curriculum turns on the degree to which the field embraces the need for evaluation and assessment. The very limited evidence for the impact and effects of clinical legal education is part of a larger, missing element in legal education generally. Assessment within the legal education community is typically limited in law school to end-of-semester course exams and then, on graduation, to the bar examination for the state where the student seeks to practise. Within clinical courses, assessment varies greatly and is very clinic specific, often including differently weighted elements such as individual reflection, graded faculty supervision, client and case management skills, course participation and a cumulative portfolio or capstone. Evidence that does exist around the longitudinal impact of clinical legal education on participants is limited to attitudinal surveys asking young lawyers their perceptions around how valuable different law school experiences, including clinics, were in their transition to practice or career choices. A growing recognition for the need for 'proof of concept' of clinical legal education, combined with the new ABA accreditation standards requiring law schools to evaluate their legal education programmes and learning outcomes offer a timely opportunity for clinical legal education to lead this process and demonstrate the benefits and advantages of clinical experiences.

Of course, recognising the need for proof of concept and compliance with the new ABA standard and actually developing meaningful assessment rubrics and instruments are two very different undertakings. Some possible effects of clinical legal education, including postgraduate employment rates, career choice, civic participation and pro bono service commitments lend themselves more readily to assessment and lack only the requisite commitment of attention and resources. The critical thinking, problem solving, and range of soft skills purportedly developed and fostered through clinical legal education are harder to assess, but more critical to demonstrating proof of concept. Researchers and learning theory experts in other fields have created mechanisms for assessing and evaluating similar skills, however, and the development of applicable models for legal education is a question more of the academy's commitment and interest than one of feasibility. Using models such as Shultz and Zedeck's lawyering factors to identify core practical skills and then developing assessments administered to all students during law school orientation would be a good starting point, for example (Shultz and Zedeck, 2011). Summative law school assessments, comparisons between students who participate in clinics and those who do not, modifications to bar examinations to evaluate practical skills, using employer feedback around new lawyers' skillsets, and more comprehensive studies of young lawyers are also possible evaluative approaches. Regardless of the precise methodology, the need for additional research into the value proposition of clinical legal education is evident and how, or whether, the field chooses to embrace this challenge will play a critical role in how the field is perceived and valued in the coming years.

Across the pond: a glimpse at clinical legal education in the UK

While many of the challenges and benefits of clinical education transcend individual legal systems or approaches to legal education, there are also marked differences in purpose and processes. In the UK, for example, the field of clinical legal education is relatively younger with less developed networks and clinical communities. The range and scope of offerings in the UK, tracing back more than 40 years and continuing to evolve, still remains less diverse than in the United States, with a heavier focus on family law and fewer clinical offerings in the criminal law realm. The emergence of the Clinical Legal Education Organisation, dedicated to fostering and promoting clinical legal education, in the 1990s and the rise in clinical offerings at UK law schools, are helping close this gap, however.

The two systems also have fundamentally different legal education systems, regulatory authorities and pathways to qualification. In the UK, law is an undergraduate degree, considered one of the options for a liberal arts education and many of the students enrol and then graduate with little intention of pursuing either of the available legal careers as a solicitor or as a barrister. The UK system also has a decidedly more vocational bent, with students required to supplement their undergraduate preparation with an overtly skills-focused training periods as part of their pathway to qualification. In the United States, by contrast, students must first attend four years of undergraduate education – in any field – before attending three years of law school. There is no mandatory training or apprenticeship in the United States legal system. UK law schools have a broader educational mission, work with younger students and are less likely to integrate clinical work across the required curriculum. In the United States, students often graduate with hundreds of thousands of dollars in debt and the economic pressures of this obligation influence both the career choices of new graduates and the cost of legal services across the market.

Conclusion

The challenges, critics and calls for reform of legal education, while ringing plangently throughout American classrooms and courtrooms, are not limited to American shores. The effects of the economic crisis, the increasing recognition of the value of experiential education, the role of law schools in preparing employment-ready lawyers, and the shifting demands of the legal profession and practice are global trends. Fortunately, so too is the spread of clinical legal education.

Whether it is phrased as a seismic shift, pivotal moment, crossroads or crisis, one thing is clear: the legal profession and the traditional legal education system are experiencing unprecedented waves of criticism and calls for reform (ABA, 2014a; Tokarz et al., 2014) And while the legal education system has long and notoriously resisted widespread innovation, the current challenges provide a unique opportunity for the academy to fundamentally rethink both how law schools educate students and the best way to prepare students for legal practice. New ABA accreditation standards requiring increased experiential education suggest that the time is ripe for a renewed and heightened consideration of the promise and potential of clinical legal education both within the United States and across the globe. How these four emerging trends, substantive reach, model evolution, standardisation and proof of concept, are encouraged and developed will shape clinical legal education, the field of legal education generally, and the legal profession for generations to come.

Bibliography

American Bar Association (2017). *2017–2018 ABA Standards for Approval of Law Schools*, https://www.americanbar.org/content/dam/aba/publications/misc/legal_education/Standards/2017-2018ABAStandardsforApprovalofLawSchools/2017_2018_ standards_chapter3.authcheckdam.pdf (accessed 8 January 2019).

American Bar Association Task Force on the Future of Legal Education (2014a). *Report and Recommendations*, https://www.americanbar.org/content/dam/aba/administrative/professional_responsibility/report_and_recommendations_of_aba_task_force.authcheckdam.pdf (accessed 4 December 2018).

American Bar Association (2014b). *Revised Standards for Approval of Law Schools*, https://www.americanbar.org/content/dam/aba/administrative/legal_education_and_admissions_to_the_bar/council_reports_and_resolutions/201406_revised_standards_clean_copy.authcheckdam.pdf (accessed 4 December 2018).

Ares, C. (1965). Legal education and the problem of the poor. *Journal of Legal Education*, 17(3), 307–310.

Barry, M., Dubin, J. and Joy, P. (2000). Clinical education for this millennium: the third wave. *Clinical Law Review*, 7(1), 5–32.

Bliss, L. and Peters, D. (2015). Delivering effective education in in-house cinics. In Maranville, D., Bliss, L. R., Kaas, C. W. and López, A. S. (eds.). *Building on Best Practices: Transforming Legal Education in a Changing World*. Durham, NC, Carolina Academic Press.

Carey, S. (2003). An essay on the evolution of clinical legal education and its impact on student trial practice. *Kansas Law Review*, 51, 509–541.

Goldfarb, P. (2012). Back to the future of clinical legal education. *Boston College Journal of Law & Social Justice*, 32(2), 279–308.

Grose, C. (2013). Beyond skills training, revisited: the clinical education spiral. *Clinical Law Review*, 19(2), 489–515.

Grossman, G. (1974). Clinical legal education: history and diagnosis. *Journal of Legal Education*, 26(2), 162–193.

Harvard Law School (n.d.). *History of Harvard Law School*, https://hls.harvard.edu/about/history/ (accessed 20 December 2018).

Haydock, R. (1983). Clinical legal education: the history and development of a law clinic. *William Mitchell Law Review*, 9(1), 103–150.

Johnstone, Q. (1951). Law School Clinics. *Journal of Legal Education*, 3(4), 535–554.

Krantz, S. and Millemann, M. (2015). Legal education in transition: trends and their implications. *Nebraska Law Review*, 94(1), 1–59.

Kuehn, R., Santacroce, D., Reuter, M. and Schechter, S. (2017). *The 2016–2017 Survey of Applied Legal Education*, http://www.csale.org/files/Report_on_2016-17_CSALE_Survey.pdf (accessed 19 December 2018).

Martini, M. (1997). *Marx Not Madison: The Crisis of American Legal Education*. Lanham, MD, University Press of America.

Mertz, E. (2007). *The Language of Law School: Learning to 'Think Like a Lawyer'*. New York, Oxford University Press.

Mlyniec, W. (2012). Where to begin? Training new teachers in the art of clinical pedagogy. *Clinical Law Review*, 18(2), 505–591.

Mlyniec, W. (1997). The intersection of three visions – Ken Pye, Bill Pincus, and Bill Greenhalgh – and the development of clinical teaching fellowships. *Tennessee Law Review*, 64(i), 963–1011.

Moliterno, J. (2013). *The American Legal Profession in Crisis: Resistance and Responses to Change*. New York, Oxford University Press.

Quigley, W. (1995). Introduction to clinical teaching for the new clinical law profession: a view from the first lloor. *Akron Law Review*, 28(3), 463–496.

Reuter, M. and Ingham, J. (2015). The practice value of experiential legal education: an examination of enrollment patterns, course intensity, and career relevance. *Clinical Law Review*, 22(1), 181–249.

Sandefur, R. and Selbin, J. (2009). The clinic effect. *Clinical Law Review*, 16(1), 57–107.

Shultz, M. and Zedeck, S. (2011). Predicting lawyer effectiveness: broadening the basis for law school admission decisions. *Law & Social Inquiry*, 36(3), 620–661.

Segal, D. (2011). Is law school a losing game? *New York Times*, 8 January, https://www.nytimes.com/2011/01/09/business/09law.html (accessed 19 December 2018).

Spencer, B. (2012). The law school critique in historical perspective. *Washington & Lee Law Review*, 69(4), 1949–2063.

Stevens, R. (1983). *Law School: Legal Education in America from the 1850s to the 1980s*. Union, NJ, Lawbook Exchange.

Stuckey, R. (2004) The evolution of legal education in the United States and the United Kingdom: how one system became more faculty-oriented while the other became more consumer-oriented. *Journal of Clinical Legal Education*, 6(1), 101–148.

Sullivan, W., Colby, A., Wegner, J. W., Bond, L. and Shulman, L. (2007). *Educating Lawyers: Preparation for the Profession of Law*, http://archive.carnegiefoundation.org/pdfs/elibrary/elibrary_pdf_632.pdf (accessed 19 December 2018).

Tokarz, K., Lopez, A., Maisel, P. and Seibel, R. (2014). Legal education at a crossroads: innovation, integration, and pluralism required! *Washington University Journal of Law & Policy*, 43(1), 11–57.

Part 5

Legal education and well-being

The following two chapters focus on student well-being, which has been the subject of an increasing amount of attention recently, both in the UK and elsewhere. In Chapter 9, Strevens looks at the ways in which multiple messages emanating from institutions of higher education and the law schools within them can affect law student well-being. Like Field and Meyer in Chapter 10, she uses Self-Determination Theory to frame her analysis. Field and Meyer themselves focus on the possibilities offered by the use of threshold concepts within the law curriculum to promote law student well-being. In both cases, the authors hope that readers will engage in a process of reflection about the ways in which legal education can hinder or promote law student well-being.

Chapter 9

The wrong message

Law student well-being in the contemporary higher education environment

Caroline Strevens

Introduction

This chapter shares a concern for the well-being of law students in common with the following chapter by Field and Meyer, and both chapters advocate the importance of self-determination theory (SDT) in exploring and addressing the issue and improving learning success. Whereas this chapter is about the institutional context and environment and its influence on the well-being of students in university law schools in England, Chapter 10 argues for curriculum reform by effectively teaching threshold concepts in law.

This chapter will not discuss the hidden curriculum. Rather, it will discuss the danger of undermining students' motivation to learn and their well-being by the messages that the law school and the university convey intentionally. In many cases, these messages are being transmitted in order to satisfy regulatory objectives and also in order to attract students and compete in the higher education marketplace. These messages are explicit and intentional and include, for example: 'the student is a consumer'; 'the relationship between the student and the university can be found described in the terms and conditions of a contract that is governed by English law'; 'choose to manage your time carefully because it's only your CV that matters'. They are conveyed through language, space and behaviour.

I am being deliberately provocative by listing some of these messages and there are, of course, some very good reasons to justify making some of them, which will be included in a balanced argument hereafter. However, I will argue that the focus of our law students is being diverted away from learning the discipline of law and towards their entitlement to consumer rights and I will mention implicit messages and one or two that ought to be here. Let us hope this need to manage her contractual rights and her future does not distract too much from the student's enjoyment of today and adversely affect her well-being. I shall enjoy pointing out some dangers of refocusing the student's attention in this way as the chapter progresses.

The messages that we send to law students and those that we do not is an important topic because of their potential to undermine intrinsic motivation to study and because of the corresponding prospect of undermining student well-being. This has the further potential to impact their achievement (Sheldon and Krieger, 2007, p.894) and their ethical decision making (Krieger, 2004).

This chapter will discuss intrinsic and extrinsic motivation and the social contexts that may hinder or promote these, making a link to well-being. It will concern itself with self-determination theory (SDT) and expound on the importance of the three basic psychological needs: autonomy support, relatedness and competence. Then there will be a discussion of the implications for levels of well-being of certain messages explicitly conveyed to law students by law schools and how some other messages, such as the need for struggle and persistence, might be more conducive to well-being. The empirical research conducted by Sheldon and Krieger (2007), based on self-determination theory, indicated that those law students with meaning in their lives and intrinsic goals of helping others had higher levels of well-being. It also found that law schools in the United States could have a profound adverse impact on law students when success was over-promoted in terms of fame and fortune pitching them into extrinsic motivation.

The growth in regulation of higher education coupled with increased competition between institutions is resulting in explicit messages that promote success in terms of winning. At the same time, messages that encourage students to take control and to enjoy themselves are missing. Although many messages may not differ by discipline, there is research to indicate a particular concern for low levels of well-being in lawyers and law students. The causes of this have been speculated about in the rich variety of research from Australia, including Kelk (2009) and elsewhere and, as neatly described by Field (2014, p.14), include the competitive nature of law school, pessimistic thinking style seeping into everyday life and the complete absence of addressing emotion within the classroom. It is a complex and changeable picture with many factors that law schools cannot control. However, we *can* control the messages that we give to students and through this do our best to promote positive motivation and well-being.

Since this chapter concerns itself with England, I must acknowledge at the outset the shortage of empirical evidence for low levels of law student well-being among the law student body in England, and thus the need to rely on international data and research analysis. I will also be drawing on such data as exists in relation to low levels of well-being in the legal profession in England and Wales.

Intrinsic motivation to learn and its link to well-being

In this section, I will cover self-determination theory, and two of its sub-theories (cognitive evaluative theory and goal content theory) and the links between well-being and motivation that these theoretical approaches explain. I will then relate this to the messages, spaces and behaviour described in the next section to highlight some of their drawbacks, before making recommendations for law schools in the final section.

Self-determination theory (SDT) is a complex theory of motivation and engagement developed using empirical studies by the eminent positive psychologists Deci and Ryan, (1985) and enhanced by many further studies (For a useful repository of the areas in which this theory has been applied and developed, see www.selfdterminationtheory.org.) In the words of Ryan and Deci (2000a, p.68) it is significant and powerful because: "It allows for prediction of social conditions that promote high quality development and performance." SDT has five sub-theories: cognitive evaluative theory; organismic integration theory; causality orientations theory; basic needs theory; and goal content theory.

The three concepts at the heart of SDT, described as basic psychological needs, are: autonomy, competency and relatedness. These concepts are explained by Krieger and Sheldon (2015) as meaning respectively authentic, effective and connected to others. SDT indicates that if the three components are absent there will be adverse consequences for mental health, persistence and achievement:

> Social contexts and individual differences that support satisfaction of the basic needs facilitate natural growth processes including intrinsically motivated behavior and integration of extrinsic motivations, whereas those that forestall autonomy, competence, or relatedness are associated with poorer motivation, performance, and well-being. (Deci and Ryan 2000, p.227)

Studies by Deci and Ryan (1985, 2000) have shown that there is a link between intrinsic motivation and higher levels of well-being. Furthermore, this results in greater persistence and achievement all of which are very desirable benefits for students.

A student can be described as intrinsically motivated where she chooses to do something for the joy of experiencing the activity as an end in itself and not because of what it might lead to in the future. Thus, she might volunteer her time to help out at a local charity because she enjoys the process of helping others and being part of a social group in which she can build fulfilling relationships. She may well be exercising a personal value, altruism, without even knowing it. Those who have not studied principles of positive psychology may have never heard of such concepts but are still capable of answering the question of what is important to them and comprehend that being able to choose activities that are important to them makes them satisfied and happy.

Deci and Ryan (2016) start from the assumption that people are all predisposed to show interest in certain activities and wish to develop themselves and their experience of and expertise in those activities because they believe them to be important. We are all intrinsically motivated to act in certain directions.

However, not all activities are inherently interesting. If we take a law school example, students are not likely to find writing a bibliography and learning correct referencing to be fun. It is a rare student who is intrinsically motivated to undertake a referencing learning task. However, a learning context that supports autonomy, relatedness and competence has a role to play in supporting the law student's motivation in this situation.

The sub-theory of SDT known as organismic integration theory (OIT) can explain how it is possible, when the three basic needs are satisfied, to move from being a-motivated, where one acts through fear of the consequences (such as you must ensure your referencing is correct or you will commit an assessment offence), to integrated motivation, where one acts in line with personal values but the motivation remains instrumental (where you learn how to reference correctly not because you enjoy it but because you have taken on the values of your lecturer and agree that it important to acknowledge other people's work in order to do well in your assessment). According to Ryan and Deci (2000b p.60):

> This problem is described within SDT in terms of fostering the internalization and integration of values and behavioral regulations (Deci & Ryan, 1985). Internalization is the process of taking in a value or regulation, and integration is the process by which individuals more fully transform the regulation into their own so that it will emanate from their sense of self.

Although a person does not have choice, their well-being is nonetheless supported since what they are being required to do chimes with their own newly adopted values. They agree that the activity is important. At one end of the scale a student can be motivated to learn through fear of failure and expulsion and thus being ostracised by family and friends. There is no choice here and in these types of condition, there is likely to be lower well-being. The student is acting in order to avoid adverse consequences. Next, a student may be motivated to learn in order to do well in a test and thus impress family or friends. Here the activity is done for personal approbation but not because the activity itself has importance. It is possible, where the three basic needs are satisfied, to move from this position to 'active personal commitment' and this is where extrinsic motivations are integrated with personal values. Thus a student may not enjoy the particular topic of study, nor have they chosen to do it, but has come to believe that it is an important and worthwhile activity. (For a full explanation and a model explaining the range of intrinsic and extrinsic motivation, see Figure 1. A taxonomy of human motivation, in Ryan and Deci 2000b, p.61). Once this is achieved SDT posits that well-being will be higher.

Constructing communities of learning and providing optimal assessment tasks with clear guidance and positive feedback are well-recognised aspects of best pedagogic practice. Lenning and Ebbers (1999) described four generic forms of learning community and these generally promote activity for learning within and outside of the classroom. The effectiveness of such communities has been explored using both empirical methods and through the application of a variety of theoretical lens (see, for instance, Bruffee, 1993; Zhao and Kuh, 2004). The importance of assessment design and feedback is well-recognised in the literature (Entwistle and Entwistle, 1991; Lizzio and Wilson, 2013; Ramsden, 2003): 'On degree programmes where the volume of formative assessment is greater, students take a deep approach to their studies to a greater extent' (Gibbs, 2012, p.34, citing Gibbs and Dunbar-Goddet, 2007). They also have powerful potential in terms of motivation of learning in our students, according to SDT, because the first satisfies the need for relatedness while the second satisfies competence. The concepts of relatedness and competence are not just an end in themselves. As explained above they have a role to play in internalisation, which results in active personal commitment and higher well-being:

> SDT proposes that people will tend naturally to internalize the values and regulations of their social groups. This tendency is facilitated by feelings of relatedness to socializing others, as well as feelings of competence with respect to the regulation being internalized. (Deci and Ryan 2000, p.238)

We are influenced, positively or negatively, by our social contexts and take on the pervading culture for better or worse. This applies to social groups including institutional norms and expectations that are conveyed in explicit messages and in images and behaviour. Ryan and Deci (2000a) highlight the distress likely to result where there is conflict between satisfaction of these basic needs (for example, in an environment where members of a group must give up autonomy in order to be fully included in the community) in addition to where the needs are not satisfied.

Messages emanating from the law school have the potential to do harm. Learning for the love of learning is a precious thing. Messages that undermine such intrinsic motivation will adversely affect well-being. Messages that endorse extrinsic values and goals may too. A controlling context may undermine intrinsic motivation where the individual experiences a reduced sense of autonomy. Empirical studies by Ryan and Deci (2000b) have shown that rewards, threats, deadlines, competition and directives can have this effect because a person perceives that they are being controlled rather than making choices. Thus we need to avoid messages that signal competition, incentives, or threats. (It should be noted, however, that the issue of rewards in particular is controversial. Conflicting research indicates (a) incentives boost performance, (b) intrinsic motivation boosts performance, and (c) incentives reduce intrinsic motivation (Black and Allen, 2018, p.208, citing Cerasoli et al., 2014, p.984).

The three concepts of autonomy, competence and relatedness are also relevant to goal content theory, since SDT also seeks to explain the implications for well-being of intrinsic and extrinsic goals, values and motivations. Sheldon and Krieger (2004, p.264 citing Kasser and Ryan, 1993, 1996) tell us that a person can be said to have intrinsic goals or values when their personal goal or value is 'intimacy, community, and personal growth' as opposed to external goals or values, which they are not able to control, such as riches and renown. A law school that consistently used messages to encourage students to take part in activities in order to enhance their CVs, because these activities were valued by potential future employers, may well be encouraging the formation of extrinsic values. Extrinsic values become problematic for well-being if they dominate in a person's value system (Krieger and Sheldon, 2015).

Kasser and Ryan (1996) conducted two empirical studies with groups of adults (the first were adults living in Rochester New York and the second were psychology undergraduates at the University of Rochester) to test their previous findings (Kasser and Ryan, 1993) that adolescents experienced lower well-being if they held stronger ambitions for money. These two studies confirmed previous results and they did so irrespective of gender, income or age. Kasser and Ryan concluded that holding extrinsic aspirations (such as financial success, beauty and fame), related negatively to well-being. They thought that this was the case because the goals relied on the reactions of others and were usually held as goals as a means to some other end and not as an end in themselves. However, intrinsic aspirations, such as health and helpfulness to others, related positively to well-being. Furthermore, research by Ryan et al. (1999) and by Kasser and Ryan (1996) indicated that attainment of extrinsic goals was not positively associated with well-being. Law schools need to be mindful of this latter point and be more wary of promoting aspirations of fame and fortune.

Messages as a result of changes in the higher education context

Frequently, the student is viewed by the university as a consumer whose rights and responsibilities are set out clearly to ensure compliance with regulation and to manage risk. Pitman (2000, citing Marceau, 1995, p.167) argues that universities have evolved into institutions that meet consumer demand and that degrees are now designed with the student as that customer in mind. Universities appear to have evolved as their funding streams have changed, to become more risk averse. Rattray (2018, p.1489) discusses the impact of the new 'risk-averse culture' on curriculum design aimed at ensuring value for money and removal of uncertainty and discomfort.

In March 2015, the Competition and Markets Authority (CMA) published guidance to higher education providers in order that they could ensure compliance with consumer protection legislation for the benefit of students (CMA, 2015). The need to protect students from unfair practices has long been the case but has somehow become more relevant in the current climate in which students are largely paying for their own education. It is only in recent years that universities have talked of managing the contractual relationship with students (Raaper, 2018). This change has not been chosen by universities but rather imposed up them by changes to the HE context (Foskett, 2010; Sonnenberg 2017). Much has been written about the implications of student fees and increased competition between universities and the transformation of education from a society aspiration into a personal investment (for example, Furedi, 2009, 2011; Naidoo and Williams, 2015; Naidoo and Williams 2017). Rather akin to amateur financial investors, consumers of higher education are perceived to be in need to help and guidance in making wise choices.

The CMA guidance (CMA, 2015) describes how consumer law applies to the student's choice of course and university. The advice that the CMA has issued to universities covers three areas: accurate and timely information, fair terms, and accessible and comprehensible complaints handling systems. Implicit in the official guidance is the notion that students are purchasing a course as described in university literature, website materials, and open day presentations. Guidance on rights and how to access them set out on the government website is addressed directly to students.

Why do we care that the student is being given messages about their consumer rights? After all, the decision whether or not to undertake a full time degree is an extremely important and one-time-only decision for most students and the balance of power and knowledge is firmly with the institution rather than the individual. Students need clear, reliable information, fair terms and a straightforward complaint process don't they?

Sonnenberg (2017) points out the dangers to both universities and students of treating the students as consumer or customer. For the university, the danger is to replace its raison d'être to merely education of the next generation in order that they are able to contribute to the economy (Collini, 2012, cited in Sonnenberg, 2017, p.269). As for the student, Sonnenberg argues, referring to her empirical studies, that 'the more pronounced a student's self-definition as a consumer, the greater his/her extrinsic motivation for entering HE.' She explains that this student will have higher expectations of their course and thus more chance of being dissatisfied and is also more likely to attribute failure to external causes such as the teaching and learning environment. Bunce et al. conducted empirical studies with students and found evidence that 'a higher consumer orientation was associated with lower academic performance' (2017, p.1958). Rattray (2018) is another advocate against treating students as consumers if this means removing risk of failure. She argues that students will be more resilient if their education exposes them to uncertainty and negative learning experiences. Citing Snyder (2002, p.1494), Rattray explains why we benefit from failure in order to learn. 'Resilience, optimism, and academic hope are not static attributes, rather they are developed over time in response to learning experiences' (Rattray, 2018, p.1494, citing Snyder et al., 2002).

The net result of this CMA guidance on departments within universities is that less information is given to applicants before enrolment and to students during their study in order to retain maximum flexibility in delivery of courses.

Open day booklets with full course structures and expansive description of assessment methods and optional subjects have been replaced with corporate PR. Module descriptions give general outlines. Programme specifications are shorter and less specific. The implications of the increased aversion to risk on staff and students in HE are discussed by Rattray (2018) and she warns that academics are discouraged from innovation in the curriculum for fear of adverse student feedback. It is inevitable that courses will evolve as new disciplines and applications of current knowledge emerge and as staff join or leave institutions. With every material change comes the requirement to consult students, which appears reasonable, but is a very bureaucratic process. Change and clarity are being impeded because of fears of the effects of consumer law.

It is unclear how these responses will assist a first-in-the-family 17-year-old to make her choice of course and institution. A key psychological need is autonomy. Niemiec, Ryan and Deci, 2010 explain that autonomy is perceived when a person is able to make meaningful choices about their behaviour and those choices align with their personal values. Reduction of information to vague generalities does not aid meaningful student choice of institution or course.

Let us hope that she will visit the university in person and meet some of her potential lecturers and tutors. The creation of a community of learning involves building relationships with trusted others. These others include your lecturers and peers. A personal visit to the institution via open day or other public event will provide an opportunity to evaluate the people. The way staff and student ambassadors behave, as opposed to what they say, convey messages about the culture of that law school. As explained, self-determination theory (Deci and Ryan, 2000) provides that one of the three basic psychological needs is relatedness – the existence of trusted relationships with people in your various communities. A sense or feel of the department about its culture of community and collegiality is an important message transmitted by the behaviour of staff and students at open days whatever limitations are placed on the words and images used.

Complaints have become a growing concern for HE institutions. The figures published by the ombudsmen show how the numbers increase year on year (OIA Annual Reports). It could be argued that one of the reasons for the increase is the increased emphasis on the student contract and the rights of the student as consumer. The consumer naturally expects a certain standard of delivery and, thanks to the internet and social media, will be swift to identify and to purse her rights. In a recent High Court decision, *Siddiqui v. The Chancellor, Masters and Scholars of the University of Oxford* [2018] EWHC 184 (QB), an Oxford graduate failed in his claim for damages for breach of contract based on poor teaching. The claim was based on teaching that had taken place in the academic year 1999/2000 and thus the teaching concerned took place before the introduction of student fees. As a result, there was no claim for a refund or reduction of fees. Rather, the remedy sought was based on both future financial loss as a result of not attaining first class honours and also on resulting psychological harm. The claim was held to be statute barred but even so the Honourable Mr Justice Foskett diligently explored the difficulties a student may face in bringing such a claim, explicitly referring to the new student fee regime:

> [T]he hurdles in establishing a claim for compensation based upon that inadequate delivery are great and often insurmountable. In this case, I have not been satisfied that the delivery of one particular feature of the Claimant's undergraduate degree course was inadequate or, in any event, that it had the consequences claimed for it.
>
> That said, in the present climate, some 17 years on from the material events in this case, when students are incurring substantial debts to pursue their university education, the quality of the education delivered will undoubtedly come under even greater scrutiny than it did in the past. There may be some rare cases where some claim for compensation for the inadequacy of the tuition provided may succeed, but it is hardly the ideal way of achieving redress. Litigation is costly, time- and emotion-consuming and runs the significant risk of failure, particularly in this area where establishing a causative link between the quality of teaching and any alleged 'injury' is fraught with difficulty. (paras 243–244)

Since that case there has been another example of litigation based on the student contract and this resulted from the Universities and Colleges Union strike action in the spring of 2018. Academic staff from a number of universities took part in strike action that resulted in thousands of students experiencing reduced contact time. Asserson Law Offices (a firm of solicitors in England and Wales regulated by the Solicitors' Regulation Authority) have established a website for students to sign up for a group action. The firm has over 6,000 students registered to claim a refund of fees and who are likely to be going through internal complaints procedures since as yet there are no reports of an action being launched. These numbers give an indication of the extent of student awareness of and association with consumer rights.

Palfreyman and Tapper (2016) have written about the difficulties faced by students in bringing a claim based on failure to delivery contracted teaching. There are many reasons why a student may underperform, quite apart from possible faulty teaching. The matter of failure to deliver contact hours may be something that, if withdrawn, can result in a cause of action.

Gibbs' influential 'Dimensions of Quality' report states that its most important conclusion is 'that what best predicts educational gain is measure of educational process: what institutions do with their resources to make the most of whatever students they have' (2012, p.43). It is clearly noted in Gibbs' report (p.21) that the number of contact hours has less correlation to learning gain than the quality of the class time. Those students who are pursing legal action for the lost strike hours may well be advised to read this report and ask for a different remedy.

This culture of risk and regulation is resulting in explicit messages that encourage the students to see themselves as a passive purchaser of a law degree. It also could be diluting the quality of information given to help student choice. Quite a perverse outcome and unlikely to increase student motivation and well-being through satisfaction of the basic psychological needs.

Spaces for learning in

What message does law school intend to convey by the construction of state-of-the-art teaching rooms, sports and social facilities and well-designed student accommodation? Again, there is much written on the investment made in recent years by vice-chancellors in the estate and the new competitive environment imperative that justifies this. Clark and Stanier (2017, p.39) question the way in which this investment inspires learning. What message do our first-in-family applicants and our freshers take in? Do they ask themselves if they fit into these gleaming imposing structures? Little or no empirical research has been conducted in this area so one can only speculate as to the message received. Images on websites, social media and in glossy brochures depict where teaching is taking place but do they show where the learning happens?

There is a missing message here as to the importance of individual engagement. Broadbent and Sellman (2013a, 2013b) discuss how images impact on student expectations and discuss the development of our new product 'the student experience'. The newly opened wing of the library at the University of Portsmouth, as described by Collinson (2008) reputedly won an award for its design because the glass walls that lit up in the evening showed the local community the presence of students long into the evening and thus influenced opinion on how hard students were working. This type of visual display, I would argue, is more likely to convey the imperative for individual student action and effort. Universities could also convey a stronger message about their learning communities through imagery, for instance, by using images of groups of students working in the newly created spaces including a member of staff as part of the group.

The raising of aspirations and the depiction of diversity provide justification for the use of these images. We are motivated in different ways by our environment and according to Kolb and Kolb (2005) different types of learning space may support different types of learner. However, students may be absorbing a different signal from walls decorated with images depicting well-known alumni or prize winners. They may conclude that success is defined by fame and high scores. The work of Krieger and Sheldon (2015) (albeit in American law schools) describes how promoting success in this way undermines intrinsic motivation with well-being levels dropping in consequence as anxiety increases in a high-stakes competitive culture.

Employment-enhancing opportunities

One of the wonderful features of a university education is the choice offered to students to take up new and unexplored activities. These may be social or educational, miserable or delightful, but many are likely to be unplanned. From the start of freshers' ,week messages are circulating about these opportunities: to join the student law society, to become a student rep, to join the mooting team, to help form a new student society, to enter a competition (usually essay writing!), to apply for a summer placement, to take a trip, often up a mountain to raise funds for charity. Have you noticed that I have been selective in my list? Well, I wished to make a point that these messages are frequently accompanied by an expression of how useful these activities would be for the CV. Anecdotally, careers advisers at the University of Portsmouth tell us that employers wish applicants to evidence active engagement across a variety of activities to develop skills and learn about the self, provide evidence of leadership, give examples of success or failure and persistence. According to a report produced for Universities UK (2015, p.23): '[T]he CBI found that between 14 and 29% of employers reported dissatisfaction with graduates' literacy, numeracy, analysis, team working, communication, problem-solving and self-management skills.' But why do we not also say that these activities are fun because you make new friends, visit new places, change your opinion and surprise yourself by hating the thing you always dreamed of doing (trying the sport of fencing, in my case) and work out what your personal values are?

Goal content theory, a part of SDT, indicates, according to Ryan, Huta and Deci (2008) that attainment of intrinsic goals is more strongly associated with well-being than attainment of extrinsic. There are good reasons to change some of our messages to promote choosing activities because a student will enjoy doing them and not because it might lead to something else. We need to remove those messages that incentivise competitions with prizes such as mini-pupillages. This provides a good example of a message that has the potential to undermine intrinsic values by promoting a performance goal as opposed to a learning goal (Dweck, 1989). Please try mooting – you might love it!

The absence of staff from their office

My final message is an implicit message. It concerns behaviour and the physical places in which students are able to find academic staff when they have a question or need help with a personal issue. Most law schools ask academic staff to act as personal tutors and this role requires face–to-face meetings, usually in staff offices, and during office hours. Many staff invite students to email to make these appointments and this invitation is fixed to their (closed) office door. All very well if your problem is not urgent and you are able to fit into an orderly schedule of meetings and appointments offered by your personal tutor. What message is being conveyed to the student with a pressing question or a delicate or embarrassing personal issue? The trend for staff to work in their offices is reducing. There are, I would argue and as explained in Wilson and Strevens (2018), a number of reasons for this: long commuting distances as staff move the location of their job but not their home; increasing workloads and expectations on staff causing them to work from home so that they can control their environments and minimise interruption; shared offices as space becomes scarce; reluctance and concern on the part of academic staff that they are not trained to deal with the serious mental health or personal issues students may declare; and fear in staff, also, of the effect of these disclosures on their own well-being.

What is the message absorbed by students seeing these empty offices? It could be that staff members are busy teaching and researching and occupied with activities that do not relate to unplanned student issues. Other matters are more important. How does this compare to the institutional celebration of Teaching Excellence Framework gold status? The dangers of a law school sending out contradictory messages about its values are pointed out by Krieger (2007). According to Wilson and Strevens (2018), this environment of empty offices impacts adversely on the well-being of academics in addition to students as it prevents the fulfilment of the basic need of relatedness. There may also be another more subtle message that is unintentionally conveyed to students seeking advice if they find mostly female academics in their offices. According to Margaret Thornton, 'dutiful daughters' are expected to undertake responsibility for the time consuming role of student pastoral support and complaints (Thornton, 1994, p.59). Does this message make it harder for male students to seek advice?

An alternative message being transmitted may be that those members of staff who are in their offices are present in order to answer student questions and it has been designed this way. Students will learn whom they can find and whom they cannot. They will receive messages about which staff are approachable and which are not. These staff members are likely to be more knowledgeable about university regulations and processes including professional support services if they are frequently answering student questions. This message from staff concerning staff personal priorities may result in differing student attendance in lectures and seminars as students 'vote with their feet' and in student feedback. This is speculative but not being physically present in your office in traditional face-to-face learning environments has strong negative implications if we are concerned with the social contexts that support student learning and the concept of relatedness (and we are very concerned about it).

Discussion and recommendations

Our messages, given mostly outside the classroom, transmitted explicitly, and through our physical spaces and behaviour, fare badly when examined through the lens of SDT because they have the potential to undermine intrinsic motivation to learn and thus to undermine student well-being. Higher well-being leads to greater persistence and achievement (Vansteenkiste, Niemiec and Soenens, 2010, p.132); an ideal goal for legal educators. Some of the messages highlighted in this chapter are transmitted at university level in order to minimise risk and also to maximise market share. I am not sure we could stop them if we wished to. So what can we do? Enjoyment of any type of learning is a precious thing. We could help our students manage anxiety by avoiding the constant preference of extrinsic goals and values the attainment or pursuit of which is largely outside their control.

Enabling informed choice and setting out realistic expectations, ensuring consistent and transparent processes are all good reasons to provide information. Indeed, the payment of student fees does result in a contractual relationship. However, the institutional message could be framed in order to empower students and to encourage them to see themselves as learners. The language used through all administrative processes should be carefully chosen to promote intrinsic goals and motivation. Identifying oneself as a consumer is unhelpful to the student. Tang and Fergusson argue that: 'There is a tendency for law schools to elevate the "law student" identity above others' (2014, p.51). The better approach, rather than yet another intervention, would be to allow space for students to develop all aspects of their identity and to explicitly recognise their own personal values.

Awards, honours and the most prestigious and renowned alumni have air space, digital space, and wall space in law school. Walk the corridors of a law school today and I would give you favourable odds that rankings will feature somewhere on the walls proclaiming success in the Teaching Excellence Framework or Research Excellence Framework or the National Student Survey. Deci and Ryan (2016, p.10) argue against seeking to increase educational achievement through testing and ranking since this is establishing a controlling environment. The danger of incentivising outcomes is that it can result in both the desired behaviour (working harder to learn) as well as the opposite behaviour (cheating or teaching to the test).

The message of persistence in the face of difficulty and the struggle to achieve being normal is missing from this imagery. Are we rewarding outcomes and not behaviour? Sheldon and Krieger (2007, p.893) warn against this if our pursuit is to improve well-being. We could make room in our corridors for more learning journeys and more public service. Why is it that so many law students wish to become commercial lawyers and earn huge salaries? Where does this message come from? Do the images we use in law schools contribute to moulding the law students' vision of success? We can do better.

Where do our messages suggest that students should take up opportunities for enjoyment and in order to gain the satisfaction of helping others? Many messages are phrased in terms of preparing for your career, improving your employability. This is advocating 'jam for tomorrow'. We can argue that these opportunities satisfy the need for competence since they afford structured learning opportunities so that students can master new skills. But there is little autonomy, authenticity or choice if a student undertakes the activity in order to please an unknown future employer and in so doing her intrinsic aspirations are subsumed by extrinsic ones. Kasser and Ryan (1996) tell us that the attainment of extrinsic goals is less highly co-related with well-being than attainment of intrinsic goals.

The empty staff offices may inform students that not all law staff prioritise learning and teaching and personal support to the same degree. Contrast this with institutional messages about gold TEF awards and we have clearly communicated contradiction about our institution's values. Research clearly indicates the benefits of enactment of one's personal values (Sheldon and Krieger, 2014, p.257) for enhanced well-being. We could all 'walk the talk' and our message to students should be consistently that they should also do this:

> Once one is aware of the importance of the basic needs, intrinsic values, and internal/identified motivations for a thriving life, one can seek out and engage in behaviors that maximize meaning and well-being in life and work.

When we can increase understanding in staff and students of these principles of SDT that apply to human nature irrespective of discipline then we can make a difference. Many law teachers hold a professional teaching qualification through the Advance HE fellowship scheme. Self-determination theory and the influence of personal values and intrinsic goals should be embedded in that teaching qualification to increase understanding of links between wellbeing and learning. As advocated by Krieger and Sheldon (2015), we could reduce levels of anxiety if our messages encourage students to redefine success in terms of pursing meaning.

I conclude with this message from Deci and Ryan (2016, p.25) made here deliberately and explicitly and in the hope it will influence behaviour and spaces in law school:

> It is our strong belief, supported by substantial empirical evidence, that, when teachers have the resources and permission to attend to the basic psychological needs of students, the students will indeed become more actively engaged in learning and will more readily internalize a value for achieving.

Bibliography

Black, S. and Allen, J. D. (2018). Part 7: rewards, motivation, and performance. *The Reference Librarian*, *59*(4), 205–218.

Boud, D. and Molloy, E. (2013). Rethinking models of feedback for learning: the challenge of design. *Assessment & Evaluation in Higher Education*, *38*(6), 698–712.

Broadbent, G. and Sellman, P. (2013a). Images of law and legal education: law school websites and the provision of information. *European Journal of Law and Technology*, *4*(1).

Broadbent, G. and Sellman, P. (2013b). Great expectations? Law schools, websites and 'the student experience'. *The Law Teacher*, *47*(1), 44–63.

Bruffee, K. A. (1993). *Collaborative Learning: Higher Education, Interdependence, and the Authority of Knowledge*. Baltimore, MD, Johns Hopkins University Press.

Bunce, L., Baird, A. and Jones, S. E. (2017). The student-as-consumer approach in higher education and its effects on academic performance. *Studies in Higher Education*, *42*(11), 1958–1978.

Clark, M. and Stanier, S. (2017). Spaces that inspire. *University Alliance Report*, https://www.unialliance.ac.uk/wp-content/uploads/2017/10/UA-technical-and-professional-excellence-perspectives-on-learning-and-teaching-WEB-FINAL.pdf, p.39.

CMA (2015). *UK higher education providers – advice on consumer protection law (CMA 33)*, https://www.gov.uk/government/publications/higher-education-consumer-law-advice-for-providers.

Collini, S. (2012). *What Are Universities For?* London, Penguin.

Collinson, T. (2008). Completing the university library at Portsmouth. *Library & Information Update*, 7(1–2),44–47.

Deci, E. L. and Ryan, R. M. (2016). Optimizing students' motivation in the era of testing and pressure: a self-determination theory perspective. In *Building Autonomous Learners*. Singapore, Springer, pp. 9–29.

Deci, E. L. and Ryan, R. M. (2000). The 'what' and 'why' of goal pursuits: human needs and the self-determination of behavior. *Psychological Inquiry*, *11*(4), 227–268.

Deci, E. L. and Ryan, R. M. (1985). Cognitive evaluation theory. In *Intrinsic Motivation and Self-Determination in Human Behavior*. Boston, MA, Springer, pp.43–85.

Deci, E. L., Olafsen, A. H. and Ryan, R. M. (2017). Self-determination theory in work organizations: the state of a science. *Annual Review of Organizational Psychology and Organizational Behavior*, *4*, 19–43.

Dweck, C. S.(1989). Motivation. In Lesgold, A.and Glaser, R. (eds.), *Foundations for a Psychology of Education*. Hillsdale, NJ, Lawrence Erlbaum Associates, pp.87–136.

Entwistle, N. J. and Entwistle, A. (1991). Contrasting forms of understanding for degree examinations: the student experience and its implications. *Higher Education*, *22*(3), 205–227.

Field, R. (2014). *Promoting law student well-being through the curriculum*. Australian Government, http://www.olt.gov.au/resource-promoting-law-student-well-being-through-curriculum.

Foskett, N. (2010). Markets, government, funding and the marketisation of UK higher education. In Molesworth, M. (ed.). *The Marketisation of Higher Education and the Student as Consumer*. Abingdon, Routledge, pp. 39–52.

Furedi, F. (2010). Introduction to the marketisation of higher education and the student as consumer. In Molesworth, M. (ed.). *The Marketisation of Higher Education and the Student as Consumer*. Abingdon, Routledge, pp.15–22.

Furedi, F. (2009). *Wasted: Why Education Isn't Educating*. London, Bloomsbury Publishing.

Gibbs, G. (2012). *Implications of 'Dimensions of Quality' in a Market Environment*. York, Higher Education Academy.

Gibbs, G. and Dunbar-Goddet, H. (2007). *The Effects of Programme Assessment Environments on Student Learning*. York, Higher Education Academy.

Kasser, T. and Ryan, R. M. (1996). Further examining the American dream: differential correlates of intrinsic and extrinsic goals. *Personality and Social Psychology Bulletin*, *22*(3), 280–287.

Kasser, T. and Ryan, R. M. (1993). A dark side of the American dream: correlates of financial success as a central life aspiration. *Journal of Personality and Social Psychology*, 65 (2), 410.

Kelk, N. (2009). *Courting the Blues: Attitudes Towards Depression in Australian Law Students and Lawyers*. Canberra, Brain and Mind Research Institute.

Kolb, A. Y. and Kolb, D. A. (2005). Learning styles and learning spaces: Enhancing experiential learning in higher education. *Academy of Management Learning & Education, 4*(2), 193–212.

Krieger, L. S. (2010). The most ethical of people, the least ethical of people: proposing self-determination theory to measure professional character formation. *University of St. Thomas Law Journal, 8*, 168.

Krieger, L. S.(2007). Human nature as a new guiding philosophy for legal education and the profession. *Washburn Law Journal*, 47, 247.

Krieger, L. S. (2004). The inseparability of professionalism and personal satisfaction: perspectives on values, integrity and happiness. *Clinical Law Review, 11*, 425.

Krieger, L. S. and Sheldon, K. M. (2015). What makes lawyers happy: a data-driven prescription to redefine professional success. *George Washington Law Review, 83*, 554.

Lenning, O. T. and Ebbers, L. H. (1999). *The Powerful Potential of Learning Communities: Improving Education for the Future. ASHE-ERIC Higher Education Report, vol. 26, no. 6.* Washington, DC, ERIC Clearinghouse on Higher Education.

Lizzio, A. and Wilson, K. (2013). First-year students' appraisal of assessment tasks: implications for efficacy, engagement and performance. *Assessment & Evaluation in Higher Education, 38*(4), 389–406.

Marceau, J. (1995). Management of higher education policy. In Rees, S. and Rodley, G. (eds.). *The Human Costs of Managerialism: Advocating the Recovery of Humanity*. Sydney, Pluto Press Australia.

Molesworth, M., Nixon, E. and Scullion, R. (2009). Having, being and higher education: the marketisation of the university and the transformation of the student into consumer. *Teaching in Higher Education, 14*(3), 277–287.

Naidoo, R. and Williams, J. (2015). The neoliberal regime in English higher education: Charters, consumers and the erosion of the public good. *Critical Studies in Education, 56*(2), 208–223.

Niemiec, C. P., Ryan, R. M. and Deci, E. L. (2010). Self-determination theory and the relation of autonomy to self-regulatory processes and personality development. In Hoyle, R. H. (ed.).*Handbook of Personality and Self-Regulation*. Oxford, Wiley-Blackwell.

OIA Annual Reports Annual reports for the Office of the Independent Adjudicator, https://www.oiahe.org.uk/resources-and-publications/annual-reports/.

Palfreyman, D. and Tapper, T. (2016). The marketization of English higher education and the financing of tuition fees. *London Review of Education, 14*(1), 47–55.

Pitman, T. (2000). Perceptions of academics and students as customers: a survey of administrative staff in higher education. *Journal of Higher Education Policy and Management, 22*(2), 165–175.

Raaper, R. (2018). Students' unions and consumerist policy discourses in English higher education. *Critical Studies in Education*, 1–17.

Ramsden, P. (2003). *Learning to Teach in Higher Education*. Abingdon, Routledge.

Rattray, J. (2018). Affect and ipsative approaches as a counter to pedagogic frailty: the guardian of traditional models of student success. *Higher Education Research & Development, 37*(7), 1489–1500.

Ryan, R. M. and Deci, E. L. (2000a). Self-determination theory and the facilitation of intrinsic motivation, social development, and well-being. *American Psychologist, 55*(1), 68.

Ryan, R. M. and Deci, E. L. (2000b). Intrinsic and extrinsic motivations: classic definitions and new directions. *Contemporary Educational Psychology, 25*(1), 54–67.

Ryan, R. M., Chirkov, V. I., Little, T. D., Sheldon, K. M., Timoshina, E. and Deci, E. L. (1999). The American dream in Russia: extrinsic aspirations and well-being in two cultures. *Personality and Social Psychology Bulletin, 25*(12), 1509–1524.

Ryan, R. M., Huta, V. and Deci, E. L. (2008). Living well: a self-determination theory perspective on eudaimonia. *Journal of Happiness Studies, 9*(1), 139–170.

Sheldon, K. M. and Krieger, L. S. (2014). Walking the talk: value importance, value enactment, and well-being. *Motivation and Emotion, 38*(5), 609–619.

Sheldon, K. M. and Krieger, L. S. (2007). Understanding the negative effects of legal education on law students: a longitudinal test of self-determination theory. *Personality and Social Psychology Bulletin, 33*(6), 883–897.

Sheldon, K. M. and Krieger, L. S. (2004). Does legal education have undermining effects on law students? Evaluating changes in motivation, values, and well-being. *Behavioral Sciences & the Law, 22*(2), 261–286.

Snyder, C. R. (2002). Hope theory: rainbows in the mind. *Psychological inquiry, 13*(4), 249–275.

Snyder, C. R., Shorey, H. S., Cheavens, J., Pulvers, K. M., Adams, V. H., III andWiklund, C. (2002). Hope and academic success in college . *Journal of Educational Psychology*, 94(4), 820–826.

Sonnenberg, S. J. (2017). Student identity and the marketisation of higher education. In *Self and Social Identity in Educational Contexts*. London, Routledge, pp. 257–276.

Tang, S. and Ferguson, A. (2014). The possibility of wellbeing: preliminary results from surveys of Australian professional legal education students. *Queensland University Law Review, 14*, 27.

Thornton, M. (1994). Discord in the Legal Academy: the case of the feminist scholar. *Australian Feminist Law Journal*, 53(3), 59.

Tomlinson, M. (2017). Student perceptions of themselves as 'consumers' of higher education. *British Journal of Sociology of Education, 38*(4), 450–467.

Tomlinson, M. (2014). *Exploring the Impacts of Policy Changes on Student Attitudes to Learning*. York, Higher Education Academy.

Universities UK (2015). *Supply and demand for higher level skills*, https://www.universitiesuk.ac.uk/policy-and-analysis/reports/Documents/2015/supply-and-demand-for-higher-level-skills.pdf.

Vansteenkiste, M., Niemiec, C. P. and Soenens, B. (2010). The development of the five mini-theories of self-determination theory: an historical overview, emerging trends, and future directions. In *The Decade Ahead: Theoretical Perspectives on Motivation and Achievement*. Bingley, Emerald Group Publishing Limited, pp. 105–165.

Williams, J. (2012). *Consuming Higher Education: Why Learning Can't Be Bought*. London, A&C Black.

Wilson, J. C. and Strevens, C. (2018). Perceptions of psychological well-being in UK law academics. *The Law Teacher, 52*(3), 335–349

Zhao, C. M. and Kuh, G. D. (2004). Adding value: learning communities and student engagement. *Research in Higher Education, 45*(2), 115–138.

Chapter 10

Threshold concepts in law

Intentional curriculum reform to support law student learning success and well-being

Rachael Field and Jan H. F. Meyer[1]

Introduction

Well-being is an important issue in contemporary education contexts because the psychological health of students, at all levels of learning, is a critical component of their capacity to learn effectively. A large body of research literature has now established that it is important that tertiary educators attend to student well-being if student learning success at university is to be adequately supported (Baik et al., 2017, and 2019). The discipline of law is no exception (Field, Duffy and James, 2016; Field, Duffy and James, 2002; Strevens and Field, 2019). Indeed, what we know about law student mental health, and the critical relationship between psychological well-being and student learning success, can be seen as creating a moral imperative for legal educators to intentionally seek to reform curricula to promote law students' well-being. We see curriculum reform beginning as a semi-continuous process of improving what we do individually to support student learning in the classroom. The focus of this process should be on activities that are directed towards issues of well-being located within the *content* of the curriculum; discrete activities that over time are integrated, consolidated and evaluated at key locations of transformational learning within the *structure* of the curriculum, thus reflecting a professional (and accountable) commitment to the aforementioned moral imperative.

In general, 'well-being' is a psychologically complex construct, and the manifestation of the condition (or not) of 'well-being' may be a function of several variables located within the personal experience of a student's engagement with both the content, and also the context, of learning. Such experience occurs in cognitive, affective and ontological domains. Apart from prior knowledge, and the driving forces of 'motivation' and 'intention' to 'learn' (to become a lawyer), such personal experience is furthermore fundamentally mediated by (variation in) the conception of 'learning' itself in a given legal education context. The conception itself reflects how 'learning' is therefore likely to function in process terms. And whatever influences the 'learning process' in context is fundamentally important, because 'process' is substantively the *mechanism of production* of learning outcome. The point is that 'well-being' can adversely influence the quality of the process (and therefore the quality of the associated outcome) but for the individual student the condition of 'well-being' itself is not attributable to or compromised by a single factor.

In contemporary times, the stressors that impact on well-being are diverse and the extent and nature of their impact on people and communities are always relative and contingent. In spite of these complexities, basic human needs theory – a sub-theory of positive psychology's meta self-determination theory (SDT) – offers law teachers (and other educators in universities across disciplines) one interpretive theoretical framework for understanding both the condition of student distress and also specific strategies for curriculum reform intended to better support student well-being and learning success (Krieger 2011; Larcombe et al., 2015).

Using SDT as a lens, this chapter proposes that the teaching of legal threshold concepts in law school offers a significant opportunity to address the basic human needs of students and contribute to the promotion of law student well-being. For this reason, we argue that a key future direction for curriculum reform in law schools is the effective teaching of key threshold concepts in law; such as, for example, 'legal reasoning' – the discursive process that introduces students to the characteristic mode of reasoning and explanation within the discipline – what it means to 'think like a lawyer'.

First, this chapter discusses what is known about law student well-being and experiences of psychological distress at law school. SDT and basic human needs theory are used to explain why law school learning environments can impact negatively on law students' psychological well-being. Second, we consider Meyer and Land's Threshold Concept Framework (2003, 2005) and the challenging nature of threshold concepts with a focus on two of their attributes; namely, 'troublesomeness' and 'liminality'. Third, we explain why effectively teaching threshold concepts in law can assist students to overcome these challenges and support the basic needs associated with 'autonomy' and 'competence' as interpreted within SDT. We conclude that the effective teaching of threshold concepts can positively impact on law students' well-being and learning outcomes, and that this process should therefore be integral to, and explicitly prioritised, in curriculum reform in law schools.

This chapter complements Chapter 9 by Caroline Strevens, which considers the connection between law student well-being, motivation and autonomy support; linking higher levels of well-being with ethical and professional behaviour. The common theme between our two chapters is the importance of SDT in informing our understanding of student well-being and learning success. As a consequence, SDT can be seen as an important theory to inform future directions for legal education that promote law student well-being.

Law student psychological distress

Members of the Australian and UK tertiary education sectors are increasingly concerned about the high levels of psychological distress being experienced by university students at large (Boon, 2018; et al., 2018; Turner et al., 2014). In Australia, Stallman's 2010 and 2011 studies, for example, showed a clear deterioration in the psychological well-being of students at university. The 2010 study by Leahy et al. across the Faculties of Psychology, Law and Mechanical Engineering at the University of Adelaide also indicated cause for concern, with 48 percent of the 955 students surveyed with the K10 instrument identified as psychologically distressed (a K10 score greater than or equal to 22) – this equating to a rate 4.4 times that of age-matched peers.

Australian scholars have been particularly active in leading enquiry and action on this important issue in the last decade (Baik et al., 2017; et al., 2012; Field et al., 2016). However, scholarship has also grown significantly globally (Ibrahim et al., 2013), with work in the UK, for example, the University Quality of Life and Learning project (Audin, Davy and Barkham, 2003), the Quality of Working Life assessment tool (Edwards et al., 2009) and the development of the Warwick-Edinburgh Mental Well-Being Scale (WEMWBS) (Tennant et al., 2007), confirming that student psychological well-being warrants careful attention in educational environments (Bewick et al., 2010).

The focus of this chapter is on the negative effect that the study of law can have on the psychological health of law students. Research and scholarship in the US have long established that legal education can have deleterious effects on law students' psychological well-being. One of the first articles on this topic was published in 1968 (Watson) and the significant body of work by Lawrence Krieger, both alone and with Kennon Sheldon (Krieger, 2011; Krieger and Sheldon, 2015; Sheldon and Krieger, 2004, 2007) and many others has offered important explanations for this distress, along with suggestions for addressing it.

The 2009 Report of Sydney University's Brain and Mind Research Institute (BMRI) *Courting the Blues*, was one of the first empirical studies in Australia to provide rigorous evidence that Australian law students suffer disproportionately high levels of psychological distress (Kelk et al., 2009). The BMRI Report found that more than one-third (35 percent) of law students surveyed suffered high to very high levels of psychological distress (Kelk et al., 2009, p.11). At the time of the release of the Report, these levels of psychological distress were 17 percent higher than those recorded for medical students, and more than 20 percent higher than those found in the general population (Kelk et al., 2009, p.11). Since the publication of that Report, Australian scholarly work in the field has continued to investigate the psychological well-being of students at a range of Australian law schools (Field et al., 2016). This body of research, including Larcombe and others' work at the University of Melbourne (Baik et al., 2019; et al., 2015), and Bergin and Pakenham's studies at universities in Queensland (2014), further confirms that law students are experiencing worryingly high levels of psychological distress (relative to the general population) after their first year of law school.

Consternation about law students' well-being inevitably quickly turns to discussion of the possible causes of the experience of psychological distress, with a view to understanding how best to formulate suitable solutions. There are several such possible causes and many scholars have sought to identify them. Daicoff, for example, has highlighted research suggesting that students who choose to study law are often high academic achievers who may have a predisposition to competitiveness, high personal expectations, perfectionism and pessimism (2004). Tani and Vines (2007) additionally found that the high levels of extrinsic motivation presenting in many law students were associated with the experience of psychological distress.

The common characteristics of individual law students are clearly only one of many possible explanations. The nature and experience of legal education itself also warrants scrutiny. A number of writers have suggested that the highly competitive nature of the learning environment at law school may be a factor causing distress, because law students feel as if they are competing not only for good grades, but also for limited jobs on graduation (Kelk et al., 2009; Stallman 2012). A body of additional literature suggests that law school may be experienced by students as adversarial, intimidating and isolating (Grover 2008; Lake 2000; Townes O'Brien et al., 2011a, 2011b), causing feelings of inferiority, inadequacy, anxiety, alienation, paranoia and depression (Benjamin et al., 1986; Hall, Townes O'Brien & Tang 2010; Hess 2002; Hess 1998). Hess has noted that law students are taught to think in ways that minimise interpersonal skill development and emphasise 'tough-minded analysis, hard facts, and cold logic' (2002, p.78; Townes O'Brien et al., 2011a, 2011b). Krieger and Silver have additionally identified that legal education requires students to think predominantly in rigorously analytical ways, with intellectual excellence rewarded at the expense of other qualities that might support well-being (Krieger 1998, p.24), such as values, morality, character, imagination and emotional intelligence (Silver, 1999).

A range of other stressors are common to the experience of legal education: a heavy, demanding and time-intensive learning workload that is specifically focused on large volumes of dense and complex reading from which personal meaning has to be extracted and developed; subject content and assessment that are sometimes intellectually difficult and challenging; high expectations that students will be internally motivated and, correspondingly, effective, self-regulated and independent learners; performance pressures in relation to self and in comparison with others; a lack of feedback (particularly a lack of positive feedback); and an absence in the curriculum of a balanced focus on real-world and life skills as well as ethical attitudes and dispositions (Krieger, 2002).

A possible consequence of such stressors is the development in students of a sense of 'imposter syndrome' (Lake, 2000). That is, a sense that they do not belong in (or merit being at) law school and will soon be found out and exposed as inadequate. It has been noted that some students respond to the stressors of law school by adopting a 'social mask' (Hall et al., 2010; Reich 1976). The 'mask' is one of strength, confidence, fortitude, action and enthusiasm. It hides the reality of the lived experience of feelings of insecurity, a lack of confidence, anxiety and uncertainty (Sheldon and Krieger, 2004).

SDT, and in particular its sub-theory about basic human needs, can partially inform the necessary understanding for the required law curriculum reform in response to this issue. SDT is an important and complex macro theory of educational and positive psychology. It seeks to explain behavioural self-motivation and self-determination (Ryan and Deci, 2008, p.654). Basic human needs theory identifies three key psychological needs if human beings are to experience self-motivation, self-determination and well-being (Niemiec, Ryan and Deci, 2010), namely: autonomy, competence, and relatedness. 'Autonomy' is experienced when a person has a sense of agency; behaviour is self-governed and volitional; and they have integrity because they are able to act in ways that are congruent with their beliefs, values and interests. 'Competence' involves feelings of ability and capability in relation to tasks and challenges, having a sense of mastery; and thus experiencing 'effective interactions with the environment' (Niemiec et al., 2010, p.176). 'Relatedness' is concerned with meaningful and reciprocal connections with key others. These connections address the human desire to bond, interact and engage with other people, and also to care for them (Niemiec et al., 2010, p.176). Strevens discusses these elements of SDT in more detail in Chapter 9 in which she argues that using an SDT lens to assess the language used in law schools, the physical spaces designed for learning and the behaviours of law staff, can assist with design and approaches that better support law student well-being.

Within the SDT model the 'basic needs' lens provides one way of understanding why the stressors of law school fail to support law student well-being and may contribute to the experience of psychological distress. The law school environment undermines student autonomy because, while students are largely held responsible for making sense of their own learning as independent learners, they are offered limited opportunities to experience agency. The competitive, adversarial nature of the learning environment and the need to wear a 'social mask' may also compromise their learning integrity and cause students to act incongruently with their beliefs and values. Further, the opaque curriculum and emphasis on student self-motivation and direction could be argued as compromising students' sense of competence. Students are often not explicitly supported to develop the capacity for independent, self-regulated learning – a (meta learning) capacity that supports competence and an understanding of expectations at law school. For some, the means for developing this capacity – becoming aware, and being in control, of self in a disciplinary learning context – is an unfortunate mystery, to be discovered at best through trial and error or through chance. 'Unfortunate' because it has been demonstrated in many empirical studies that the means for developing this capacity can be integrated into the learning experiences of, in particular, the concepts that 'really matter' within the discipline. (A detailed qualitative and quantitative study by Meyer, Ward and Latreille (2009) operationalises meta learning in the specific context of a threshold concept in economics.) Furthermore, the impact of 'imposter syndrome' when present exacerbates feelings of inadequacy and inability, fuelling a sense of not belonging or fitting in. Finally, the discussion of the law school learning environment above indicates that it can be isolating, and negatively impact opportunities for relatedness with others, because stressors such as heavy workload and complex subject matter cause students to feel as if they have significantly less time for family, friends and recreation than before they attended law school (Segerstrom, 1996, p.602).

If we intentionally begin to reform curricula with the three basic needs of autonomy, competence and relatedness in mind, and with the purpose of harnessing students' intrinsic motivations, then curriculum support for student well-being comes into view. However, it is important to note that not just any curriculum reform will do. Tang reminds us that curriculum reform intending to promote student well-being must be deeply justifiable, carefully and intentionally chosen, and informed by evidenced-based practice (Tang, 2014). In the next section, we explain how effectively teaching legal threshold concepts is one such justified reform, because it can support the three basic human needs of law students and, in particular, their autonomy and competence. We begin by explaining threshold concepts. We then discuss why teaching threshold concepts well in law is important to the student experience of autonomy and competence, and thus an effective curriculum strategy for the promotion of law student well-being.

Threshold concepts

Meyer first proposed the notion of a 'threshold concept' at a research project meeting held at the University of Edinburgh in February 2001 (Meyer, 2014, p.5). This notion was subsequently developed and formally expressed in two seminal papers (Meyer and Land, 2003, 2005). A basic introduction is that, in many disciplines, one can associate transformational learning experiences (involving, in particular, cognitive and ontological shifts) with a particular class of concepts, the apprehension and internalisation of which can be likened to a journey through a 'liminal' space towards a 'conceptual gateway':

> [A] portal, opening up a new and previously inaccessible way of thinking about something. It represents a transformed way of understanding, or interpreting, or viewing something without which the learner cannot progress. As a consequence of comprehending a threshold concept there may thus be a transformed internal view of subject matter, subject landscape, or even world view. This transformation may be sudden, or it may

> be protracted over a considerable period of time, with the transition to understanding proving troublesome. Such a transformed view or landscape may represent how people 'think' in a particular discipline, or how they perceive, apprehend, or experience particular phenomena within that discipline (or more generally). (Meyer and Land, 2003, p.1).

As Åkerlind et al. (2010, p.2) explain, the transformative nature of threshold concepts relates to the way in which understanding them 'enables students to coherently integrate what were previously seen as unrelated aspects of the subject, providing a new way of thinking about it'; and Davies has stated: 'when an individual acquires a threshold concept the ideas and procedures of the subject make sense to them when before they seemed alien' (2006, p.74). Threshold concepts have been called the 'jewels in the curriculum' (Land et al., 2005, p.5), playing a 'diagnostic role' in curriculum design 'highlighting for teachers areas that deserve special attention, not only because they represent transformative learning points, but because this is where students are most likely to experience difficulties in their learning' (Åkerlind et al., 2010, p.2).

There has been relatively little consideration of legal threshold concepts in the vast threshold concepts literature (see, however, for example, Åkerlind et al., 2011; Huxley-Binns, 2016; Steele, 2019; Steele, 2013). Nevertheless, a number of threshold concepts for law are identifiable that satisfy the key characteristics of being experienced in varying degrees (attributable to, for example prior knowledge) as transformative, irreversible, integrative, bounded and troublesome (Meyer and Land, 2003). For example, concepts such as the rule of law, and the notion of precedent. One of the most critical threshold concepts for law, however, is legal reasoning (Åkerlind et al., 2010, p.3) because it is the foundation on which the law curriculum, and indeed legal practice, is constructed.

Understanding and being able to enact legal reasoning is transformative because it provides students with a sense of self-identity as a lawyer. A student who can effectively conduct legal reasoning has passed through a portal of knowing what it means *to be* a lawyer. Once inducted into legal reasoning, a student is able to formulate and assess arguments from multiple perspectives. They can accept nuance and uncertainty in legal argument and they can manipulate legal information to be persuasive. Being proficient at legal reasoning helps students comfortably to problematise and question facts as well as the boundaries and limits of issues. However, the transformative nature of legal reasoning is iterative, sometimes taking three or four semesters (or a lifetime) to master. The teaching of the concept in the first year is a critical first step on that pathway.

Legal reasoning is integrative because it facilitates student understanding about what lawyers *do*. Learning legal reasoning inculcates students into the integrated nature of the culture and discourse of legal argument and the importance of authority and evidence to its efficacy. The ability to engage in legal reasoning is also irreversible. Once a student is able to reason, analyse, argue like a lawyer, and use authority to provide evidence for a position and assertions, they are unable to undo that skill.

Perhaps most importantly for the purposes of this chapter, legal reasoning is a troublesome concept because it contradicts some of the students' prior assumptions (or the everyday 'ways of knowing' the things they were familiar with up to the point of entry to law school) and asks them to *think differently*. For this reason, it takes them out of their comfort zone, forcing students to reconsider, and possibly change, their preconceptions about what law is, what it can achieve and who they might become as a lawyer.

Threshold concepts, psychological distress and learning success

The 'troublesome' but 'transformative' nature of a threshold concept such as legal reasoning, and the fact that learning such a concept may involve a protracted process over time, provides insight, we believe, into understanding law student psychological distress.

As law students struggle to understand threshold concepts, such as legal reasoning, particularly in their first year, they may experience feelings of uncertainty, ambiguity and disorientation. The Threshold Concept Framework has used the notion (taken from anthropology) of 'liminality' to explain why these feelings are associated with learning such concepts. Arnold van Gennep (1909) introduced the concept of liminality when he found that people going through transitional life states shared certain characteristics. The idea was later taken up by Turner (1959), who viewed it as a state of being, or space, where the transitioning person may experience disconnection, having 'lost' their previously settled state but not having achieved a new one to replace it. Connecting this with threshold concept theorising, Land (2014) has described the state of liminality as follows:

> [L]iminality is a kind of flux. It is a space provoked by some encounter with a threshold concept and it renders things fluid, less certain than they used to be, and it starts to transform the learner … it is a suspended state in which students can sometimes struggle to cope … it often feels like a space where you are losing things … where you have to let go of your prevailing way of seeing, your prior understanding and your prior schema … Letting go in that way is challenging and I think that is one of the key sources of troublesomeness. (p.1)

Considering these descriptions of liminality through the lens of SDT, it is apparent that a student in these 'stuck places' of doubt, confusion and uncertainty is the very converse of a 'self-determining individual' with autonomy and a sense of competence. For this reason, sites of liminality offer useful explanations of student distress, but also opportunities to further explore teaching approaches that seek to preserve student well-being.

Although a first thought may be to seek strategies to bypass the liminal stage, this would be to misunderstand its nature. It is a period of transition that should not, indeed cannot, be eliminated. As Land (2014) states:

> Liminality is a difficult space, but it is also a space of emergence in which emergent entities (in this case thoughts or states) 'arise' out of more fundamental entities and yet are 'novel' or 'irreducible' with respect to them. (p.2)
>
> In the end hopefully these signs will coalesce and students will gain a transformed understanding. But there will be, while that is happening, a period of conceptual uncertainty. (p.7)

Threshold concepts may well be troublesome, casting students into a liminal space of uncertainty and anxiety, but they are also transformative, and this is why they hold the key to law student learning success and well-being. That is, the experience of liminality and dissonance, in relation to learning legal threshold concepts such as legal reasoning, is a critical aspect of the epistemological change necessary for successful learning on the path to *becoming* and *thinking* like a lawyer because learning success is what results from the 'dissonance' and liminal state.

Meyer and Timmermans (2016, p.28) further unpack this point:

> 'Troublesome' concepts can unlock developmental progression, their power being that "they trigger dissonance not only at the cognitive and affective levels, but also dissonance at the epistemological level, calling upon learners to 'change their minds', not by supplanting *what* they know, but by transforming *how* they know". (citing Timmermans, 2010, pp.10–11).

Meyer and Timmermans (2016, p.28) comment further that:

> 'Troublesomeness', for example, can be used deliberately to provoke the condition of a liminal state that captures inter-individual variation across cognitive, epistemic and ontological dimensions. That is, variation in those critical features of threshold concepts that might be apprehended or experienced by students as weird, illogical, counter-intuitive, unsettling and alien, leading to 'stuck places'.

The words 'weird', 'illogical', 'counter-intuitive', 'unsettling' and 'alien' powerfully evoke a range of uncomfortable, even distressing, feelings that students may experience while attempting to engage with threshold concepts. This supports the conjecture that there is an association between particular states of liminality and (the evidence we have of) the decline in the psychological well-being of law students. Auton-Cuff and Gruenhage's 2014 study, 'Stories of persistence: the liminal journeys of first-generation university graduates' gives further credence to this conjecture, as does Timmermans and Meyer's recent work on linking cognition, emotion, and learning (2020) in which they emphasise that 'more integrative conceptions of learning that capture the process of covariation between cognition and affect may allow us better to acknowledge the 'whole person' (2020, p.53), and thus reform curriculum to support student well-being through connecting the students' whole selves with their cognitive states (2020, p.53). Such approaches clearly can support student autonomy, competence and relatedness because they recognise how affective troublesomeness is joined up with cognitive troublesomeness (2020, p.56). As Rattray (2016, p.73) states, learners who are supported to believe that:

> [T]hey are capable of understanding new ideas (self-efficacy), who make positive attributions in relation to their potential for success (optimism), who can monitor and re-align goals and the pathways to attaining these goals (hope) and who do not give up in spite of the difficulties they encounter with the new knowledge (resilience) may be able to cope with liminality more effectively than those who lack these affective assets.

The curriculum reform key here is to explicitly teach both legal threshold concepts well, as well as the affective assets to make the most of that learning. The core affective asset is the ability to accept the experience of 'liminality' as an episodic compromise of well-being, one that – in terms of the full degree and achievement of inculcation into a discipline – is also an experience that can ultimately, with appropriate support, explicit explanation and understanding, be positively harnessed.

Encounters with threshold concepts and associated transitions of liminality may invoke feelings of distress and uncertainty, that, ethically, legal educators are compelled to respond to. 'Ethically' because theoretically underpinned approaches to so respond are known and are increasingly being documented in relation to curriculum reform and associated teaching strategies. Students need to know that their learning well-being is valued. But they also need to know that, although there will be obstacles to learning that might compromise their well-being, there will also be in place a supportive environment intended to empower them to take control of their learning behaviour and self-initiate change in managing these challenging, and hopefully transient, learning episodes. Meyer and Timmermans trenchantly comment that 'dissonance' may be 'deliberately provoked' to propel the student into the state of liminality; a state that offers an opportunity to simultaneously address issues of autonomy, competence and relationality in an integrated manner. The principle of 'do no harm' is important – but some supported challenges may be necessary on the way to a sustained future of 'thinking like a lawyer' and *becoming a lawyer*.

The manifestations of cognitive and affective well-being experiences that were earlier discussed from the STD perspective deserve further comment here.

Some of the constructs involved have been extensively used, in both the qualitative investigation, and in the quantitative (statistical) modelling, of (variation in) the quality of learning outcomes. Simply put, some constructs – for example, reproductive and externally regulated learning processes, external forms of motivation and intentions to reproduce rather than understand learned material, coupled with perceptions of a heavy workload – constitute theoretically 'at risk' dimensions of variation in learning behaviour. More complex *dissonant* patterns of variation are defined by combinations of constructs that are conceptually and theoretically incompatible. Meyer and Shanahan (2003) further demonstrate that dissonant learning processes (embodying contrasting forms of 'memorising' and 'repetition') can be explicitly modelled. The challenge for legal education is that, for some students the aforementioned patterns may be persistent, preventing, by definition, progression to transformational learning outcomes.

Such persistence effectively puts students in distressed conflict with their learning environments, precluding contextualised deep-level, integrative learning within the discipline. Acknowledging these dim realities creates an imperative for legal educators both to better understand the student experience, and especially so in terms of interpretive and explanatory models of student learning that are *discipline specific*. The real challenge is to focus on those transformational learning experiences that really matter; those learning episodes that capture the quintessential essence of the liminal process of becoming, self-identifying as, and transforming into, a lawyer. It is self-evident that purposeful, congruent intention and self-regulated process towards achieving this outcome must be reflected within the curriculum rather than outside it in some 'bolt-on' tinkering. Intentional curriculum reform is therefore the mechanism for influencing and guiding students in ways intended to promote student learning well-being in the most fundamental sense (Field and Kift, 2010; Field and Kift, 2008).

Concluding discussion

The law curriculum offers a rich environment for the development of strategies to support law student well-being. While extra-curricular strategies in universities – such as study skills programmes, counselling, peer support and mental health and wellness initiatives – will always be important, the curriculum provides a site for the foregrounding of student well-being, meeting the students where they are, and normalising the importance of attending to wellness for the sake of achieving student learning success.

The Threshold Concept Framework provides an important lens on positive ways to make direct links between curriculum content (what we teach), teachers (and their practice) and the student learning experience (which directly influences well-being). The transformational and irreversible nature of threshold concepts means that, when taught effectively, they can facilitate and promote student well-being, because they support autonomy and competence. The transformative nature of threshold concepts, and the often troublesome cognitive and affective learning episodes that are associated with them, present challenges for learners and teachers alike. Left unsupported, some students will experience the liminal journey as traversing terrain that is perceived to be alien and threatening. And yet Timmermans and Meyer emphasise that: 'One of the great strengths and contributions of the Threshold Concepts Framework is that it puts learning at the centre of teaching. Yet, do we sometimes lose sight of the very human learner who is the location of this learning?' (2020, p.51).

Here then, in the spirit of promoting learning well-being, lies a challenge to change the alien and threatening into the exotic but alluring – a challenge that, for the individual teacher may appear daunting. So, where to start? And how might a productive analysis for, and of, a threshold concept within the curriculum translate into a deeper understanding of student learning well-being in relation to that concept, informing in turn a change of practice as a first step in curriculum reform? A detailed case study by Meyer (2016) – referencing earlier work by Meyer (alone, and with colleagues) – provides discursive account of threshold concepts analysis and clarification of some associated terminology. With a threshold concept 'in hand', and harnessing the notion of 'Integrated Threshold Concept Knowledge' as proposed by Meyer and Timmermans (2016) (see also Timmermans and Meyer, 2017), it becomes possible to envisage ways of teaching threshold concepts through novel, and theoretically underpinned, methods for effective learning and teaching purposes and with a view to improving student engagement, satisfaction, performance and well-being. This, we believe, is an important future direction for legal education.

Note

1 The authors acknowledge with gratitude the contribution of Dr Rosalind McCulloch to earlier versions of this chapter.

References

Åkerlind, G. et al. (2011). *A threshold concepts focus to curriculum reform: supporting student learning through application of variation theory. Final report to the Australian Learning and Teaching Council.* Sydney, ALTC.

Åkerlind, G. et al. (2010). A threshold concepts focus to first year law curriculum reform: supporting student learning using variation theory, paper presented to the 2010 First Year in Higher Education Conference, Adelaide, July.

Audin, K., Davy, J. and Barkham, M. (2003). University quality of life and learning (UNIQoLL): an approach to student well-being, satisfaction and institutional change. *Journal of Further and Higher Education*, 27(4), 365.

Auton-Cuff, F. and Gruenhage, J. (2014). Stories of persistence: The liminal journeys of first generation university graduates, paper presented to the International Research Conference, Lancaster, July.

Baik, C., Larcombe, W. and Brooker, A. (2019). How universities can enhance student mental wellbeing: the student perspective. *Higher Education Research & Development*, 1.

Baik, C., Larcombe, W. and Brooker, A. (2017). *Enhancing Student Mental Wellbeing: A Handbook for Academic Educators*. Melbourne, University of Melbourne Press.

Benjamin, A., Kaszniak, A., Sales, B. and Shanfield, S. B. (1986). The role of legal education in producing psychological distress among law students and lawyers. *American Bar Foundation Research Journal*, 11(2), 225.

Bergin, A. and Pakenham, K. (2014). Law student stress: relationships between academic demands, social isolation, career pressure, study/life imbalance and adjustment outcomes in law students. *Psychiatry, Psychology and Law*, 1.

Bewick, B., Koutsopoulou, G., Miles, J., Slaa, S. and Barkham, M. (2010). Changes in undergraduate students' psychological well-being as they progress through university. *Studies in Higher Education*, 35(6), 633.

Boon, H. J. (2018). Preliminary findings from an international study of subjective wellbeing in tertiary students. *International Journal of Innovation, Creativity and Change*, 3(3), 29.

Clough, B. A., Nazareth, S. M., Day, J. J. and Casey, L. M. (2018). A comparison of mental health literacy, attitudes, and help-seeking intentions among domestic and international tertiary students. *British Journal of Guidance & Counselling*, 1.

Cranney, J., Andrews, A. and Morris, S. (2012). *Curriculum Renewal to Build Student Resilience and Success*. Sydney, OLT.

Daicoff, S. (2004). *Lawyer, Know Thyself: A Psychological Analysis of Personality Strengths and Weaknesses*. Washington, DC, American Psychological Association.

Davies, P. (2006). Threshold concepts: how can we recognize them? In Meyer, J. H. F. and Land, R. (eds.). *Threshold Concepts and Troublesome Knowledge*. Abingdon, Routledge, p. 70.

Edwards, J. A., Van Laar, D., Easton, S. and Kinman, G. (2009). The work-related quality of life scale for higher education employees. *Quality in Higher Education*, 15(3), 207.

Field, R. and Kift, S. (2010). Addressing the high levels of psychological distress in law students through intentional assessment and feedback reform in the first-year law curriculum. *International Journal of the First Year in Higher Education*, 1(1), 65.

Field, R., Duffy, J. and James, C. (eds.) (2016). *Promoting Law Student and Lawyer Well-Being in Australia and Beyond*. Abingdon, Routledge.

Grover, S. (2008). Personal integration and outsider status as factors in law student well-being. *Washburn Law Journal*, 47, 419.

Hall, K., Townes O'Brien, M. and Tang, S. (2010). Developing a professional identity in law schools: a view from Australia. *Phoenix Law Review*, 4, 19.

Hess, G. F. (2002). Heads and hearts: the teaching and learning environment in law school. *Journal of Legal Education*, 52, 75.

Huxley-Binns, R. (2016). Tripping over thresholds: a reflection on legal andragogy. *The Law Teacher*, 50, 1.

Ibrahim, A., Kelly, S. J. and Adams, C. E. (2013). A systematic review of studies of depression prevalence in university students. *Journal of Psychiatric Research*, 47(3), 391.

Iijima, A. L. (1998). Lessons learned: legal education and law student dysfunction. *Journal of Legal Education*, 48, 524.

Kelk, N., Luscombe, G., Medlow, S. and Hickie, I. (2009). *Courting the Blues: Attitudes Towards Depression in Australian Law Students and Legal Practitioners*. Sydney, Brain & Mind Research Institute, University of Sydney.

Kift, S. (2008). 21st century climate for change: curriculum reform for quality learning engagement in law. *Legal Education Review*, 18(1 and 2), 1.

Krieger, L. S. (2011). The most ethical of people, the least ethical of people: proposing self-determination theory to measure professional character formation. *University of Saint Thomas Law Journal*, 8, 168.

Krieger, L. S. (2002). Psychological insights: why our students and graduates suffer, and what we might do about it. *Journal of the Association of Legal Writing Directors*, 1, 258.

Krieger, L. S. (1998). What we're not telling law students – and lawyers – that they really need to know: some thoughts-in-action toward revitalizing the profession from its roots. *Journal of Law & Health*, 13, 1.

Krieger, L. S. and Sheldon, K. M. (2015). What makes lawyers happy? A data-driven prescription to redefine professional success. *George Washington Law Review*, 83, 554.

Lake, P. (2000). When fear knocks: the myths and realities of law school. *Stetson Law Review*, 29, 1015.

Land, R. (2014). A closer look at liminality: Incorrigibles and threshold capital, keynote presentation to the Fourth Biennial Conference *on* Threshold Concepts, NAIRTL, Ireland.

Land, R., Cousins, G., Meyer, J. H. F. and Davies, P. (2005). Threshold concepts and troublesome knowledge (3): implications for course reform and evaluation. In Rust, C. (ed.). *Improving Student Learning: Diversity and Inclusivity*. Oxford, Oxford Centre for Staff and Learning Development.

Larcombe, W., Finch, S. and Sore, R. (2015). Who's distressed-not only law students: psychological distress levels in university students across diverse fields of study. *Sydney Law Review*, 37, 243.

Leahy, C., Peterson R. F., Wilson, I. G., Newbury, J. W., Tonkin, A. L. and Turnbull, D. (2010). Distress levels and self-reported treatment rates for medicine, law, psychology and mechanical engineering students: cross-sectional study. *Australian and New Zealand Journal of Psychiatry*, 44, (7), 608.

Meyer, J. H. F. (2016). Threshold concepts and pedagogic representation. *Education + Training*', 58(5), 463.

Meyer, J. H. F. (2014). Foreward. *Waikato Journal of Education*, 19(2), 5.

Meyer, J. H. F. and Land, R. (2005). Threshold concepts and troublesome knowledge (2): epistemological considerations and a conceptual framework for teaching and learning. *Higher Education*, 49(3), 373.

Meyer J. H. F. and Land, R. (2003). Threshold concepts and troublesome knowledge (1): linkages to ways of thinking and practicing within the disciplines in Rust, C. (ed.). *Improving Student Learning: Theory and Practice Ten Years On*. Oxford, Oxford Centre for Staff and Learning Development, p.412.

Meyer, J. H. F. and Shanahan, M. P. (2003). Dissonant forms of 'memorizing' and 'repetition'. *Studies in Higher Education*, 28(1), 5.

Meyer, J. H. F. and Timmermans, J. A. (2016). Integrated threshold concept knowledge. In Land, R., Meyer, J. H. F. and Flanagan, M. T. (edss.). *Threshold Concepts in Practice*Rotterdam, Sense Publishers, p.25.

Meyer, J. H. F., Ward, S. C. and Latreille, P. (2009). Threshold concepts and metalearning capacity. *International Review of Economics Education*, 8(1), 132.

Niemiec, C., Ryan, R. and Deci, E. (2010). Self-determination theory and the relation of autonomy to self-regulatory processes and personality development. In Hoyle, R. (ed.). *Handbook of Personality and Self-Regulation*. Chichester, Wiley-Blackwell, p. 169.

Rattray, J. (2016). Affective dimensions of liminality. In Land, R., Meyer, J. H. F. and Flanagan, M. T. (eds.). *Threshold Concepts in Practice*. Rotterdam, Sense Publishers, p.67.

Reich, R. (1976). California psychological inventory: profile of a sample of first-year law students. *Psychology Reporter*, 39, 873.

Ryan, R. M. and Deci, E. L. (2008). Self-determination theory and the role of basic psychological needs in personality and the organization of behavior. In Oliver, J. P., Robins, R. W. and Pervin, L. A. (eds.) *Handbook of Personality: Theory and Research*, 3rd edn. New York, Guilford Press, p.654.

Segerstrom, S. C. (1996). Perceptions of stress and control in the first semester of law school. *Willamette Law Review*, 32, 593.

Sheldon, K. M. and Krieger, L. S. (2007). Understanding the negative effects of legal education on law students: a longitudinal test of self-determination theory. *Personality and Social Psychology Bulletin*, v33(6), 883.

Sheldon, K. M. and Krieger, L. S. (2004). Does legal education have undermining effects on law students? Evaluating changes in motivation, values, and well-being. *Behavioral Sciences & the Law*, 22(2), 261.

Silver, M. (1999). Emotional intelligence and legal education. *Psychology, Public Policy and Law*, 5(4), 1173.

Stallman, H. (2012). A qualitative evaluation of perceptions of the role of competition in the success and distress of law students. *Higher Education Research and Development*, 31(6), 891.

Stallman, H. (2011). Embedding resilience within the tertiary curriculum: a feasibility study. *Higher Education Research and Development*, 30(2), 121.

Stallman, H. (2010). Psychological distress in university students: a comparison with general population data. *Australian Psychologist*, 45(4), 286.

Steele, A. (2019). Succeed, question, repeat: threshold concepts and variation theory in understanding how law students build competency. *The Law Teacher*, 53(3), 1.

Strevens, C. and Field, R. (2019). *Educating for Well-Being in Law: Positive Professional Identities and Practices*. Abingdon, Routledge.

Tang, S. (2014). What works? Critically evaluating and applying psychological interventions in the legal education or practice environment, plenary address, Wellness for Law Forum, Queensland University of Technology, Brisbane.

Tani, M. and Vines, P. (2007). Law students' attitudes to education: Pointers to depression in the legal academy and the profession? *Legal Education Review*, 19(1), 3.

Tennant, R. Hiller, L., Fishwick, R., Platt, S., Joseph, S., Weich, S. et al. (2007). The Warwick-Edinburgh mental well-being scale (WEMWBS): development and UK validation. *Health and Quality of Life Outcomes*, 5(1), 1.

Timmermans, J. A. (2010). Changing our minds: the developmental potential of threshold concepts. In Meyer, J. H. F., Land, R. and Baillie, C. (eds.). *Threshold Concepts and Transformational Learning*. Rotterdam, Sense Publishers, p.3.

Timmermans , J. A. and Meyer , J. H. F. (2020). Embedding affect in the Threshold Concepts Framework. In Land, R. and Timmermans, J. A. (eds.). *Threshold Concepts on the Edge*. Rotterdam, Brill, p.51.

Timmermans, J. A. and Meyer, J. H. F. (2017). A framework for working with university teachers to create and embed 'Integrated Threshold Concept Knowledge' (ITCK) in their practice. *International Journal for Academic Development*, 1.

Townes O'Brien, M., Tang, S. and Hall, K. (2011a). Changing our thinking: empirical research on law student well-being, thinking styles and the law curriculum. *Legal Education Review*, 21(2), 149.

Townes O'Brien, M., Tang, S. and Hall, K. (2011b)No time to lose: negative impact on law student well-being may begin in year one. *International Journal of the First Year in Higher Education*, 2(2), 49.

Turner, I., Reynolds, K. J., Lee, E., Subasic, E. and Bromhead, D. (2014). Well-being, school climate and the social identity process: a latent growth model study of bullying perpetration and peer victimization. *School Psychology Quarterly*, 29(3), 320.

Turner, V. (1959). *The Ritual Process: Structure and Anti-Structure*. Chicago, Aldine.

Van Gennep, A. (1909/1972)*The Rites of Passage*, trans. M. Visedon and G. Caffee. Chicago, University of Chicago Press.

Watson, A. S. (1968). The quest for professional competence: psychological aspects of legal education. *Cincinnati Law Review*, 37, 93.

Weresh, M. H. (2013). Stargate: malleability as a threshold concept in legal education. *Journal of Legal Education*, 63, 689.

Part 6

Legal education and skills

In the following two chapters, Solomon and Guth focus on concerns about the teaching of academic legal skills within the law curriculum. In Chapter 12, Solomon calls for an integrative approach to the teaching of legal skills in Nigeria, while in Chapter 11, Guth uses William Twining's article 'Legal skills and legal education' to ground her analysis of some key issues facing the teaching of legal skills in the UK. The concerns of these authors clearly resonate with each other, and together these chapters provide stimulating consideration of the longstanding issues surrounding the place of legal skills within the law curriculum.

Chapter 11

The pasts and futures of legal skills in English law schools

Jessica Guth

Introduction

The discussion of the place of (legal) skills in legal education and training seems somehow timeless and, as the contribution to this volume by Solomon shows, it also transcends jurisdictions. The issues of concern and for debate remain remarkably constant. Students' critical thinking, analysis, reading and writing skills are bemoaned as inadequate, students should or should not be taught practical legal skills as part of their undergraduate (UG) degrees and graduates apparently lack and have always lacked the basic skills expected for entry into the labour market. While the emphasis may have shifted, the core issues have not. Skills teaching in law remains contentious. This chapter takes Twining's now 30-year-old paper 'Legal skills and legal education' (Twining, 1988) as its starting and reference point and briefly introduces some of the key debates relating to legal skills and considers what we can learn from them to shape the future. The chapter begins with a brief outline of what legal skills are considered to be for the purposes of this discussion. It then examines some of the debates about legal skills teaching before considering how those debates shape legal skills now and into the future.

What are legal skills?

Legal skills are not easy to define. Even the seemingly simple distinction between knowledge and skills easily becomes blurred and does not easily capture the overlap and connections between the two. Solomon, for example, in this volume, refers to functioning legal skills to distinguish them from practical skills, which is perhaps a helpful starting point. Broadly however, in this chapter, skills are conceptualised as learning about how to do things rather than learning about things (Twining, 1988). If skills then are about learning how rather than learning about, what might be considered *legal* skills? It is now fashionable to speak of threshold concepts (Huxley-Binns, 2016; Huxley-Binns, 2019) – what knowledge and skills are the key to unlocking the discipline in question? In this volume, Field and Meyer emphasise the importance of these in promoting law student well-being. However, thinking about threshold concepts might also help determine the most crucial skills in the discipline of law. The most crucial skills will be determined by the focus taken: what can law students and law graduates do that defines them as belonging to the discipline? Should the focus be on skills required to be a successful law student and, if so, how might one define a successful law student and does that definition hold true across the sector or differ from institution to institution? Alternatively, should the focus be on skills required to be a successful law graduate and how, if at all, are these different from those required to be a student? Or should we be concerned with skills for the enormous variety of roles in the legal services market or maybe even the labour market generally? The definition of threshold concepts and what skills are included in that and which should additionally be taught will depend on one's view of the discipline of law, its purpose, its place in the university and the particular level and type of course one is concerned with. Some of these questions and issues are examined further below. Suffice it to say for now that in this chapter, as in Twining's 1988 paper, it is tempting to focus only on those skills required for the study of law. However, the current picture of skills teaching in law schools is more complex than that so, for the purposes of the chapter, legal skills are those related to how to do things within the discipline of law broadly defined. This admittedly very broad definition allows the exploration of a variety of debates that impact on what law schools do now and might do in the future.

Key debates about legal skills

Arguments about legal skills and their place in the law school curriculum appear to be firmly embedded in wider debates about legal education. In particular they seem inextricably linked to the age-old question 'what are law schools for?' The place of legal skills overall and practical legal skills, (those of relevance to those working in the legal services sector), in particular depends on whether law schools train future lawyers or provide a more liberal legal education. The place of legal skills is caught up in arguments about how academic or vocational a programme is, how doctrinal or contextual, how socio-legal, how interdisciplinary and/or how liberal. Obviously perhaps, the skills emphasised depend on which approach or combination of approaches is favoured but might also determine whether one thinks skills should be taught at all. This section therefore considers whether skills should be taught at all and whether doing so is compatible with a liberal legal education. It then examines how, when and at what level skills should be taught.

Should skills be explicitly taught at all?

The fundamental question is whether the incorporation of explicit skills teaching is something that should be done in law schools at all. While

Twining (1988) noted significant resistance to such inclusion in his article, this sort of opposition now appears less strong. Teaching students how to do things is now a mostly accepted part of a law teacher's job and an explicit part of the law school curriculum (see, for example, Boon, 1998; Huxley-Binns, 2011; Webb, 2015). The consensus now appears to be that students should not be required to learn the basic skills (or maybe threshold concepts) by osmosis as was previously expected (Thornton, 2012). This shift towards skills could have many reasons and arguable has gone too far leading '[a]cademic education [to] become skills driven' (van Klink and De Vries, 2016, p.3) and students "to imagine themselves as bundles of skills" (Thornton, 2012, p.81; Urciuoli, 2010, p.162). The increased focus on skills might simply be a symptom of the neoliberal and marketised university as Thornton (2012) argues but there may also be other reasons including that the skills of incoming law students can no longer be taken for granted because the pool from which those students are drawn is becoming significantly larger and more diverse (Sommerlad, et al., 2015; Thornton, 2012) as the massification of HE continues (Kogan and Hanney, 2000). In addition, the nature of knowledge and the availability of information have changed dramatically in recent years and knowledge is no longer the privilege of those with access to the dusty books stored in awe-inspiring university libraries (Hazleton, 2012). A full exploration of these reasons is beyond the scope of this chapter but we will return to some of the issues below.

Twining (1988, p.4) comments that some argue that 'emphasis on skills in legal education is necessarily illiberal, amoral, narrow, reactionary, anti-intellectual, impractical, or unnecessary.' It is an argument made less frequently and perhaps in a more specific context now than it was then. It appears to most often rear its head in relation to the introduction of employability skills to the undergraduate curriculum. Thornton notes that law schools are under pressure to include more practical 'how to' skills and that 'the acquisition of skills is equated with modernisation and success' (Thornton, 2012, p.81). This kind of skills focus is arguably not compatible with a liberal legal education. Nonetheless, Twining was right in noting that the overall argument that skills teaching does not belong in a liberal legal education is the 'Luddite Fallacy' (Twining, 1988, p.4). Learning how to locate, access, read and use specific information and as well as learning how to think about particular issues in certain ways and construct cogent arguments about those issues are in fact the essence of a liberal education. These things alongside the knowledge help students to 'call their minds their own' (Nussbaum, 1997, p.295). The teaching of skills therefore is not contrary to the ethos of any academic law degree (see also Solomon in this volume), even the most liberal ones. The arguments to be had here are about what sort of skills should be taught, when and how.

What, how and when?

While it now seems clear that skills ought to be actually taught rather than just expected, there is little consensus on the best way to teach skills. English law schools deal with the teaching of skills at undergraduate level in a variety of ways. Some include specific skills modules, usually in the first semester of the programme, others incorporate skills teaching into an English legal systems or similar modules and others still focus intensively on skills during induction and then integrate skills development into the curriculum. Even where there is no obvious skills content evident from the module names, the learning objectives of first-year modules often suggest at least some skills-focused content and anecdotal evidence from teaching on such courses and discussing them with colleagues suggest that this is true.

In our system (as in the Nigerian one as outlined by Solomon in this volume), where an academic stage is followed by a vocational one, logic might dictate that an undergraduate law curriculum focuses on basic legal academic skills such as finding, reading and using legal materials as well as legal writing for academic purposes. Further it might seem obvious that legal research skills become more dominant as students' progress through the levels, perhaps even culminating in advanced research methods courses at doctoral level and that vocational courses provide training in skills required for legal practice such as client interviewing, negotiation or advocacy, not to mention form filling and basic accounts handling. However, these seemingly obvious boundaries have become, or perhaps always were, blurred (Twining, 1988) and in an age of employability skills where universities are expected to produce market-ready graduates (whatever that may mean) that blurring is exacerbated (Bothwell, 2015; Thornton, 2012).

Conversations about the teaching of legal skills often focus on the first year of the undergraduate law degree or the vocational courses in relation to practical legal skills in particular. Beyond the undergraduate degree the focus of skills very much depends on the type of programme. For vocational programmes the focus is in fact, rightly, on those skills required for work in the legal services sector although it is arguable whether we currently accurately capture the nature of those skills, given the rapidly changing legal services market (Francis, 2011, Susskind, 2017). Academic programmes either focus on the (mostly implicit) further development of legal reasoning skills in order to examine areas of law in more detail or shift the focus to research skills that are broader than just legal research and acknowledge – for example, the contributions social science methodologies and methods can make to our understanding of law (Hutchinson, 2016; Watkins and Burton, 2017). A full discussion of these areas is beyond the scope of this chapter. Overall, however, it seems that the skills that should be focused on at postgraduate academic level are less contentious than the undergraduate level and that there is little argument that vocational courses should develop practical legal skills even where there may be some argument about what practical legal skills are.

Most of the contentious questions therefore appear to arise at undergraduate level. In spite of the lack of empirical work on the ways in which legal skills are taught, what does appear striking when looking at LLB structures on university websites (although also in need of systematic examination) is that explicit skills modules all but disappear after the first year of undergraduate programmes. The dominant assumption in programme design appears to be that legal skills have been acquired at Level 4 and need not be further developed explicitly. Interestingly, however, the inclusion of employability skills, both generic and legal, seems quite widespread across the curriculum and we return to this issue further below. A focus on practical skills has brought with it an approach based on the notion that 'you cannot learn to ride a bike by reading about riding a bike' and that therefore skills teaching must be practical in nature. It is difficult to argue with that. It is hard to imagine teaching someone to write a persuasive legal argument without asking them to write, for example. However, the argument for a practical approach sometimes appears to be taken to mean that the skill in question must be taught in a practical context and that skills cannot be learned in lecture halls and tutorial rooms (see Solomon in this volume for a helpful critique). The argument is that skills are best acquired and developed in 'real-life' situations (even if simulated) so skills teaching should ideally take place in relation to legal simulations or law clinic type activities (see Alexander and Boothby, 2018; Grimes and Gibbons, 2016). This suggests a particular view of skills and of academia (see Thornton, 2012). Critical thinking, reading, interpreting and applying statutes and case law and crafting cogent arguments are the real-life skills of academic lawyers, teaching these skills in an academic context is no less practical, in the sense that it is about how to do something and learn it by doing it, than any of the other possible approaches and all of them should be underpinned by relevant learning theories (see Wallace, 2018). While there are several studies that suggest things that can be done in order to enhance students' legal skills, they are usually small scale and their success may well be context and cohort dependent (see, for recent examples, Del Mar, 2016; Killian and Summerville, 2018; Bulley, 2016) and many are concerned with practical skills (for example, Knox and Stone, 2019; Turner, Bone and Ashton, 2018) and only a few with academic skills (Tyrell and Jowitt, 2018; Wallace, 2018). In order to really understand what works best for what sort of skills teaching we need a much more systematic exploration of how things are done now and what the impact of that is.

As these debates about what should be taught, by whom, where and how continue much as they have for decades, with a little change in emphasis and nuance here and there, the only thing that is really clear is that we do not know enough about what is currently done, how it is done, whether it works and how it could be different. What the patchy and mostly anecdotal evidence suggests is that legal skills are conceptualised and taught in a variety of different ways with different approaches and aims and that should make it the perfect site for a detailed empirical examination that could provide some answers to some of the questions posed so far.

The futures of legal skills

The preceding section has introduced, albeit very briefly, some of the debates about legal skills. This section of the chapter considers what this might mean for legal skills in the future. It seems likely that law schools will continue to conceptualise legal skills differently and teach the skills they choose to prioritise in different ways. This is perhaps obvious, but there are five issues which are worth exploring: the continuing creep of the employability agenda, the Solicitors Qualifying Examination, the changing nature of knowledge and availability of information, the neglect of the affective domain and the fact that in all law schools there are pockets of resistance challenging the neoliberal and market driven narratives and practices of universities and their law schools. Each of these points is dealt with briefly below.

The continuing creep of the employability agenda

Should law degrees include the sort of generic skills that arguably help graduates get jobs? One view is that undergraduate degrees should not concern themselves with such skills at the expense of intellectual skills and knowledge (see Furedi, 2011). Law degrees are, after all, academic qualifications focused on acquiring and developing academic intellectual skills and knowledge in the discipline of law. They are not per se preparation for the labour market. Nonetheless, all universities have an employability strategy of some kind and law schools are not immune from those and some have argued for the inclusion of skills that go beyond purely legal skills (Huxley-Binns, 2011; Knox and Stone, 2019) because they help students develop attributes employers want (see, for example, Liverpool John Moores' 'Career focused teaching for work-ready graduates', 2019). However, the employability agenda is fundamentally flawed and could lead to a future where employability skills take centre stage, where legal knowledge and specific legal skills are built around an employability focus or agenda and where they, rather than the employability skills, become the add-ons. The example outlined by Knox and Stone (2019), who write about the further inclusion of employability skills in an LLB and GDL curriculum in a vocationally focused law school (BPP), suggests that in some cases this already happens. While employability is oft cited there is actually little clarity over what employability skills are. Self-management, good time keeping, personal presentation (which is, of course, highly racialised and gendered (Moreau and Leathwood, 2006), good communication skills and a personable manner have all been given as examples of such skills (Knox and Stone, 2019) or, even more obscurely, commercial awareness (Huxley-Binns, 2011). The inclusion of these skills, even if they did, in fact, enhance the employability of graduates, which is doubtful, risks the pushing out of those intellectual skills that make the law degree a valuable qualification in the first place. As Sanders notes 'academic education is supposed to challenge the status quo, not simply to equip students with the skills to leech off it' (Sanders, 2015, p.154). But even if one takes the view that law degrees should prepare graduates for the general labour market, focusing on employability as opposed to general legal skills is probably counterproductive (Moorhead, 2013; Sanders, 2015) and other skills such as, for example, using social science methodologies and knowledge may be more important (see Hutchinson, 2016) for one example). Law degrees are valued because of the qualities of mind they encourage in students and because graduates have intellectual independence, the ability to think clearly and critically and provide cogent arguments based on an analysis of information from a variety of sources (see QAA, 2015). They may or may not be someone who cares to be on time and dress in a particular way, but they are likely to have made their mind their own and thus have the ability to make that choice for themselves. The focus on employability skills takes up time that is then no longer available to encourage students to think. The future might, therefore, be one dominated by teaching the sort of skills that encourage students to follow instructions, look the part and not question too much, which might, of course, be exactly what the labour market wants.

The Solicitors Qualifying Examination

The rise of employability skills, or at least practical legal skills, is likely to be exacerbated by the introduction of the Solicitors Qualifying Examination (SQE) in 2021. Knox and Stone (2019, p.10) note: 'Designing and delivering courses with explicitly embedded employability skills now could be seen as laying important groundwork for delivery of law courses in the post-SQE landscape.' As discussed in Unger's contribution to this volume, the SQE will replace the current pathways for qualifying as a solicitor, making up part of the qualification requirements alongside supervised work experience and being of suitable character and takes the form of a two-part examination. The first consists of a series of multiple-choice examinations covering the knowledge stipulated by the Statement of Legal Knowledge and its application, while the second tests practical legal skills. It is likely that in vocationally oriented degree programmes, the focus will shift to these practical legal skills at the expense of other skills in order to ensure students are as prepared as they can be for the SQE. While it is difficult to see how the vast content of the knowledge statement as well as intellectual and practical legal skills could all be taught at undergraduate level, some law schools have indicated that this is exactly what they propose to do.

Those institutions that decide, foolishly perhaps (see Bradney, 2018), to offer SQE-aligned or even SQE-ready degree programmes are not only like to shift the focus to those practical legal skills required by the SQE 2 but also to change the sort of skills they teach generally. In fact, the skills required to be a successful law student on an SQE-aligned degree programme might be rather different from the skills required to be a successful law student on a programme that does not align to the SQE and will certainly be different from the skills required to successfully study a liberal law degree (seeMason, 2018; Mason and Guth, 2018; Morrison, 2018). The SQE 1 focuses on legal and procedural knowledge and its application. It is concerned with the learning of facts and processes as they are now and their application. It is about finding the correct answer in an already known and carefully defined area of law (which may cover more than one specific topic of course but is still narrowly drawn) and it therefore requires skills aimed at finding out (and remembering) what the law is now and how it can be applied to what is likely to be a fairly standard scenario. Skills that are concerned with thinking about law, why it is as it is, whether it should be as it is or how it could be will not be relevant to students studying SQE-aligned degrees and therefore are likely to be sidelined or pushed out altogether. Of course, one might argue that such a degree would not be compliant with the QAA benchmark statement for law (QAA, 2015), but even if this were true there is no guarantee that the benchmark statement will remain as it is or that the priorities currently included in it will not change in line with continuing marketisation of higher education. In some institutions, the SQE will be the death of academic/intellectual skills development.

The changing nature of knowledge and information

There is no doubt that the 'digital revolution' has changed the availability, form and accessibility of information quite dramatically. This has, of course, also impacted on education including legal education. The volume edited by Rubin (2012) explores some of these issues from an American perspective including contributions looking at digital course books and materials (Cunningham, 2012; Palfrey, 2012; Reese, 2012; Vladeck, 2012), law games (Silverman, 2012) and the place of law libraries in this new digital age (Hazleton, 2012). Maharg (2007) hints at some of these issues but from a more critical and theoretical perspective and there are numerous articles dealing with the challenges and opportunities of technology and availability of information (for recent examples, see Allbon, 2016; Jones, Gadallah and Lazem, 2019; Moffett, Cubie and Godden, 2017; Newbery-Jones, 2016; Halder in this volume; Ryan and McFaul in this volume). There is, however, less research on how the availability of information and the easily searchable nature of it changes the nature of knowledge and our relationship, and that of our students in particular, to knowledge. Anecdotal evidence suggests that students find it increasingly difficult to free themselves from the notion that there is 'a right answer' and that they see legal reasoning, at least initially as a formulistic way of achieving the right answer (Bleekers, 2016) rather than as a way of learning to arrive at reasoned conclusions by arguing in a particular way (see Wallace, 2018). This is nothing new, but the digital age might make this worse. Students are used to being able to access information at the click of the button and having answers to their questions within seconds. This necessarily shapes the questions asked and the sort of answers they are used to and expect. Having information at our fingertips can make us lazy. It can make us stop when we have an answer, possibly even before we have thought much about whether the answer is plausible or stands up to scrutiny. Searching for information, evidence or alternative views is alien in a world where we are constantly bombarded with social media soundbites and easy web searches. We cannot ignore this in legal education and as there is no sign of the information or social media overload slowing down, our best hope to encourage students to think deeply, develop their information literacy and ability to distinguish quality information from soundbites and to consider evidence and a variety of views is to foster their curiosity, spark their interest and push them to want to know more – not because it leads to a right answer, or even an answer at all, but because it develops the qualities of mind important for the study of law and for meaningful engagement with the world around us. More research is needed on how we equip students with the skills to navigate the web of (mis)information so that they can begin to think about, rather than just absorb, the many sources of law and commentary on law available to them.

The neglect of the affective domain

In his 1988 article, Twining contrasts the legal skills he is concerned with, with the affective domain (Twining, 1988, p.13). Until quite recently very little attention had been paid to affect in legal education. However, the importance of emotion in learning and teaching in law is becoming more widely researched and better understood (see Jones, 2018a, 2018b, 2018c; Maharg and Maughan, 2011) as are aspects of emotional labour in law (Westaby, 2014; Westaby and Jones, 2018). It seems likely that law schools will have to think more carefully about how to deal with the affective domain in terms of teaching both knowledge and skills, about how it can help and what challenges it poses. It also seems likely that law schools or at least universities more widely will have to make provision for skills teaching that helps students (and teachers?) deal more effectively with affect. A better understanding of emotion in legal learning and teaching could lead to better programme design to enhance learning and skills development. It may also help address some of the well-being debates in legal education (Strevens and Wilson, 2016; Field and Meyer in this volume; Strevens in this volume) as it provides a more holistic picture of learning and teaching law that challenges the dominant view of law as objective, rational and emotionless. A full exploration is beyond the scope of this chapter, but skills drawn from the affective domain as well as taking the affective domain into account when teaching legal skills is likely to play a larger role in the future than it currently does.

Resistance is not futile

There are pockets of resistance to the neoliberal turn and the marketisation of higher education (see Bradney, 2016; Brown, 2013; Cheng, 2010; Giroux,

2014; Giroux, 2008; Molesworth, Nixon and Scullion, 2011;) as well as the SQE (Bradney, 2018; and Dutton, 2018; Mason, 2018; Mason and Guth, 2018; Morrison, 2018). These pockets of resistance spell hope for the future of legal skills (rather than employability skills) in English law schools. Some institutions, most obviously perhaps Russell Group Universities, will change very little in response to the SQE and for those institutions the focus will remain on legal education as opposed to training and on academic and intellectual skills. At the other end of the spectrum in mostly vocationally focused law schools (and often new universities) that are at the coal face of marketisation and widening participation and under extreme and increasing pressure to move up rankings, get graduates into graduate jobs and satisfy employability and other student-related key performance indicators (see Guth and Dutton, 2018) there are always individuals or groups committed to the key legal skills Twining outlined over 30 years ago (Twining, 1988). After all 'for academics it is their own sense of worth of what they have done that matters more and it is easy to find academic lives where individuals have pursued what they thought was important even at the expense of personal preferment' (Bradney, 2016, p.94; Bradney, 2011). And many academics agree that 'reasoning and analysis are central to the discipline of law' (Twining, 1988, p.13) and form the basis of what it means to study law and to be a lawyer (broadly defined).

This chapter has picked up some of the discussions started by William Twining over 30 years ago to argue that while skills teaching has a place in undergraduate legal education, skills have been rather hijacked by an agenda that is focused on marketisation and employability rather than on the development of intellectual skills. While this is of concern, particularly in light of the SQE, we should not underestimate the resistance to this agenda and the broader neoliberal context within which it sits, or the risks that law schools would take by following it.

Bibliography

Alexander, J. andBoothby, C. (2018). Stakeholder perceptions of Clinical Legal Education within an employability context. *International Journal of Clinical Legal Education, 25(3)*, http://dx.doi.org/10.19164/ijcle.v25i3.768 (accessed 1 March 2019).

Allbon, E. (2016). Seeing is believing: we are all converging. *The Law Teacher*, 50(1), 44–60.

Bleekers, T. (2016). Epilogue: an overview, reflections and a student's perspective. In Van Klink, B. and de Vries, U. (eds.). *Academic Learning Law. Theoretical Positions, Teaching Experiments and Learning Experiences*. Cheltenham, Edward Elgar,pp.288–313.

Boon, A. (1998). History is past politics: a critique of the legal skills movement in England and Wales. *Journal of Law and Society, 25*(1), 151–169.

Bothwell, E. (2015). Should UK universities do more to create work-ready graduates? *Times Higher*, 11 November,https://www.timeshighereducation.com/blog/should-uk-universi ties-be-doing-more-produce-work-ready-graduates (accessed 20 January 2019).

Bradney, A. (2018). The success of university law schools in England and Wales: or how to fail. *The Law Teacher, 52*(4), 490–498.

Bradney, A. (2016). The necessary loneliness of teaching (and of being a legal academic). In Van Klink, B. and de Vries, U. (eds.). *Academic Learning Law. Theoretical Positions, Teaching Experiments and Learning Experiences*. Cheltenham, Edward Elgar, pp. 79–95.

Bradney, A. (2011). Instead of a career: work, love and art in university law schools. In Maharg, P. andMaughan, C. (eds.). *Affect and Legal Education: Emotion in Learning and Teaching the Law*. Farnham, Ashgate, pp. 109–124.

Brown, R. (2013). *Everything for Sale? The Marketization of UK Higher Education*. Abingdon, Routledge.

Cheng, M. (2010). Audit cultures and quality assurance mechanisms in England: a study of their perceived impact on the work of academics. *Teaching in Higher Education, 15*(3), 259–271.

Cunningham, L. A. (2012). Digital evolution in law school course books: trade-offs, opportunities, and vigilance. In Rubin, E. (ed.). *Legal Education in the Digital Age*. Cambridge, Cambridge University Press, pp. 81–105.

Del Mar, M. (2016). Learning how to read cases: resources from the visual and dramatic arts. In Van Klink, B. and de Vries, U. (eds.). *Academic Learning Law. Theoretical Positions, Teaching Experiments and Learning Experiences*. Cheltenham, Edward Elgar, pp. 244–266.

Francis, A. (2011). *At the Edge of Law. Emergent and Divergent Models of Legal Professionalism*. Abingdon, Routledge.

Furedi, F. (2011). *Wasted. Why Education Isn't Educating*. London, Continuum.

Giroux, H. A. (2014). *Neoliberalim's War on Higher Education*. Chicago, IL, Haymarket Books.

Grimes, R. and Gibbons, J. (2016). Assessing experiential learning – us, them and the others. *International Journal of Clinical Legal Education, 23(*1), http://dx.doi.org/10.19164/ijcle.v23i1.492 (accessed 1 March 2019).

Guth, J. andDutton, K. (2018). SQE-ezed out: SRA, status and stasis. *The Law Teacher, 52*(4), 425–438.

Hazleton, P. A. (2012). Law students and the new law library: an old paradigm. In Rubin, E. (ed.). *Legal Education in the Digital Age*. Cambridge: Cambridge University Press, pp. 158–182.

Hutchinson, T. (2016). Empirical methodologies knowledge and expertise: a 'necessary' skill for lawyers? In Van Klink, B. and de Vries, U. (eds.). *Academic Learning Law. Theoretical Positions, Teaching Experiments and Learning Experiences*. Cheltenham, Edward Elgar, pp. 1–11.

Huxley-Binns, R. (2016). Tripping over thresholds: a reflection on legal andragogy. *Law Teacher*, 50(1), 1–14.

Huxley-Binns, R. (2011). What's the Q for? *The Law Teacher, 45*(3), 294–309.

Jones, B., Gadallah, Y. andLazem, S. (2019). Facebook debate: facilitating international, intercultural knowledge exchange and collaboration in the field of international intellectual property law. *The Law Teacher*, https://doi.org/10.1080/03069400.2018.1537170 (accessed 12 March 2019).

Jones, E. (2018a). Transforming legal education through emotions. *Legal Studies, 38*(3), 450–479.

Jones, E. (2018b). Making practice more affective: Emotional intelligence as a legal meta-competency. *European Journal of Current Legal Issues, 24*(1), articleno.2.

Jones, E. (2018c). Affective or defective? Exploring the LETR's characterisation of affect and its translation into practice. *The Law Teacher, 52*(4), 478–489.

Killian, R. andSummerville, R. (2019). Creative podcasting as a tool for legal knowledge and skills development. *The Law Teacher.* https://www.tandfonline.com/doi/full/10.1080/03069400.2019.1568675 (accessed 1 March 2019).

Knox, J. andStone, M. (2019). Embedding employability skills for the legal professionals of the future. *The Law Teacher, 53*(1), 90–101.

Kogan, M. andHanney, S. (2000). *Reforming Higher Education.* London, Jessica Kingsley.

Kolsaker, A. (2008). Academic professionalism in the managerialist era: a study of English universities. *Studies in Higher Education, 33*(5), 513–525.

Liverpool John Moores University (2019). *Career Focused Teaching for Work-ready Graduates,* https://www.ljmuisc.com/news/career-focused-teaching-for-work-ready-graduates (accessed 20 March 2019).

Maharg, P. (2007). *Transforming Legal Education: Learning and Teaching the Law in the Early Twenty-first Century.* Abingdon, Routledge.

Maharg, P. andMaughan , C. (eds.) (2011). *Affect and Legal Education: Emotion in Learning and Teaching the Law.* Abingdon, Routledge.

Mason, L. (2018). SQEezing the jurisprudence out of the SRA's super exam: the SQE's Bleak Legal Realism and the rejection of law's multimodal truth. *The Law Teacher, 52* (4), 409–424.

Mason, L. andGuth, J. (2018). Re-claiming our discipline. *The Law Teacher, 52*(4), 379–383.

Moffett, L., Cubie, D. andGodden, A. (2017). Bringing the battlefield into the classroom: using video games to teach and assess international humanitarian law. *The Law Teacher, 51*(4), 499–514.

Molesworth, M., Nixon, E. andScullion, R. (eds.) (2011). *The Marketization of Higher Education and the Student as a Consumer.* Abingdon, Routledge.

Moorhead, R. (2013). LETR II: employability may not be what employers really want. *Lawyerwatch,* https://lawyerwatch.blog/2013/06/27/letr-ii-employability-may-not-be-what-really-employers-want/ (accessed 5 January 2019).

Moreau, M. and Leathwood, C. (2006). Graduates' employment and the discourse of employability: a critical analysis. *Journal of Education and Work,* 19*(*4),305–324.

Morrison, D. (2018). The SQE and creativity: a race to the bottom? *The Law Teacher,* 53 (4), 467–477.

Newbery-Jones, C. (2016). Ethical experiments with the D-pad: exploring the potential of video games as a phenomenological tool for experiential legal education. *The Law Teacher,* 50(1), 61–68.

Nussbaum, M. C. (1997). *Cultivating Humanity.* London, Harvard University Press.

Palfrey, J. (2012). Smarter law school casebooks. In Rubin, E. (ed.). *Legal Education in the Digital Age.* Cambridge, Cambridge University Press, pp. 106–129.

Quality Assurance Agency (QAA) (2015). *Subject Benchmark Statement for Law,* https://www.qaa.ac.uk/docs/qaa/subject-benchmark-statements/sbs-law-15.pdf?sfvrsn=ff99f781_8 (accessed 18 December 2018).

Reese, R. A. (2012). Copyright and innovation in legal course materials. In Rubin, E. (ed.). *Legal Education in the Digital Age.* Cambridge, Cambridge University Press, pp. 60–80.

Rubin, E. (ed.) (2012). *Legal Education in the Digital Age.* Cambridge, Cambridge University Press.

Sanders, A. (2015). Poor thinking, poor outcomes? The future of the law degree after the legal education and training review and the case for socio-legalism. In Sommerlad, H., Harris-Short, S., Vaughan, S. andYoung, R. (eds). *The Futures of Legal Education and the Legal Profession*. Oxford, Hart Publishing, pp. 139–168.

Silverman, G. (2012). Law games: the importance of virtual worlds and serious video games for the future of legal education. In Rubin, E. (ed.). *Legal Education in the Digital Age*. Cambridge, Cambridge University Press, pp. 130–157.

Sokhi-Bulley, S. (2016). Learning law differently: the importance of theory and methodology. In Van Klink, B. andde Vries, U. (eds.). *Academic Learning Law. Theoretical Positions, Teaching Experiments and Learning Experiences*. Cheltenham, Edward Elgar, pp. 121–141.

Sommerlad, H., Harris-Short, S., Vaughan, S. andYoung, R. (2015). The futures of legal education and the legal profession. In Sommerlad, H., Harris-Short, S., Vaughan, S. andYoung, R. (eds.). *The Futures of Legal Education and the Legal Profession*. Oxford, Hart Publishing, pp. 1–22.

Steel, A.(2019). Succeed, question, repeat: threshold concepts and variation theory in understanding how law students build competency. *Law Teacher*, 53(3), 231–244.

Strevens, C. andWilson, C. (2016). Law student wellbeing in the UK: a call for curriculum intervention. *Journal of Commonwealth Law and Legal Education*, 11(1), 44–56.

Susskind, R. (2017). *Tomorrow's Lawyers. An Introduction to Your Future*, 2nd edn. Oxford, Oxford University Press.

Thornton, M. (2012). *Privatising the Public University: The Case of Law*. Abingdon, Routledge.

Turner, J., Bone, A. andAshton, J. (2018). Reasons why law students should have access to learning law through a skills-based approach. *The Law Teacher*, 52(1), 1–16.

Twining, W. (1988). Legal skills and legal education. *The Law Teacher*, 22(1), 4–13.

Tyrell, H. and Jowitt, J. (2018). A bridge over troubled water: addressing the skills gap between school and degree level learning, Society of Legal Scholars, Annual Conference.

Urciuoli, B. (2010). Neoliberal education: preparing the student for the new workplace. In Greenhouse, C. J. (ed.). *Ethnographies of Neoliberalism*. Philadelphia, PA, University of Pennsylvania Press.

Van Klink, B. andde Vries, U. (2016). Introduction: rethinking academic legal education. In Van Klink, B. and de Vries, U. (eds.). *Academic Learning Law. Theoretical Positions, Teaching Experiments and Learning Experiences*. Cheltenham, Edward Elgar, pp. 1–11.

Vladeck, D. C. (2012). Law school 2.0: course books in the digital age. In Rubin, E. (ed.). *Legal Education in the Digital Age*. Cambridge, Cambridge University Press, pp. 185–199.

Wallace, C. J.(2018). The pedagogy of legal reasoning: democracy, discourse and community. *Law Teacher*, 52(3), 260–271.

Watkins, D. and Burton, M. (2017). *Research Methods in Law*. Abingdon, Routledge.

Webb, J. (2015). The LETRs (still) in the post: the legal education and training review and the reform of legal services education and training – a personal (re)view. In Sommerlad, H., Harris-Short, S., Vaughan, S. andYoung, R. (eds.). *The Futures of Legal Education and the Legal Profession*. Oxford, Hart Publishing, pp. 97–138.

Westaby, C. (2014). A qualitative study of the impact of law clinics on students' perceptions of emotional labour expectations. *The Law Teacher*, 48(3), 248–280.

Westaby, C. andJones, E. (2018). Empathy: an essential element of legal practice or 'never the twain shall meet'? *International Journal of the Legal Profession*, 25(1), 107–124.

Chapter 12

Legal skills

Making a real change in Nigerian legal education

Ekokoi Solomon

Introduction

The unswerving need for improvement in legal education is a reflection of the internationalisation of law, a phenomenon that has been intensified by legal globalisation, as depicted by the globalisation of legal standards and practices. In Nigeria, this phenomenon has undoubtedly influenced the teaching of law at the postgraduate level, which has, over the past few years, become more interdisciplinary, comparative and international in approach (Ako and Olawuyi, 2017, p.227). This is, however, not the case for the LLB programme. Thus, law teachers and undergraduate law students cannot continue to teach and learn law only in the local and national contexts (Ako and Olawuyi, 2017, p.227).

There is an ongoing debate on the need to reform or transform legal education in Nigeria to reposition it to equip law students with requisite legal skills. At the core of the debate is the call for an integrative and comprehensive system of legal education that focuses on the teaching of legal doctrines and skills that are needed to equip law students who seek to become members of the legal profession (Ojukwu, 2017, p.197), as academic and vocational legal education appear to be at odds with one another.

The need for a robust legal education in Nigeria cannot be overemphasised. This is in view of its feeder role for the legal profession and the society at large, for to equip law students with legal skills is to ensure 'good general education in the discipline of law' (Twining, 1988, p.5), the maintenance of standard in the legal profession, and the safeguard of the interest of the public that consumes and benefits from legal services. It is the concern for public interest that led Woodward and Dalton (1990, p.130) to argue that the idea of legal education goes beyond law. As the failure to ensure effective legal education is tantamount to failure of the legal profession of which the society becomes the ultimate victim. This depicts the important role of legal education and lawyers in the ordering of society (Ndulo, 2002, p.488). To drive home the point, in comparison with other disciplines, the study and practice of law are held in very high esteem in Nigeria, as is the case in the United Kingdom (Slapper, 2011, p. 11; Udombana, 2017), and to use the words of Slapper (2011, p.9), the law degree and legal studies are 'the most versatile of academic qualifications and the most popular undergraduate subject' in Nigeria.

Philosophy of legal education

In Nigeria, legal education is a two-tier system, as it is in many Commonwealth countries, and is one that takes place through structured curricula in law faculties of Nigerian universities and the Nigerian Law School. This demarcation creates a dichotomy between the educational objectives of acquiring knowledge of legal theories and skills. Carter notes that the development of skills may not require cognition and may, in some cases, flourish in the absence of cognitive abilities. He argues that the acquisition of skills may, however, be made much easier by having good cognitive knowledge, but insists that proficiency is only attained through diligent practice and feedback (Carter, 1985, p.140).

The dichotomy in Nigerian legal education creates incidental challenges that have developed from the notion that academic legal education, through the plain teaching and learning of the law, should merely introduce law students to legal doctrines and teach them to reason like legal practitioners (Azinge, 2017, p.8), while vocational legal education should concentrate on training and preparing law students for the legal profession (Denning Committee Report, 1961, pp.60–62, 85). This notion inhibits rather than accentuates the teaching of legal skills in Nigerian legal education and promotes a compartmentalised system that has been described by Ojukwu (2013, pp.311–312) as the 'oil and water approach' to legal education. Nevertheless, the suggestion that the teaching of legal skills at the academic legal education stage is necessarily impractical or unnecessary has been rejected as fallacious and a demonstration of the attitude of the 'diffused resistance to talk of skills' (Twining, 1988, p.4). The point here is that the idea of acquiring legal skills is central in the taxonomy of legal education and crucial to the discipline of law as an academic field of study, as well as a vocational training that is aimed at aiding the practice of law.

In order, therefore, to bridge the gap created by the compartmentalised system of legal education in Nigeria, it is imperative to equip law students with skills with which 'to organise and process ideas [...] through interaction with and feedback to the student[s] in an ongoing process of supervised trial and error' (Petter, 1982, p.86) at the academic legal education stage. This may explain why, in 2006, after a collaborative brainstorming session organised by the Nigerian Bar Association and the Office of the Attorney General of the Federation, a communique was issued calling for the teaching of law to be less theoretical and more practical. For, according to Ojo, practicality entails the teaching of law with the aim of shifting the focus from litigation to a broader practice of development lawyering (Ojo, 2006).

Teaching/learning methods and legal skills

The chapter adopts, in its entirety, the definition of legal skills as provided by Guth in this volume. Therefore, the issue of definition of what legal skills are will not be belaboured. Rather, the chapter continues with the examination of the various methods of teaching and learning legal skills in Nigerian legal education. There is an ongoing debate in the Nigerian legal academy as to the effectiveness of the existing instructional methods in Nigerian legal education. Omoragbon, however, argues that the global trend points toward 'a shift from transmission of knowledge to construction of knowledge, from direct instruction to inquiry and independent projects' (Omoragbon, 2014, p.23). This suggests that for any pedagogy to be effective, it must be capable of enhancing students' experience and performance, encouraging creativeness in students, offering students the opportunity of self-expression and participation, as well as building the capacity of students to develop critical thinking and problem-solving skills (Adekoya, 2017, p.82).

Lecture method

The lecture method is the most widely used instructional method in Nigerian legal education. A lecture is an 'educational talk to an audience especially of students in a university' (Soanes and Stevenson, 2006, p.812) and is effective in the teaching of doctrines and theories of law (Cooper, 2002, pp.54–55). Its application is predicated on the assumption that the law is certain. Yet, often we find that there is *no* certainty in the law. In relation to legal education, there are certain flaws associated with the lecture method (Adekoya, 2017, pp.69–74). The problem with the predominant use of the lecture method is evident in its inability to enhance the development of knowledge of the law and competencies in law students (Cooper, 2002, p.55; Ojukwu, 2017, p.194). In fact, the lecture method encourages law students to devote much of their time 'memoris[ing] large numbers of rules which are organised into categorical systems' of doctrines and theories that inhibit critical arguments and analyses (Ndulo, 2002, p.492). This explains why it has been argued that the lecture method should not be used in isolation of other teaching methods (Ojukwu, 2017, p.194).

Thus, in the late 1980s, the National Universities Commission (NUC) introduced some reforms in Nigerian legal education through the Benchmark Minimum Academic Standards (BMAS) for Undergraduate Programmes in Nigerian Universities. That BMAS for the law programme highlighted the objective of the LLB programme, which sought to enable law students to have a clear perspective and understanding of the place, importance and role of law in society. It emphasised the need for legal education to act as a stimulus to stir law students into critical analysis and examination of the social systems around them (NUC, 1988, pp.2–4). The reform conceived the use of tutorials in addition to the lecture method as a complete package in the teaching of law. Tutorials were meant to complement the lecture method and enable law students express and build on knowledge of legal doctrines acquired during lectures.

When used effectively, tutorials are capable of enhancing the ability of law students to analyse cases, statutes and legal principles and to apply these to new facts. This is because tutorials are supposed to be interactive in nature, allowing students to express their understanding of legal doctrines and principles and stimulating their critical thinking and analytical skills using hypothetical or practical situations. Through the exchange of ideas and the discussions that ensue during tutorials, students should be able to appreciate the law and how it can be used to solve problems (Manteaw, 2008, p.944). Unfortunately, however, tutorial sessions have lost their significance in Nigerian legal education because they have been turned into extensions of the lecture method. This has made it impossible to realise the objectives of the first NUC reform in Nigerian legal education, as law teachers doggedly embraced the use of the lecture method (Ojukwu, 2003, p.138, 2006, p.3, 2017, p.194).

Clinical methods

There is no clear definition of what constitutes clinical method of teaching/ learning, as there are aggregate instructional approaches and processes that are comprised in clinical methods. According to Feldman (1985, p.611), clinical methods refer to a 'wide range of tenuously related educational approaches and processes', which promote experiential learning. They transcend traditional classroom activities to experiential activities such as research, writing, etc. In legal education, clinical methods aid in the expression of knowledge of the law and legal skills of law students. For, as Wade (1994, p.191) notes, skills are shallow and transient without doctrines, and without the expression of skills the knowledge of doctrines become insignificant. Law clinics and the pupillage programme are the two main clinical approaches in Nigerian legal education.

Law clinics

A law clinic is a medium used to expose law students to the impact of law within the society where it is located. A law clinic provides opportunity for law students to 'use [their] legal expertise to address issues of social concern' (Barry, 2007, p.35). It is a platform for the application of acquired legal knowledge and skills and an integrative approach for the realisation of the goal of clinical legal education (Ojukwu, Erugo and Adekoya, 2013, p.7). According to Ojukwu et al. (2013, p.10): '[I]n a law clinic, a law student is expected to demonstrate the ability to function like a lawyer after going through the academic component of the programme and incrementally learning from experience.' As laudable as the goal of law clinics may be, law students will not be effective if they lack functional legal skills.

At present, there are 22 law clinics based in 17 law faculties of Nigerian universities and five campuses of the Nigerian Law School (Lagi, 2017, p.16; Ojukwu, Lagi and Yusuf, 2014, p.5). The existence of these law clinics is a testament to the efforts of the Network of Universities Legal Aid Institutions, Nigeria with the support and partnership of the Open Society Foundations and MacArthur Foundation. The law clinic approach commenced with four pilot law clinics in 2004 with the aim of promoting clinical legal education in Nigeria (Lagi, 2018, pp.15–16; Ojukwu, Erugo and Adekoya, 2013, p.5). Regrettably, only a negligible number of students take part in law clinic activities because participation is not compulsory for all law students – only fourth-year law students who offer the non-compulsory law course generally referred to as 'Introduction to legal practice' and very few final-year students who engage in moot court competitions participate in law clinic activities. The fact that greater emphasis is placed on the summative examination, which is taken at the end of each of the two semesters in which the course is taught, makes the goal of passing examination to appear to outweigh the need to learn legal skills.

Pupillage programme

In Nigeria, the pupillage programme for law students is organised and supervised by the Council of Legal Education (Nigerian Law School). It is predicated on the assumption of complementarity, whereby law students engage in some legal work in law offices and courts for a fixed period of time for free. In return, senior lawyers and judges in law offices and courts respectively are supposed to teach the pupils law office and courtroom crafts. The pupillage programme would appear, in theory, to be a good idea but, in practice, it appears to be ineffective and deficient. It is a good idea because it is a clinical approach that seeks to equip law students with secondary legal skills (e.g. interviewing, negotiating, case management, litigation and advocacy and courtroom skills) before they are called to the Nigerian bar.

The pupillage programme is, however, ineffective and deficient because many law students are unable to utilise the pupillage programme to their benefit as they lack functional legal skills. It is also ineffective and deficient because of the structure and organisation of the programme. For example, a careful review of the log books of many law students on the programme will expose their lack of functional legal skills. The author vividly recalls his experience at the Nigerian Law School some years ago. After completion of the pupillage internship, many students returned to the campus with blank log books and copied the contents of the log books of their friends for the purpose of assessment. Due to the large number of students admitted into the Nigerian Law School each year, many students are thus able to circumvent the assessment process. There is also the issue of lack of collaboration and interface between the Nigerian Law School and law offices/courts. Additionally, many law offices in Nigeria can hardly be classified as standard law offices, as they lack well-equipped libraries. Senior lawyers in the law offices are seldom prepared to teach pupils how to engage in legal research and drafting of legal documents, as they consider these to be the responsibilities of law teachers (da Rocha, 2002, p.6).

Developing functional legal skills in law students

For the fact that law students are 'initiate novice practitioners' seeking to enter the legal profession, they must not only be taught legal doctrines, they must also be taught 'to think, to perform, and to conduct themselves like professionals' (Sullivan et al., 2007, p.22). As such, they must be equipped with both theoretical knowledge of the law, as well as legal skills (Jessup, 2002, p.400). In recognition of this fact, it would appear, the NUC, in early 2018, released a new draft BMAS for the law programme that now provides for the teaching of legal research and writing, and clinical training in Nigerian universities (NUC, 2018, p.27). The proposed BMAS for the LLB programme seeks to enrich and enhance the study of law in a manner that will develop in law students the requisite legal skills that are capable of addressing national and global challenges through intellectual rigour, analytical and critical engagement. The objective is to imbue in law students knowledge of the law and produce law graduates who are intellectually competent to apply legal knowledge, research and analytical skills to solve theoretical and practical legal, social, economic and political problems (NUC, 2018, p.2). This suggests that the NUC seeks to promote the use of integrative teaching/learning in the training of law students for cognitive and skills acquisition. This is in view of the widening scope of the subject matter of law, which makes it impossible for any system of legal education, before qualification, to possibly cover the full extent of law without being utterly superficial and useless in approach (Ormrod Report, 1971).

Wade (1994, p.180) has categorised legal skills into three groups – the first, second and third categories of skill. According to Wade, the first category of legal skills is the traditional and dominant skill sets that most law schools seek to enhance through the 'ability to manipulate and critique rules in thought, word and writing', while the second and third category of skills, which include interviewing, negotiating, advocacy and the ability to spot ethical issues and devise appropriate responses, entail skills that are developed in the course of clinical legal education to give expression to the first category of skills. The first category of legal skills may be referred to as functional legal skills. This is because they are relevant and applicable to both the discipline and practice of law, unlike the second and third categories of legal skills, which are applicable to only the practice of law.

Legal research skills

According to Smits (2014, pp.76–79), there are four interrelated developments that confront and threaten the foundation of legal education, namely (i) the increasing complexity, specialisation and fragmentation of law, (ii) the evolving nature of legal studies, which is becoming less doctrinal and more interdisciplinary and scientific in approach, (iii) the 'increasing separation of research and teaching and the ensuing concern that law graduates are no longer sufficiently qualified for legal practice' and (iv) the internationalisation of law resulting in the standardisation of legal aid, which is likely to result in the outsourcing of legal work and increase in the demand for specialised legal services. The impact of these developments is being felt in Nigerian legal education and there is no doubt that they require equal measure of response from law teachers and policymakers. Equipping law students with legal research skills is one measure with which to tackle these threats to Nigerian legal education. This is because law students (apprentice practitioners) and lawyers (professionals) can truly be up to date with developments in the law and effectively discharge their obligations only if they possess legal research skills which serve as tool for problem solving and seeking to apply original perspectives that provide understanding for applying law in society (Seims, 2008, p.148).

Legal writing skills

Another measure with which law teachers and policymakers in Nigeria can mitigate the growing threats to legal education is to teach and promote the teaching of legal writing skills to law students respectively. Writing is an art that requires intellectual depth and flair in language (Constable, 2014; Worika, 2004, p.353). To effectively engage in legal writing, law students must have analytical skills, and the ability to convey their thoughts using straightforward language. This means that language skills must also be given priority in the teaching of legal writing. This is, however, not the case in law faculties of Nigerian universities, even though law students in Nigeria are required to study and taught subjects such as 'Use of English' and 'Literature' in the first year of the law programme (University of Uyo, 2015–2017, pp.24–25). The reality is that 'the actual teaching [of the subjects is] done without any serious attempt at achieving any educational goal' (Ojukwu, 2017, p.192).

In Nigeria, English is the official language and the language of the law (*Ojengbede v. Esan* [2001] 18 NWLR (Pt. 746) 771, 790), despite its acculturation occasioned by the influence of the mother tongue (Jowitt, 1991, pp.1–149). Yet, it has been asserted that the teaching of English language to law students is not the responsibility of law teachers and that the issue of efficiency in the use of English language should not be used to determine the level of efficiency of law students in Nigeria (Azinge 2017, pp.8–9). It is also the case that the teaching of legal writing and use of the English language to law students have not been emphasised as much as they should be, even when it is not in doubt that English language is an important element in Nigerian legal education. For, according to Constable (2014, p.64): '[L]aw is fundamentally a matter of language and there are some things one cannot understand about law if one does not understand language – and the limits of speech [as well as thought].' And to effectively engage in the study and practice of law, students and practitioners must have sufficient facility of writing in the language of the law. It is, therefore, imperative that law students in Nigeria are properly taught language, the skill of its usage and how to understand the meaning it expresses.

Udombana (2017, p.28) provides a blunt reflection of the consequences of the dearth of legal writing skills and the effective use of the English language, which give rise to the ignominious practice of 'copy and paste' by many law students in Nigeria. The problem of this practice seems to have extended into the professional careers of many law graduates who are unable to engage in effective legal writing such as research reports/papers, pleadings, legal decisions and other documents, such as office memos, minutes of meetings, etc.

Critical thinking and analytical skills

Critical thinking may be defined as the ability to engage in independent and reflective thinking. It is an intellectual mechanism for the 'exploration of theory and practice' (Moon, 2008). Critical thinking skills such as reflection, analysis, interpretation, evaluation, inference, etc. encourage students to be active learners rather than passive recipients of knowledge. In terms of legal education, critical thinking skills entail the intellectual ability to orchestrate, coordinate and analyse legal information in a proficient manner as possible (Gold, 1983, p.251). Critical thinking skills enable law students to engage in the intellectual process of synthesising legal doctrines for the purpose of problem-solving. Analytical skills, by way of contrast, allow for a syllogistic approach to solving legal problems, as analytical skills are at the root of effective lawyering (Gold, 1983, p.251). To equip law students with critical thinking and analytical skills is to enhance their innovation and adaptation to legal theory that is both deductive and analogical (Worika, 2004, p.368). The fact that effective legal writing is a function of critical thinking and analytical skills, law students who lack these skills will not be able to engage in effective legal writing irrespective of the amount of knowledge of law that they possess (Rowe, 2009, p.13).

Regrettably, due to the predominant use of the lecture method of teaching in Nigerian legal education, law students are not encouraged to have reflective and intellectual thoughts of their own on what they are being taught. For, insofar as law is a factual and normative discipline, it is also a critical and an analytical subject (Dubber, 2012, p.3), and a legal education system that merely seeks to transfer cognitive knowledge to students cannot enhance their critical thinking and analytical abilities and skills (de Bono, 1971, p.7).

Therefore, if the goal of Nigerian legal education is to produce law graduates who will develop the capacity to solve social, economic and political problems, attention must be given to the teaching of critical thinking and analytical skills that are important ingredients for the development of perspective in this era of globalisation (Manteaw, 2008, p.941). Additionally, if the goal of teaching critical thinking and analytical skills to law students is to liberate their legal mind, elaborate existing legal doctrines and concepts – with the prospect of determining their deficiencies through the linkage of theory and application of law in a manner that produces alternative theories – such teaching activity must engage both left and right cerebral hemispheres of the brain. Law teachers in Nigeria must come to the realisation that since the formality of law accentuates left-side functions and conceals the wholesome influence of right-side functions, the continued fixation with teaching methods that offer little truly scientific rigour and perpetuate left-hand functions quite freely should be reconsidered (Woodward and Dalton, 1990, p.131).

Challenges to the teaching of legal skills

The teaching of legal skills to law students, as Guth has rightly argued in her chapter on legal skills in this volume, is confronted with certain challenges posed by neoliberal and market-focused agenda. In the case of Nigerian legal education, however, these challenges manifest in the continual offload of the cost of legal education, so that there appears to be increasing attempt to privatise legal education because it is no longer considered, *stricto sensu*, as a tool for social development but merely as another market commodity. This challenge gives rise to the manifestations that are examined below.

Contents versus method

It has been suggested that not much has been done to review the course contents of legal studies and the teaching method in Nigerian legal education (Bukar, 2014, pp.594–595; Udombana, 2017, p.43). With regard to course contents, Nigerian legal education curriculum lacks educational modules which ensure the teaching/learning of functional legal skills. The NUC only recently proposed the teaching of legal research and writing as a non-compulsory module (NUC, 2018, p.27). In view of the fact that law students in Nigeria now have to deal with the significant expansion in the body of legal knowledge due to the evolving nature and specialised fields of law (Bukar, 2014, pp.594, 596; Ndulo, 2002, p.487), it is unfathomable that the teaching/learning of legal research and writing is being proposed as an elective module.

By the same token, it may be argued that the method of teaching is a serious factor militating against functional legal skills in Nigerian legal education. In an effort to address the problem, Ernest Ojukwu, through the Network of University Legal Aid Institutions Nigeria, which was established in 2003, has been a leading advocate in promoting change in the method of teaching law in

Nigeria. His theory of change is anchored on the 'reform of legal education for social justice and community development' through a change in the attitudes of policy makers, law teachers and law students toward legal education (NULAI Nigeria, 2013, p.1). And going by Ojukwu's presentation at the 51st Annual Conference of the Nigerian Association of Law Teachers 2018, it is apparent that his advocacy is not necessarily for change in the curriculum of legal education but for a change in the method of teaching in law faculties of Nigerian universities. Accordingly, it will be futile to institute any change in the legal profession without foundational reforms in how the LLB students are being taught (Ojukwu, 2018).

Systemic problems

Another challenge militating against the teaching of legal skills in Nigeria is the lack of adequate funding of legal education. The miserable funding of legal education in Nigeria has resulted in the lack of facilities and infrastructures such as functional libraries, computers and internet facilities, conducive lecture halls, as well as the lack of incentives by way of training, research funding and respectable remuneration for law teachers. The above factors are compounded by the large and unsustainable number of law students who are admitted into the various law faculties each year. Ojukwu (2006, p.4) records that there are as many as 150 to 300 law students in any one class in a Nigerian university. This is because many universities offer admission to applicants beyond the approved quotas set by the Council of Legal Education.

Also, there is the issue of the competency of law teachers in Nigeria. Many law teachers lack the knowledge and expertise to teach functional legal skills, considering the fact that they are themselves products of the same system that is more inclined to the teaching of doctrines and theories of law. This explains why many law teachers find it difficult or impossible to undertake legal research that has practical relevance to the problems confronting the country.

In Nigeria, as in many countries on the African continent, the challenges to legal skills teaching appear to be growing in proportion. This is because of the shift in policy focus that has resulted in very little attention being given to the notion of using legal education as an instrument of social transformation. This has ultimately resulted in the growing indifference to public funding of legal education in Nigeria. Therefore, for real change to occur in Nigerian legal education, this trend must be reversed.

Concluding remarks

Kneebone (2016) has lamented the withering of the dexterity of surgeons in the United Kingdom due to the use of computers in surgical operations. Acknowledging that modern surgery is a performative practice, he proposes the teaching of skills applied by stand-up magicians and puppeteers in the training of medical students in the UK. Law teachers and policymakers in Nigerian legal education have a lesson to learn from this proposal to rejuvenate the teaching of skills to medical students who are being trained to become surgeons. This is because law, like medicine, is a discipline whose intellectual and institutional history predates the classic disciplines of the nineteenth century (Valverde, 2014, p.60). It is, therefore, imperative that Nigerian legal education shifts its focus from the current practice of training for legal practice to training for competency, as the failure of legal education to equip law students with functional legal skills has resulted in the training of many lawyers who lack the capacity to engage in independent legal research, effective legal writing and critical and logical analysis.

Nigerian legal education cannot afford to limit the measure of its success or failure to the litigation game (i.e. the ability of lawyers to present legal arguments in courts and for judges to make judicial decisions based only on precedents), as this is a misconception of the function of lawyers in society. Litigation must not be seen as the core objective and end of legal education (Gower, 1967, pp.131–132). The ends of legal education should be to equip initiates with legal knowledge and functional legal skills for the benefit of clients and the society, as there is something for everyone and everything for society in the discipline of law (Slapper, 2011, p.10). It must be realised that at some point, every lawyer will be required to research, analyse and write, whether in a law firm, government agency or public organisation, private company, the academia or the judiciary (Rowe, 2009, pp.22–23). Nigerian legal education must now aspire to countermand the prevailing legal practitioner model of legal education, which is predicated on the assumption that functional legal skills would naturally be learned by law graduates in the course of their professional careers (Ako and Olawuyi, 2017, p.228).

Bibliography

Adekoya, C. O. (2017). Clinical legal education: human rights and justice-based approach to legal training. In Erugo, S. and Adekoya, C. O. (eds.). *Lawyering with Integrity: Essays in Honour of Ernest Ojukwu, SAN*. Raleigh, NC, Lulu Press Inc., pp. 67–105

Ako, R. and Olawuyi, D. S. (2017). Methodology, theoretical framework and scholarly significance: an overview of international best practices in legal research. *Afe Babalola University: Journal of Sustainable Development Law & Policy*, 8(2), 225–241.

Azinge, E. (17 October 2017). Interview. *This Day Lawyer*. Lagos.

Barry, M. (2007). Clinical legal education in the law university: goals and challenges. *International Journal of Legal Education*, 27–50.

Bukar, B. A. (2014). Legal education and challenges of contemporary developments in Nigeria. *International Journal of Clinical Legal Education*, 20(2), 593–601.

Carter, R. (1985). A taxonomy of objectives for professional education. *Students in Higher Education*, 10, 135.

Committee on Legal Education (March, 1971). *The Ormrod Report*. London, HMSO Cmnd No. 4595.
Committee on Legal Education for Students from Africa (1961). *Denning Committee Report*. London, HMSO. Cmnd No. 1255.
Constable, M. (2014). Law as language. *Critical Analysis of Law*, 1(1), 63–74.
Cooper, B. D. (2002). The integration of theory, doctrine, and practice in legal education. *Journal of the Association of Legal Writing Directors*, 1(1), 50.
Da Rocha, B. J. (2002). The future of professional legal education in Ghana. *Ghana School Law Journal*, 1, 1.
Dagan, H. and Kreitner, R. (2014). The interdisciplinary party. *Critical Analysis of Law*, 1(1), 23–31.
De Bono, E. (1971). *Practical Thinking*. London, Penguin Books.
Dubber, M. D. (2012). *Critical Analysis of Law: Interdisciplinarity, Contextuality, and the Future of Legal Studies. CAL Manifesto*, http://cal.library.utoronto.ca/public/journals/99/CAL.pdf (accessed 4 November 2018).
Feldman, M. (1985). On the margins of legal education. *New York University Review of Law & Social Change*, 13, 607.
Gold, N. (1983). The professional legal training program: training for competence. *The Advocate (Canada)*, 41, 247.
Gower, L. C. B. (1967). *Independent Africa: The Challenge to the Legal Profession*. London, Oxford University Press.
Jessup, G. (2002). Symbiotic relations: clinical methodology – fostering new paradigms in African legal education. *Clinical Law Review*, 8, 377.
Jowitt, D. (1991). *Nigerian English Usage: An Introduction*. Ikeja, Learn Africa Plc.
Kneebone, R. L. (2016). Performing surgery: commonalities with performers outside medicine. *Frontiers of Psychology*, 7(1233), 1–17, https://www.ncbi.nlm.nih.gov/pmc/articles/PMC5006638/pdf/fpsyg-07-01233.pdf (accessed 27 October 2018).
Lagi, O. (2017). Chronicling the development of clinical legal education in Nigeria. In Erugo, S. and Adekoya, C. O. (eds.). *Lawyering with Integrity: Essays in Honour of Ernest Ojukwu, SAN*. Raleigh, NC, Lulu Press Inc., pp. 13–27.
Manteaw, S. (2008). Legal education in Africa: What type of lawyer does Africa need? *McGeorge Law Review*, 39, 903–976.
Moon, J. (2008). *Critical Thinking*. Abingdon, Routledge.
National Universities Commission (2018). *Benchmark Minimum Academic Standards for Undergraduate Programmes in Nigerian Universities – Law*. Abuja, National Universities Commission.
National Universities Commission (1988). *Minimum Academic Standards in Law for all Nigerian Universities*. Lagos, National Universities Commission.
Ndulo, M. (2002). Legal education in Africa in the era of globalization and structural adjustment. *Penn State International Law Review*, 20(3), 487–503.
NULAI Nigeria (2013). *NULAI Nigeria 2008–2012 Activities Report*. Abuja: Network of University Legal Aid Institutions.
Ojo, B. (9 May 2006). Rethinking legal education in Nigeria. A paper presented at a two-day summit. *Guardian Newspaper*. Lagos.
Ojukwu, E. (2018). Practicing law in a regulated environment: what we need to know, paper presented at the Nigerian Bar Association Section on Legal Practice Conference, Port Harcourt.

Ojukwu, E. (2017) Making a real change: legal education in Nigeria – partly re-imagined? In Grimes, R. (ed.). *Re-thinking Legal Education Under the Civil and Common Law: A Road Map for Constructive Change*. Abingdon, Routledge, pp. 192–201.

Ojukwu, E. (2013). *Legal Education in Nigeria: A Chronicle of Reforms and Transformation Under Tahir Mamman*. Abuja, Council of Legal Education.

Ojukwu, E. (2006). *Clinical Legal Education Curriculum for Nigerian Universities' Law Faculties/Clinics*. Abuja, Network of University Legal Aid Institutions Nigeria.

Ojukwu, E. (2003). Trends in legal education: A comparative analysis of Nigeria, U.S.A, U.K and South Africa. In Mamman, T. *et al.* (eds.). *Nigerian Law School: Four Decades of Service to the Legal Profession*. Abuja, Council of Legal Education, pp. 133–141.

Ojukwu, E., Erugo, S. and Adekoya, C. (2013). *Clinical Legal Education: Curriculum Lessons and Materials*. Abuja, Network of University Legal Aid Institutions Nigeria.

Ojukwu, E., Lagi, O. and Yusuf, M. (2014). *Compendium of Campus Based Law Clinics in Nigeria*. Abuja, Network of University Legal Aid Institutions Nigeria.

Omoragbon, K. M. (2014). Theorizing clinical legal education: An evaluation of the pedagogy versus andragogy debate in the constructivist paradigm. *African Journal of Clinical Legal Education and Access to Justice*, 3, 1–25.

Petter, A. (1982). A closet within the house: learning objectives and the law school curriculum. In: Gold, N. (ed.). *Essays on Legal Education*. Toronto, Butterworths, p. 77.

Rowe, S. E. (2009). Legal research, legal writing, and legal analysis: putting law school into practice. *Stetson Law Review*, 1–23.

Seims, M. M. (2008). Legal originality. *Oxford Journal of Legal Studies*, 28, 147–164.

Slapper, G. J. (2011). The history of legal education. *Journal of Commonwealth Law and Legal Education*, 8(1), 9–21.

Smits, J. M. (2014). Law and interdisciplinarity: on the inevitable normativity of legal studies. *Critical Analysis of Law*, 1(1), 75–86.

Soanes, C. and Stevenson, A. (2006). *Concise Oxford English Dictionary*, 11th edn. Oxford, Oxford University Press.

Sullivan, W. M., Colby, A., Wegner, J. W. and Bond, L. (2007). *Educating Lawyers: Preparing for the Profession of Law*. Hoboken, NJ, Jossey-Bass (John Wiley & Sons, Inc.)

Twining, W. (1988). Legal skills and legal education. *Law Teacher*, 22(1), 1.

Udombana, N. J. (2017). The noble profession in the dock, a lecture delivered in honour of the retiring Chief Judge of Akwa Ibom State, Hon. Justice Stephen E. Okon, Uyo.

University of Uyo (2015–2017). *Faculty of Law Academic Programme 2015–2017*.

Valverde, M. (2014). Between a rock and a hard place: legal studies beyond both disciplinarity and interdisciplinarity. *Critical Analysis of Law*, 1(1), 51–62.

Wade, J. H. (1994). Legal skills training: Some thoughts on terminology and ongoing challenges. *Legal Education Review*, 5, 173–193.

Woodward, P. and Dalton, P. (1990). Green papers, black letters, grey matter. *Journal of the Association of Law Teachers*, 124–136.

Worika, I. L. (2004). Writing research papers, dissertations and thesis: from choice of topic to final work. In Nwosu, K. N. (ed.). *Legal Practice Skills & Ethics in Nigeria*. Lagos, DCONconsulting, pp. 353–379.

Conclusion

What are university law schools for?

Anthony Bradney

Introduction

Each of the essays in this volume demonstrates, in various different ways, that the pressing question for every analysis of university legal education is always first and foremost, what is it that university law schools are supposed to do. The focus of a writer may be on the assessment of students, the financing of law schools or any of the many other things that have been the subject of study in the vast literature that there is on university legal education. Nevertheless, ideas about the purpose of university law schools are always foundational, whether explicitly or implicitly, in investigations into university legal education.

Occasionally the matter of purpose for a law school can be seen as being obvious and unproblematic. Thus, in this volume Arthurs writes that '[i]n the United States, the charge of law schools is quite clear – to prepare lawyers.' For some in the USA, Arthurs' assertion will be uncontroversial. After all, the MacCrate Report on American lawyers observed several decades ago that '[t]he skills and values of the competent lawyer are developed along a continuum that … reaches its most formative and intensive stage during the law school experience' (MacCrate, 1992, p.3). Nevertheless, even in the context of the USA, that which is 'clear' to one person may the converse of the truth for another. Thus, for example, Fiss' final contribution to the 'Of law and the river' exchange about United States law schools ends by stating that:

> [L]aw professors are not paid to train lawyers but to study law and to teach their students what they happen to discover. The law school is an integral part of the university … and by virtue of that membership and all the commitments it entails must be pure in its academic obligations. (Martin, 1985, p.26)

Fiss directly rebuts the position taken by Arthurs. Others in the USA have been more equivocal. Appleman, for example, has suggested that the historical development of American law schools has meant that in the USA legal academics become part of two scholarly communities: 'the legal community and the university community' (Appleman, 2004–2005, p.300).

In any event, usually the question and therefore the answer as to the purpose of a university law school is seen to be difficult and problematic in one way or another as once again contributions to this collection demonstrate. Thus Solomon in this volume writes that 'academic and vocational legal education appear to be at odds with each other' while de Vries contends that 'the vocational aspect of legal education is over-emphasised, at the cost of legal learning as an academic pursuit.' Also in this volume, Zhou and Palmer observe that in China 'there is no clear and positive relationship between formal legal education on the one hand and the administration of justice and professional practice of law on the other.' Others in this volume make similar points, as we can see in the following.

Even if university law schools are there 'to prepare lawyers', as Arthurs suggests, who, in the twenty-first century, counts as being a lawyer? If the '[t]he market for legal services is changing rapidly', as Ryan and McFaul maintain, or if 'the legal landscape is changing dramatically' as Burton and Watkins, echoing de Vries, ask, what does the term lawyer now mean? Bok, writing over 30 years ago, responding to the suggestion that American law schools do not simply train lawyers but prepare 'leaders of the bar', argued that '[l]aw schools will need to take the initiative in educating [students] for a broader range of legal needs in our society' (Bok, 1983, p.583). What lawyers are and what they do is, in the twenty-first century, as problematic as what law schools should do.

There is a long history of debating the role of university law schools. Dicey's lecture 'Can English law be taught at the universities' was given and published in 1883 (Dicey, 1883). There is analysis of university legal education in academic law journals in the United Kingdom in the late nineteenth and early twentieth centuries (Cownie and Bradney, 2017, S130–S131). The same thing is true in some other countries. In the USA, for example, Thayer's article 'The teaching of law at university' was published in 1895 (Thayer, 1895). From then until now there has been constant consideration and reconsideration of the function of university law schools. The fact that this question as to purpose has been asked for so many years does not alter its saliency in the present day. There is a constant need for each university law school and each individual legal academic to decide what it is that they should do in the light of the prevailing conditions which they find themselves in. The twin obligations of the professional ideal and academic freedom mean that academics must both take personal responsibility for 'the quality of [their] work' (Freidson, 2001, p.200) and also do what they believe to be 'important and true' (Dworkin, 1996, p.189).

One final point remains to be noted. While it is true that there are many contenders for selection as the role or roles for a university law school and equally many reasons as to why one role or another should be chosen, this does not mean that the choice can be either a matter of whim, simple self-interest or obedience to the diktats of others. Instead the wealth of literature noted above means that to justify the conclusion drawn as to purpose there must be a reaction to and reflection on that literature. If that is not done the claims that academics make for a professionalism that is based, in part, on the possession of 'specialized bodies of knowledge and skill' (Freidson, 2001, p.213) will be lost.

What is at issue?

The way in which the question as to the purpose of the university law school is framed is important. The question at issue is what should a university law school do? It is not, at least in the first analysis, what would prospective university law students like to do? It is not how do we produce more able lawyers? It is not what would governments like university law schools to do? It is not even what would university administrations like law schools to do? All of these questions and other similar suggestions might be relevant to what university law schools should do. Nonetheless to ask any of these questions first or to ask them in isolation is to prejudge what the focus of university law schools is to be. Thus, for example, whatever the merits of Frank's article 'A plea for lawyer-schools', it rests on the unexamined premise that university legal education is about lawyers (Frank, 1947). His arguments are compromised by the assumptions that he makes. But analysing the purpose of university law schools entails a different line of reasoning which, insofar as is possible, critically assesses all possibilities.

University law schools are precisely that; schools, departments or faculties that are part of a university. Were they independent entities, wholly different questions about their purpose and focus might be appropriate. However, university law schools have elected to be part of a university and the starting point for analysis must then be first what is it that universities should do? After that has been ascertained the question then becomes how then do law schools fit within a university that takes this form? Indeed, even more fundamentally, given Veblen's remark about universities needing a law school as much as they need as school of fencing (Veblen, 1919, p.211), can they in fact fit within a university? In a similar fashion those working in a university law school as academics have decided to be part of a university. What does this membership say about what it is that they should do? This latter imperative also extends to those who do not accept the description of academic, instead styling themselves, for example, as clinicians. If they have an academic contract and have thus made 'a conscious choice has been made to enter academia' they are then bound by the obligations inherent in being in academia (Blackburn, 2018, p.182).

The literature on the purpose and function of universities is even larger than the literature on university law schools. The issue is and always has been contentious. This, however, does not mean that the term university is indeterminate. Equally, it does not mean that every institution that decides to call itself a university is in fact worthy of that title or that every department that call itself a university law school is in fact a university law school. The terms 'university' and 'university law school' both carry with them a certain status. Institutions may seek to benefit from that status without in fact doing anything to live up to the reality of the thing that they claim to be. There may, for example, be a commercial advantage in attracting students if a body uses the university title. The fact that an institution finds it profitable to call itself a university does not, of itself, mean that it is a university.

Research and the university

A central question about universities that is of great importance to law schools is the place of research in the university. Newman, in his classic work on the nature of universities first published in 1852, was clear that universities were concerned with 'the diffusion and extension of knowledge rather than the advancement' (Newman, 1960, p.xxxvii). Teaching not research was, in Newman's view, what universities should be focused on. However, in the Western world, the influence of American and, more importantly, German universities in the nineteenth and twentieth centuries has resulted in a much greater focus on research in universities in the present day (Clark, 2006; Howard, 2006). Noting Newman's view about research and universities, Flexner argued for what he described as 'the idea of a *modern* university' (Flexner, 1930, p.3; emphasis in original). Although, for Flexner, research was not the only purpose of the modern university he suggested that in such universities one found 'the overwhelming and increasing importance of the study and solution of problems and advancement of knowledge' (Flexner, 1930, p.8). Research has now become a central part of the role of universities (Harris, 2005, p.426). In many countries for academics '[i]n the world of scholarship we are what we write' (Kennedy, 1997, p.186).

If research is so vital to the modern university mission, it will be difficult for law schools to evade this obligation and still remain other than nominally a part of the university. Indeed, there is little evidence that the majority of legal academics would wish to do so. Thus, for example, the majority of respondents in Cownie's survey of English university law schools were engaged in research and all but one enjoyed it (Cownie, 2004, p.133). In McBorrow and Baldwin's study of retired American law professors 23.08 percent of respondents spent a 'great deal of time' doing research and writing while 39.42 percent 'sometimes' engaged in such work (McMorrow and Baldwin, 1991, p.416). Blackburn argues that even clinicians, if they have an academic contract, should engage in research (Blackburn, 2018, pp.185–189). Yet, even if research is an accepted and even enjoyable part of legal academics' role, questions for law schools remain.

In the 1990s, Edwards criticised research done in American university law schools that was motivated simply by the researcher's individual fascination with the subject of the research and which served 'no social purpose' or which not 'useful to practicing lawyers, judges, administrators, and legislators' (Edwards, 1993, p.36, 1993, p.2195). In a similar fashion in the United Kingdom, Birks argued that in law schools research should not be 'detached from what the courts do' (Birks, 1998, p.406). Yet, as both Edwards and Birks acknowledge, it is not difficult to find legal academics whose research is solely motived by what interests them and others who have no concern at all with what courts do. Research for some legal academics is 'done for no other purpose than the exploration of new ideas' (Bradney, 2003, p.125). Who research should be done for is a question for law schools that divides those in university law schools as much as others in their parent universities. Something that is sometimes regarded as equally problematic is the spirit in which the research has to be done. In the 1980s Carrington controversially suggested that 'the nihilist who must profess that legal principle does not matter has an ethical duty to depart the law school' (Carrington, 1984, p.227). Elsewhere Birks argued that '[t]he lawyer must be committed to the law and the legal system, albeit not uncritically' (Birks, 1996, p.xiv). Again, however, it is not difficult to think of legal scholars in many jurisdictions who are either not committed to the law of their state, believing for example that it is fundamentally unjust, are not committed to the notion that state law can ever be valuable, preferring non-state legal systems or anarchist alternatives or who do not accept that there are settled principles that underlie the law. The publications of such academics will inevitably reflect their positions.

The centrality that research has in the work of most university law schools can have an impact on other things that the law school can and should do. In the early 1970s, Trow argued that one result of a move from a system of elite higher education to a system of mass higher education was that academics began to 'spend less time in their offices and more time at home' (Trow, 1973, p.3). In this volume, Strevens argues that the absence of academics from their offices is damaging to the well-being of law students in a number of ways. Yet, even if this were true, given the research mission of university law schools, how far is this avoidable? Modern universities can rarely offer academic staff the necessary conditions that are conducive to reflection and writing. If academics can supply such things themselves how far is it feasible to suggest that they should not do so, particularly if they are driven by the need, both personally and institutionally, to produce ever greater quantities of research? More than this, if academics are appointed because of their potential with respect to research and teaching will they necessarily have the knowledge, skills or temperament to deal with the issues that Strevens raises? It has been suggested that the personal tutor role that Strevens writes about requires counselling skills on the part of the tutor (McFarlane, 2016, p.79). However, the response of academics might be simply that they are not counsellors (Stephen, O'Connell and Hall, 2008, p.456). Even if the role of the university encompasses protecting student well-being, it does not therefore follow that the role of legal academics, appointed because of their research and teaching abilities, stretches this far.

A vocational law school?

One of the central issues in debates on the nature of a university, and one of the issues most pertinent to law schools, is to what extent, if any, can a university pursue vocational aims? It is important to note that the question here is about aims not ends or outcomes. Thus, for example, the possession of a university law degree in the United Kingdom clearly leads to a vocational advantage, at least if that advantage is measured in salary terms. Research has consistently shown that law graduates will tend to earn more than graduates from many other disciplines (Belfield et al., 2018; Walker and Zhu, 2010, pp.13–14). However, Cownie in her study of legal academics in English university law schools observes that none of the respondents to her survey mentioned teaching vocational skills (Cownie, 2004, p.77). Law graduates in England have a vocational advantage but that does not mean that law schools aim to give them that advantage through vocational teaching. What a university and its law school seek to do and what happens because of what it aims to do and does do can be very different matters. Equally a vocational advantage, again if measured in salary terms, if found is not necessarily a benefit. Thoreau's nineteenth-century argument that participating in commonly accepted patterns of work lead most people to 'lives of quiet desperation' (Thoreau, 1948, p.5) is to some extent repeated in Graeber's recent critique of the prevalence of 'bullshit jobs'; jobs, exemplified for Graeber by working as a corporate lawyer, that are, among other things, 'pointless, unnecessary, or pernicious' (Graeber, 2018, pp.xiii, 9). Bullshit jobs, whether or not gained because of the possession of a university degree, even if they entail a large salary may not be fulfilling for those who have them (Graeber, 2018, p.67). Higher earnings are not necessarily the same thing as higher personal satisfaction or happiness: '[C]hoosing courses with low pecuniary returns is potentially rational [for students]' (Green and Zhu, 2010, p.760).

The extent to which it is legitimate for universities to pursue vocational ends has long been the subject of significant debate. If universities are pre-eminently concerned with the pursuit of knowledge and cultivating humanity (Nussbaum, 1997) how can they also focus on vocational matters? This notwithstanding, it is clear that in the United Kingdom successive governments with differing political backgrounds from the 1980s onwards have sought to persuade universities to do more to produce graduates whose knowledge and skills are such as to make them employable. However, almost every statement and paper that has put forward this policy has been accompanied by a disclaimer accepting that the pursuit of knowledge for its own sake is a legitimate goal for universities, academics and students. Thus, for example the relatively recent 2011 White Paper *Higher Education: Students at the Heart of the System* stated that '[o]ur reforms aim to make the English higher education system more responsive to students and employers' but also said that '[h]igher education is a good thing in itself. Students may study a subject because they love it regardless of what it means for their earnings' (Higher Education, 2011, pp.27, 38).

Statements that vocational aspirations are the only thing that universities should have are relatively rare; suggestions for a vocational turn to the mission of universities usually have a degree of ambivalence to them. At the same time attempts by governments to redirect the goals of universities in a vocational direction have been met with resistance on the part of academics (Cheng, 2010; Collini, 2017). The very fact that the need for universities to change their mission has been a mantra for governments for over three decades in the United Kingdom does not suggest that governments themselves regard their policies as having had the impact that they wished for. Similar stories can be told about universities and their law schools in other countries.

On the face of it, university law schools might seem to be one part of the university that would find it easiest to accommodate a vocational mission. Stolker suggests that for university law schools the 'primary focus is on training young people to become lawyers' (Stolker, 2014, p.373). However, even for those in a law school who would accept that at least one of the things that law schools are for is to educate lawyers, the vocational nature of law schools is treated with caution. For example Maharg, in a book that argues for the need to reappraise the traditional notion of a liberal education that he sees as underlying the learning and teaching usually done in law schools, writes that moving away from liberal education as the defining feature of the law school does not mean that 'we ought to turn our law schools into vocational schools … we ought rigorously to reject such an approach' (Maharg, 2007, p.7). Grimes in this volume, who sees clinical legal education as a way of providing graduates who are 'work-ready employees', notes that clinical legal education is 'necessarily a balancing act between education and public service functions'. Similarly, Arthurs in this volume, who sees clinical legal education as a way 'to graduate lawyers who possess the skills and competencies to be practice ready', also observes that taking part in clinical legal education 'requires a corresponding decrease in the strictly academic, or intellectual study of law. This tension is often reduced to a purported election between law schools as intellectual proving grounds and law schools as trade schools.' These doubts and hesitations are to some extent mirrored in wider work on the nature of the university. Flexner, for example, was clear that it was not the role of universities to provide 'secondary, technical, *vocational*, nor popular education' (Flexner, 1930, pp.27–28; emphasis added). However, he went on to add that '[o]f the professional faculties, a clear case can, I think, be made out for law and medicine' (Flexner, 1930, p.29).

A key distinction for those who argue for university law schools educating lawyers might lie in the potential difference between an occupation and a profession. Thus, for example, the Arthurs Report on Canadian legal education said that: 'Canadian law schools imagine themselves to be offering a legal education that is humane and professional, rather than narrowly vocational' (Arthurs, 1983, p.47). Savage and Watt, who have argued for the university law school to be 'a house of intellect', see this house as being not for lawyers per se but for the legal profession, which is for them a 'learned profession' that consists of both 'scholar jurist and practitioner jurist' (Savage and Watt, 1996, p.49). Bright, similarly, has argued that law schools have grown out of professional education and that in teaching in law schools '[t]he subjects and methods that are used to achieve ... [the] enlargement of the mind are largely irrelevant provided that the orientation of the educative process is on the ordering of thought, rigorous logical analysis and the faculties of perception and persuasion' (Bright, 1991, pp.12, 20). Professional education for lawyers can, for Bright, take place at the same time as the 'enlargement of the mind'. Flexner, when thinking about the university, argued, echoing notions of the professional ideal, that the '[p]rofessions are learned, because they have their roots in deep and idealistic soil' and that '[p]rofessions have primarily objective, intellectual and altruistic purposes' (Flexner, 1930, pp.29, 30). These are arguments not for straightforwardly vocational education in the university but for education for what Flexner describes 'a caste' (Flexner, 1930, p.30). Such arguments about universities and law schools raise two immediate questions in the twenty-first century. First, is it true to say every subject can be taught in such a way as to allow for the enlargement of the mind, particularly if that learning is also directed to making graduates 'work-ready employees'? The Arthurs Report, for example, suggested that the Canadian experience was that there was 'an apparent tension between the human-intellectual goals of a law faculty and its professional-training activities' (Arthurs Report, 1983, p.49). De Vries and Solomon make similar points in this volume about the tensions between academic and vocational legal education in the Netherlands and Nigeria respectively. Second, is the occupation of lawyer still in any meaningful sense a profession? If '[t]he very language used in these [large law] firms has changed: law is a *business* and has to be explicitly *managed*, "practice development" is "marketing", "professional development" is "training", and so on' (Greenwood, 2007, p.190) is this commensurate with law being a profession in the sense that Flexner understood the term? Is Bright's 'enlargement of the mind' commensurable with acquiring 'professionalism as a commitment to commercially focused expertise' (Greenwood, 2007, p.194)? If lawyers now are 'pursuing profit above all' (Edwards, 1992, p.34) should law schools still educate them?

Decisions as to the ends they pursue made by universities and their law schools must in the final analysis be justified on intellectual and theoretical grounds. Neither university nor university law school is a business with a primary concern for making a profit. Nevertheless, even if they are not businesses, universities must be run in a business-like way (Pillay, 2009, p.66). Universities must be clear on what their costs are as well as what their sources of income are, even though this does not mean they should therefore necessarily pursue the most lucrative opportunities open to them or refuse to do things on grounds of expense. Thus, as Grimes observes in this volume, clinical legal education is undoubtedly expensive to deliver. This does not mean that law schools should not use such methods. However, it does mean that the quality of any evidence of its benefits will have to be looked at in the context of the fact of its relatively high cost.

Unger in this volume suggests that market considerations may lead law schools to alter their curricula in order to match changes to examinations leading to professional qualification. The example, however, of law schools in the USA in the recent past may suggest a different lesson about the dictates of the market. There is no question that in the past, whatever legal academics have seen their role as, law schools in the USA have marketed themselves to prospective students as places from which, as graduates, they would be able to secure relatively high-paying employment (Tamanaha, 2012, p.137). This was true in the case of non-elite law schools as well as in the case of elite law schools (Tejani, 2017, p.88). Whatever the merits of the arguments for doing this the collapse of the market for lawyers in the USA after 2008 meant that many law graduates could not find the employment that would allow them to repay the debts they had acquired in being students (Campos, 2012, pp.198–204; Shah, 2010, p.844). Applications to American university law schools fell by 38 percent between 2010 and 2013 (Schrag, 2013, p.408). This suggests that from a pragmatic, commercial perspective, it is risky for law schools to tie themselves into a particular employment market, particularly if that market might shrink.

The USA is not the only country where law graduates can find it difficult to find jobs as lawyers. In this volume, Zhou and Palmer observe that this is the case in China, while in England and Wales, there have always been significant numbers of law graduates who have found employment as something other than a lawyer (Wilson, 1966, p.55). In recent years only one-third of law graduates have become either solicitors or barristers (Bar Standards Board, 2018; Law Society, 201 8). However, in England and Wales, unlike the USA, the number of students recruited into law schools has continued to rise. In 2010, there were 103,900 applications to university law schools in England and Wales while in 2019 the figure was 133,470 applications (UCAS, 2019). A liberal law degree not tied to a particular employment market offers students the possibility of an education that will enable them 'to call their mind their own' (Nussbaum, 1997, p.295). At the same time, as Guth observes in this volume, they will have acquired both the habits of mind and general intellectual skills that will allow them to choose employment in a variety of areas.

Conclusion

The primary duty that a university law school has is towards its university. This duty can be discharged in a number of different ways. The financial support that it can often offer to other parts of the university that are not so profitable is, for example, not unimportant. However financial support is not enough. In the Western tradition, there is a long history of the study of law being part of the university (Mitchell, 1937, p.24). Yet, despite this, law schools and legal academics are often still viewed with suspicion by academics in other parts of the university. In addition to Veblen's view noted above, Becher, in the United Kingdom, has said that they are seen as being 'arcane, distant and alien: an appendage to the university world' (Becher, 1989, p.30). Others have expressed similar doubts about the place of law schools and legal academics in the university. This context means that the decisions by legal academics and university law schools as to what they do are of especial significance. They must be choices that are such as to convince others in the university that law can add to the intellectual life of the university; that it earns rather than buys its place in the university. Students, lawyers and governments may like what law schools do but a more important question is will universities approve of what law schools do?

Bibliography

Appleman, L. (2004–2005). The rise of the modern American law school: how professionalization, German scholarship and legal reform shaped our system. *New England Law Review*, 39(2), 251–306.

Arthurs Report: Law and Learning (1983). Ottawa, Social Sciences and Humanities Research Council of Canada.

Bar Standards Board (2018). *Statistics*, https://www.barstandardsboard.org.uk/media-centre/research-and-statistics/statistics/pupillage-statistics/.

Becher, T (1989). *Academic Tribes and Territories: Intellectual Enquiry and the Cultures of Disciplines*. Milton Keynes, SRHE and the Open University Press.

Belfield, C., Britton, J., Buscha, F., Dearden, L., Dickson, M., van der Erve, M. et al. (2018). *The Impact of Undergraduate Degrees on Early-Career Earnings: Research Report*. London, Institute for Fiscal Studies.

Birks, P. (1998). The academic and the practitioner. *Legal Studies*, 18(4), 397–414.

Birks, P. (1996). Editor's preface. In Birks, P. (ed.). *Pressing Problems in the Law Volume 2 What Are Law Schools For?*Oxford, Oxford University Press.

Blackburn, L. (2018). Reimagining the clinician profile. In Thomas, L., Vaighan, S., Malkani, B. and Lynch, T. (eds.). *Reimagining Clinical Legal Education*. Oxford, Hart Publishing.

Bok, D. (1983). A flawed system of law practice and training. *Journal of Legal Education*, 33(4), 570–585.

Bradney, A. (2003). *Conversations, Chances and Choices: The Liberal Law School in the Twenty-First Century*. Oxford, Hart Publishing.

Bright, S. (1991). What, and how, should we be teaching? *The Law Teacher*, 25(1), 11–25.

Campos, P. (2012). The crisis of the American law school. *University of Michigan Journal of Law Reform*, 46(1), 177–224.

Carrington, P. (1984). Of law and the river *Journal of Legal Education*, 34(2), 222–228.

Cheng, M. (2010). Audit cultures and quality assurance mechanisms in England: a study of their perceived impact on the work of academics. *Teaching in Higher Education*, 15, 259–271.

Clark, W. (2006). *Academic Charisma and the Origins of the Research University*. Chicago, University of Chicago Press.

Collini, S. (2017). *Speaking of Universities*. London, Verso.
Cownie, F. (2004). *Legal Academics: Culture and Identities*. Oxford, Hart Publishing.
Cownie, F. and Bradney, A. (2107). An examined life: research into university legal education in the United Kingdom. *Journal of Law and Society*, 44(S1), S129–S143.
Dicey, A. V. (1883). *Can English Law Be Taught at the Universities?*London, Macmillan.
Dworkin, R. (1996). A new interpretation of academic freedom. In Menard, L. (ed.). *The Future of Academic Freedom*. Chicago, University of Chicago Press.
Edwards, H. (1993). The growing disjunction between legal education and the legal profession: a postscript. *Michigan Law Review*, 91(8), 2191–2219.
Edwards, H. (1991). The growing disjunction between legal education and the legal profession. *Michigan Law Review*, 91(1), 34–78.
Flexner, A. (1930). *Universities: American, English, German*. New York, Oxford University Press.
Frank, J. (1947). A plea for lawyer-schools. *Yale Law Journal*, 56(8), 1305–1344.
Freidson, C. (2001). *Professionalism: The Third Logic*. Cambridge, Polity Press.
Graeber, D. (2018). *Bullshit Jobs: A Theory*. London, Allen Lane.
Green, F. and Zhu, Y. (2010). Overqualification, job dissatisfaction, and increasing dispersion in the returns to graduate qualification. *Oxford Economic Papers*, 62, 740–763.
Greenwood, R. (2007). Redefining professionalism? The impact of management change. In Empson, L. (ed.). *Managing the Modern Law Firm*. Oxford, Oxford University Press.
Harris, S. (2005). Rethinking academic identities in neo-liberal times. *Teaching in Higher Education*, 10(4), 421–433.
Higher Education: Students at the Heart of the System (2011). London, HMSO. Cm 8122.
Howard, T. (2006) *Protestant Theology and the Making of the modern German University*. Oxford, Oxford University Press.
Kennedy, D. (1997). *Academic Duty*. Cambridge, MA, Harvard University Press.
Law Society (2018). *Trends in the Solicitors' Profession: Annual Statistical Report 2017. Executive Summary*, http://www.lawsociety.org.uk/support-services/research-trends/annual-statistics-report-2017.
MacCrate Report (1992). *Legal Education and Professional Development – An Educational Continuum*. Chicago, American Bar Association.
Maharg, P. (2007). *Transforming Legal Education: Learning and Teaching the Law in the Early Twenty-first Century*. Aldershot, Ashgate.
Martin, P (ed.) (1985). Of law and the river and of nihilism and academic freedom. *Journal of Legal Education*, 35(1), 1–26.
McFarlane, K. (2016). Tutoring the tutors: supporting effective personal tutoring. *Active Learning in Higher Education*, 717(1), 7–88.
McMorrow, J. and Baldwin, A. (1991). Life after law school: on being a retired law professor. *Journal of Legal Education*, 41(2), 407–421.
Mitchell, R. (1937). Scottish law students in Italy in the later Middle Ages. *Juridical Review*, 49(1), 19–24.
Newman, J. (1960). *The Idea of a University*. New York, Holt, Rinehart & Winston.
Nussbaum, M. (1997). *Cultivating Humanity: A Classical Defense of Reform in Liberal Education*. Cambridge, MA, Harvard University Press.
Pillay, G. (2009). Valuing higher education. *Higher Education Review*, 42(1), 64–76.
Savage, N. and Watt, G. (1996). A house of intellect for the profession. In Birks, P. (ed.). *Pressing Problems in the Law Volume 2 What Are Law Schools For?*Oxford, Oxford University Press.

Schrag, P. (2013). Failing law schools – Brian Tamanaha's misguided missile. *Georgetown Journal of Legal Ethics*, 26(3), 387–422.

Shah, M. (2010). The legal education bubble: how law schools should respond to changes in the legal market. *Georgetown Journal of Legal Ethics*, 23(3), 843–845.

Stephen, D. O'Connell, P. and Hall, M. (2008). 'Going the extra mile', 'fire-fighting' or laissez-faire? Re-evaluating personal tutoring relationships within mass higher education. *Teaching in Higher Education*, 13(4), 449–460.

Stolker, C. (2014). *Rethinking the Law School: Education, Research, Outreach and Governance*. Cambridge, Cambridge University Press.

Tamanaha, B. (2012). *Failing Law Schools*. Chicago, University of Chicago Press.

Tejani, R. (2017). *Law Mart: Justice, Access and For-Profit Law Schools*. Stanford, CA, Stanford University Press.

Thayer, J. B. (1895). The teaching of law at university. *Harvard Law Review*, IX(3), 169–184.

Thoreau, H. (1948). *Walden*. New York, Rinehart & Co.

Trow, M. (1973). *Problems in the Transition from Elite to Mass Higher Education*. Berkeley, CA, Carnegie Commission on Higher Education.

UCAS (2019). *Applications*, https://www.ucas.com/data-and-analysis/undergraduate-statistics-and-reports/ucas-undergraduate-releases/applicant-releases-2019-cycle/2019-cycle-applicant-figures-january-deadline.

Veblen, T. (1919). *The Higher Learning in America*. New York, August M. Kelley.

Walker, I. and Zhu, Y. (2010). *Differences by Degree: Evidence of the Net Financial Rates of Return to Undergraduate Study for England and Wales*. Lancaster, Lancaster University Management School.

Wilson, J. (1966). A survey of legal education in the United Kingdom. *Journal of the Society of Public Teachers of Law (New Series)*, 9(1), 1–144.

Index

Page numbers in italics refer to figures.

For Product Safety Concerns and Information please contact our EU representative GPSR@taylorandfrancis.com
Taylor & Francis Verlag GmbH, Kaufingerstraße 24, 80331 München, Germany

www.ingramcontent.com/pod-product-compliance
Ingram Content Group UK Ltd.
Pitfield, Milton Keynes, MK11 3LW, UK
UKHW021302190926
475701UK00009B/580

* 9 7 8 1 0 3 2 1 7 5 0 4 1 *